Ruby Programming for the Absolute Beginner

JERRY LEE FORD, JR.

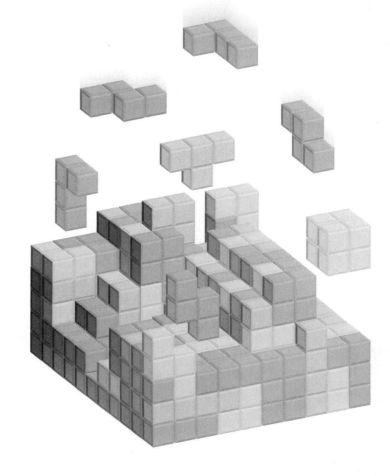

THOMSON

COURSE TECHNOLOGY

Professional ■ Technical ■ Reference

Important: Thomson Course Technology PTR cannot provide software support. Please contact the appropriate software manufacturer's technical support line or Web site for assistance.

Thomson Course Technology PTR and the author have attempted throughout this book to distinguish proprietary trademarks from descriptive terms by following the capitalization style used by the manufacturer.

Information contained in this book has been obtained by Thomson Course Technology PTR from sources believed to be reliable. However, because of the possibility of human or mechanical error by our sources, Thomson Course Technology PTR, or others, the Publisher does not guarantee the accuracy, adequacy, or completeness of any information and is not responsible for any errors or omissions or the results obtained from use of such information. Readers should be particularly aware of the fact that the Internet is an ever-changing entity. Some facts may have changed since this book went to press.

Educational facilities, companies, and organizations interested in multiple copies or licensing of this book should contact the Publisher for quantity discount information. Training manuals, CD-ROMs, and portions of this book are also available individually or can be tailored for specific needs.

ISBN-10: 1-59863-397-X
ISBN-13: 9-781-59863-397-9

Library of Congress Catalog Card Number: 2007927293

Printed in the United States of America

08 09 10 11 12 TW 10 9 8 7 6 5 4 3 2 1

Publisher and General Manager, Thomson Course Technology PTR:
Stacy L. Hiquet

Associate Director of Marketing:
Sarah O'Donnell

Manager of Editorial Services:
Heather Talbot

Marketing Manager:
Mark Hughes

Acquisitions Editor:
Mitzi Koontz

Project Editor:
Jenny Davidson

Technical Reviewer:
Deepak Vohra

PTR Editorial Services Coordinator:
Erin Johnson

Interior Layout Tech:
Value-Chain Intl.

Cover Designer:
Mike Tanamachi

Indexer:
Sharon Shock

Proofreader:
Brad Crawford

THOMSON

COURSE TECHNOLOGY

Professional ■ Technical ■ Reference
Thomson Course Technology PTR,
a division of Thomson Learning Inc.
25 Thomson Place
Boston, MA 02210
http://www.courseptr.com

To my mother and father for always being there for me, and to my wonderful children, Alexander, William, and Molly, and my beautiful wife, Mary.

ACKNOWLEDGMENTS

This book would never have been possible without the hard work and dedication of a number of individuals to whom I own many thanks. For starters, I would like to thank the book's acquisitions editor, Mitzi Koontz, for working behind the scenes to help make this book a reality. Special thanks also go out to Jenny Davidson. Jenny served as this book's project editor and copy editor and spent many long and difficult hours working to ensure that everything came together like it was supposed to. I also wish to thank Deepak Vohra, who served as the book's technical editor, providing me with invaluable insight and guidance. Finally, I wish to acknowledge and thank everyone who works at Thomson Course Technology PTR for their contributions and hard work.

ABOUT THE AUTHOR

Jerry Lee Ford, Jr. is an author, educator, and IT professional with over 18 years' experience in information technology, including roles as an automation analyst, technical manager, technical support analyst, automation engineer, and security analyst. Jerry has a master's degree in business administration from Virginia Commonwealth University in Richmond, Virginia. He is the author of 22 other books and co-author of 2 additional books. His published works include *AppleScript Studio Programming for the Absolute Beginner, Microsoft Windows Shell Scripting for the Absolute Beginner, Perl Programming for the Absolute Beginner, Beginning REALbasic, Microsoft Windows Shell Scripting and WSH Administrator's Guide, VBScript Professional Projects*, and *Microsoft Visual Basic 2005 Express Edition Programming for the Absolute Beginner*. He has over five years' experience as an adjunct instructor teaching networking courses in information technology. Jerry lives in Richmond, Virginia, with his wife, Mary, and their children, William, Alexander, and Molly.

TABLE OF CONTENTS

Chapter 6   WORKING WITH COLLECTIONS OF DATA..................... 163

INTRODUCTION

Welcome to *Ruby Programming for the Absolute Beginner*. Ruby is an object-oriented interpreted scripting language. It is *object oriented* in that Ruby views everything that it sees and interacts with as an object. This sets Ruby apart from most other scripting languages. Ruby is also *interpreted*, which means that Ruby scripts are compiled and executed by an interpreter at runtime. This allows you to make changes to your Ruby scripts, and immediately run them to see how things work without having to go through an extensive compilation process like so many other programming languages require.

Ruby is also a cross-platform programming language, meaning that you can develop and execute Ruby scripts that can run on Windows, Mac OS X, UNIX, Linux, and many other operating systems. Therefore, you will be able to leverage your Ruby programming skills across a host of different operating system platforms, thus maximizing the investment in time and effort that you will make in learning Ruby. You can even apply your Ruby programming skills to the development of web applications, using a specialized Ruby framework known as Ruby on Rails.

Ruby is easy to learn and yet quite powerful. This makes Ruby a wonderful choice for first-time programmers. It is a great programming language for tackling all kinds of small tasks. At the same time, Ruby is more than robust and powerful enough to support the development of the most complicated programming tasks, making it a great language to learn for experienced programmers looking for an advanced object-oriented programming language.

Ruby is immensely popular. As of the writing of this book, Ruby was listed as one of the 10 most popular programming languages in the world by Tiobe Software, which specializes in accessing and tracking the quality of software. Ruby is on track to become more popular than both JavaScript and Python (http://www.tiobe.com/tpci.htm).

Best of all, Ruby is free. If you are running a UNIX or Linux operating system, Ruby may already be installed. If not, you can easily download and install it directly from the Internet. Free installation packages are available for Microsoft Windows as well. This book is dedicated to teaching you what you need to know to begin programming with Ruby. By the time you have reached the end of this book, you will have developed a solid understanding of the fundamentals of Ruby programming and will have a foundation upon which you can build to become an effective Ruby programmer.

WHY RUBY?

Ruby is a free programming language. It runs on Windows, Mac OS X, UNIX, Linux, and numerous other operating systems. By learning to program with Ruby, you will not only develop a completely new set of skills but also end up with programming skills that can be applied to many different programming environments. Ruby's growing popularity and acceptance as a programming language can ultimately translate into a lucrative programming career if that is what interests you. Alternatively, if you are just in it for fun, you'll be quite pleased with not only what you can do with Ruby but also with how fun and satisfying it can be to work with. Since Ruby is object-oriented, the programming skills that you will learn will lend themselves well to other object-oriented programming languages like Visual Basic and Visual C++.

Ruby has a simple syntax. It is very adept at dealing with tasks like text processing, database administration, networking programming, and system administration. Of course, as this book will demonstrate, it can also be used to develop computer games. In addition to the aforementioned uses, Ruby has also begun to play a major role as a web-development programming language in the form of a web application development framework referred to as Ruby on Rails. Although not specifically covered in this book, by learning the fundamentals of Ruby programming, you will lay the foundation required to get started with web development using Ruby on Rails.

As programming languages go, Ruby is relatively new, having first appeared on the scene in 1995. As a scripting language, Ruby supports rapid application development, eliminating the compilation requirement of other traditional programming languages. Ruby can be used to create everything from small scripts made up of a few lines to full-featured applications made up of many thousands of program statements.

Ruby shines when compared with other scripting languages like Perl and Python. Its syntax is much easier to learn and yet it is just as powerful and effective. Unlike Perl, Ruby is fully object oriented. Ruby scripts are usually smaller than Python scripts and tend to run faster as well.

As I mentioned, Ruby makes for a great first programming language. Yet it is robust and powerful enough to satisfy the demands of professional programmers. It can be used to quickly build prototype applications or to build complete stand-alone applications. Regardless of which operating system you work with, Ruby is available. The same cannot be said for many other programming languages like Microsoft's Visual Basic or Apple's AppleScript programming language.

As this book will demonstrate, learning how to program with Ruby can be both fun and satisfying. Learning Ruby makes for a great first step into the world of programming. Of course, Ruby also makes a great second programming language for any professional programmer. So regardless of whether you just want to learn Ruby as a hobby or are looking to begin a new career as a professional programmer, Ruby will serve you well.

WHO SHOULD READ THIS BOOK?

One of my primary goals in writing this book is not only to teach you how to program using Ruby but also to teach you how to become an effective programmer. There is no requirement for you to have previous programming experience. In fact, my only expectation is that you have basic knowledge of how to use a computer and are interested in learning how to become a Ruby programmer.

I hope that you will find this book's approach to teaching programming principles through the development of computer games to be refreshing, fun, and effective. First-time programmers and computer hobbyists should find the systematic, hands-on instructional approach used by this book to be very effective. The information and programming skills that you learn from this book will lay a foundation upon which you can build and will prepare the way for you to begin to use Ruby to tackle a variety of challenges. At the same time, professional programmers looking to expand their toolset will find Ruby to be a great second or third programming language. As such, this book will serve as a great Ruby primer and quick-reference guide.

WHAT YOU NEED TO BEGIN

Ruby runs on most computer operating systems, including Windows, Mac OS X, UNIX, and Linux, as well as many other operating systems like OS2 and BeOS. In addition to having access to a computer running one of these operating systems, you will need to install Ruby, if it is not already installed. Ruby can be downloaded and installed free from http://www.ruby-lang.org. You will find instructions for installing Ruby in Chapter 1, "Ruby Basics."

Ruby scripts are created as plain text files. Therefore, you will need to have a plain text file editor installed on your computer. On Windows, you can use the Notepad application. On Mac OS X, you can use TextEdit, provided you configure it to save out as plain text. On UNIX and Linux, you can use vi or any other text editor that may be installed.

Instead of using a regular text-editing application, you may instead want to use a specialized Ruby-integrated development environment, or IDE, when creating and testing your Ruby scripts. An *IDE* is a specialized editor that is specifically designed to support script or application development. An example of one such IDE is FreeRIDE. *FreeRIDE* is a Ruby-specific code editor that provides syntax color-coding and the ability to test the execution of your Ruby scripts from within the IDE, saving you the hassle of having to switch between an editor and the command line. Like Ruby, FreeRIDE is cross platform and it is free. There are versions of FreeRIDE for Windows, Mac OS X, and various flavors of UNIX and Linux. As of the writing of this book, you could download an installation package for FreeRIDE at http://rubyforge.org/projects/freeride/ or http://freeride.rubyforge.org/wiki/wiki.pl.

How This Book Is Organized

I wrote this book with the intention that it be read from cover to cover. However, if you have previous programming experience and are reading this book because you are interested in adding another programming language to your arsenal of development tools, you may instead want to skip around and focus on topics of particular interest to you. Still, I recommend that you take the time to read the first two chapters as they contain a lot of foundational information. In addition, you should at least glance through Chapters 3 to 6. These chapters provide you with a review of the basic language components that make up the Ruby programming language.

Ruby Programming for the Absolute Beginner is organized into four major parts. Part I consists of two chapters that provide basic information about Ruby and its development environment. This includes a review of Ruby's features and capabilities. It also includes learning how to install and interact with Ruby, as well as learning how to save and execute Ruby scripts.

Part II consists of four chapters that provide complete coverage of the Ruby programming language. You will learn how to formulate script statements and to understand statement syntax. You will learn how to work with variables, conditional logic, loops, arrays, hashes, and all of the programming elements that make up the Ruby programming language.

Part III consists of four chapters, each of which addresses an advanced programming topic. These topics include learning how to work with regular expressions as well as how to use Ruby to develop basic system file and network administration scripts. You will also learn more about object-oriented programming and the basic steps involved in tracking down and eliminating script errors that inevitably work their way into just about every script and application.

Part IV is made up of two appendices and a glossary. The first appendix provides you with an overview of the source code from this book, which you can download from this book's companion website (www.courseptr.com/downloads). The second appendix is designed to help you further your Ruby programming knowledge once you have finished reading this book by providing you with information on Ruby books that have more advanced instruction aimed at intermediate and professional programmers. You will also find suggestions about Ruby websites, newsgroups, and mailing lists. Finally, the Glossary provides you with a complete listing of all the terms that are used throughout the book.

A high-level overview of each chapter in this book and the topics that are covered is provided here:

- **Chapter 1, "Ruby Basics."** This chapter will provide you with a high-level overview of Ruby programming, including a little information about its history, major features, and capabilities. You will also learn how to install Ruby and to create and execute your first Ruby Script, the Ruby Joke game.

- **Chapter 2, "Interacting with Ruby."** In this chapter, you will learn how to interact with Ruby from the command line. In addition, you will learn how to use interactive Ruby shell, also known as the irb. In doing so, you will begin to learn about Ruby's syntax and its built-in support for object-oriented programming. You will create the Ruby Tall Tale game in this chapter.

- **Chapter 3, "Working with Objects, Strings, and Variables."** In this chapter, you will learn how to work with and manipulate string and numeric data. You will also learn how to define variables and objects and use them to store and retrieve data. You will create the Ruby Virtual Crazy 8 Ball game in this chapter.

- **Chapter 4, "Implementing Conditional Logic."** In this chapter, you will learn how to use conditional logic as a tool for analyzing data and controlling the logical execution of script statements. You will then apply what you have learned through the development of the Ruby Typing Challenge game.

- **Chapter 5, "Working with Loops."** In this chapter, you will learn how to formulate and control the execution of loops. In doing so, you will learn how to create Ruby scripts that are capable of processing enormous amounts of data or performing repetitive tasks. In this chapter you will create the Superman Movie Trivia Quiz.

- **Chapter 6, "Working with Collections of Data."** In this chapter, you will learn how to store and process related collections of data more efficiently. This will include learning how to store data in indexed lists that can then be processed efficiently using loops. You will also learn how to define data in hashes, which provide an efficient means of storing large collections of data in key-value pairs. You will create the Ruby Number Guessing game in this chapter.

- **Chapter 7, "Working with Regular Expressions."** In this chapter, you will learn how to use regular expressions to evaluate and manipulate string content. This will lay the foundation you need to begin to dissect user input and file contents. You will create the Word Guessing game in this chapter.

- **Chapter 8, "Object-Oriented Programming."** In this chapter, you will learn more about Ruby's support for object-oriented programming. This includes learning about Ruby's support for encapsulation, polymorphism, and inheritance. You will also learn how to create modules and work with namespaces. You will create the Ruby Rock, Paper, Scissors game in this chapter.

- **Chapter 9, "File and Folder Administration."** In this chapter, you will learn how to access and manage file system resources. You will learn to read from and write to files and to access system and network data and resources.

- **Chapter 10, "Debugging."** In this chapter, you will learn how to find and fix script errors. You will learn how to develop exception handlers that trap and deal with errors, preventing them from terminating your Ruby scripts. You will also learn how to work with Ruby's integrated debugger to exercise detailed control over the execution of your Ruby scripts, while tracking their logical execution.

- **Appendix A, "What's on the Companion Website?"** This appendix provides a review of all the Ruby game scripts that are developed in this book and made available as downloads on this book's companion website (www.courseptr.com/downloads).

- **Appendix B, "What Next?"** This appendix provides you with helpful information that you can use to continue your Ruby programming education. This includes information about other Ruby programming books as well as Ruby websites, newsgroups, blogs, and mailing lists.

- **Glossary.** This unit provides a glossary of terms used throughout the book.

CONVENTIONS USED IN THIS BOOK

To provide the best possible learning experience and to make this book as easy to read and understand as possible, I have implemented a number of helpful conventions to help emphasize certain points. These conventions are outlined and described below.

Hints provide you with tips for doing things differently and point out things that you can do to become a more proficient Ruby programmer.

Traps point out areas where problems are likely to occur and then provide you with advice on how to stay away from or deal with those problems, hopefully saving you the pain of learning about them the hard way.

Tricks share with you programming shortcuts designed to help make you a better and more efficient programmer.

CHALLENGES

Each chapter in this book ends with a series of challenges intended to improve chapter game projects and further your programming skills.

Part

I

Introducing Ruby

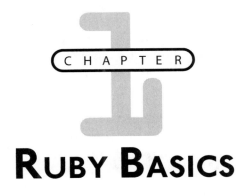

RUBY BASICS

R uby is an object-oriented scripting language originally developed in 1993 to run on UNIX. However, it has since been ported to many other popular operating systems, including Microsoft Windows, Mac OS X, and Linux. Ruby is distributed under an open-source license, allowing anyone to freely install and use it. In this chapter, you will learn background information required to begin working with Ruby and to use it to create and execute Ruby scripts. You will also learn how to use Ruby to create the first of a number of computer games presented in this book.

Specifically, you will learn:

- Basic information about Ruby and its capabilities
- How to determine if Ruby is already installed on your computer
- How to install Ruby on your computer
- How to interact with Ruby from the command line
- How to save and execute Ruby scripts

PROJECT PREVIEW: THE RUBY JOKE GAME

In this chapter and in each chapter that follows, you will learn how to create a new computer game. By following along and creating your own copies of these games, you will gain practical, hands-on experience programming with Ruby, and you will develop a foundation upon which you can build and move on to developing larger and more complex Ruby projects, such as system and network administration scripts or the development of website applications.

In this chapter's game project, the Ruby Joke game, you will learn the basic steps involved in writing a Ruby script. When the game is first started, the screen shown in Figure 1.1 displays, prompting the player for permission to begin telling jokes.

FIGURE 1.1

The player may elect to play the game or quit.

If the player enters a value of n, the game responds by displaying a message that invites the player to return to play another time. However, if the player enters a value of y, the game responds by displaying the first of a series of jokes, as demonstrated in Figure 1.2.

FIGURE 1.2

The player must press Enter to advance from screen to screen during game play.

In order to view the first joke's punch line, the player must press the Enter key, after which the screen shown in Figure 1.3 displays.

FIGURE 1.3

The punch line for
the game's first
joke.

To advance to and view successive jokes, the player must continue to press the Enter key. Once the game's final joke has been told, the screen shown in Figure 1.4 displays, thanking the player for playing the game.

FIGURE 1.4

The game ends by
thanking the
player.

In the previous set of screen prints, you saw what the Ruby Joke game looks like when executed on a computer running Microsoft Windows. Of course, since Ruby is a cross-platform programming language that runs on a number of different operating systems, you can just as easily create and run this game on a different operating system. For example, Figure 1.5 shows an example of how the game would look if it were run on Mac OS X.

By the time you have completed the development of the Ruby Joke game, you will have a good understanding of the basic mechanics involved in creating Ruby scripts, and you will be ready to move on and tackle more challenging projects.

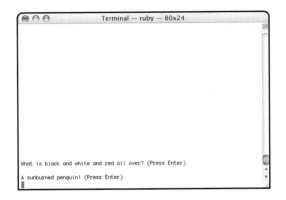

FIGURE 1.5

The Ruby Joke
game runs exactly
the same
regardless of
which operating
system it is run on.

INTRODUCING RUBY

Ruby is a modern, object-oriented scripting language created by a Japanese computer scientist named Yukihiro Matsumoto, better known within the Ruby community as Matz. Matz created Ruby to address the shortcomings he found in other programming languages, which he viewed as overly complex and difficult to work with. Instead, as he set out to create what would become Ruby, he did so with the intention of making programming less difficult and fun again.

Matz ultimately named his new programming language Ruby after joking with a friend about the Perl language name. As such, Ruby is the actual name of the scripting language and not just a clever acronym. As a relatively new programming language, Ruby represents lessons learned from many other programming languages. For example, rather than integrating support for object-oriented programming long after the language was originally created, as is being done with Perl, Ruby was created from the ground up with object-oriented programming in mind.

As he worked on creating his new programming language, Matz was heavily influenced by Smalltalk, a pure object-oriented programming language created in the 1970s. Unlike Ruby, Smalltalk programs tended to be cryptic, lacking Ruby's naturalistic programming style and syntax. Matz also drew heavily on another scripting language, Perl. Unlike Ruby, Perl was not originally designed to support object-oriented programming. In slowly changing to include object-oriented programming and other modern programming features, Perl's syntax has become cryptic and inconsistent. Other programming languages to which Matz attributed inspiration include Python, C++, Lisp, and ADA.

HINT   Because of their influence on the overall design of Ruby, programmers with previous experience with Perl and Smalltalk, and to a somewhat lesser extent, Python, C++, Lisp, and ADA, should find many similarities between Ruby and these languages, making for a shorter learning curve. Perl programmers in particular will quickly appreciate the many similarities between Perl and Ruby syntax as well as the many Perl-like regular expressions that Ruby provides.

Matz began working on Ruby in February of 1993 and released his first version in December of 1995. It quickly gained notice and popularity in Japan. However, elsewhere few people gave it attention. Ruby 1.0 was released a year later, in December 1996. A big reason for the slow recognition of Ruby in its first few years was the lack of non-Japanese documentation. It was not until the end of 1998 that the ruby-talk mailing list was created that Ruby began to be promoted in English. Later, in 1999, www.ruby-lang.org, shown in Figure 1.6, was set up as the official English-language website for Ruby.

FIGURE 1.6

www.ruby-lang.org is the official English website for Ruby.

Despite its obvious power and capabilities, Ruby still lacked the notoriety and popularity of other scripting languages like Perl and Python. What Ruby needed, but did not have yet, was a killer application that demonstrated Ruby's capabilities and got everybody's attention.

Then, with the introduction of Ruby on Rails, everything changed. Suddenly, programmers all over the world began to take notice of Ruby and recognize its capabilities, both as a general-purpose scripting language and as a web development language.

Ruby on Rails, sometimes just referred to as *Rails,* is a web-based application development framework that allows programmers to build website applications using Ruby. It facilitates the development of database-driven applications. Ruby on Rails was first released in 2004 and, like Ruby, it is free. Although coverage of Ruby on Rails is beyond the scope of this book, you will find that the Ruby programming foundation that you build by reading this book will prepare you well, should you decide to later make the jump to Ruby on Rails.

As of the writing of this book, the current stable version of Ruby is version 1.8.6. This version is considered by the Ruby community to be the current general release version of the language. Version 1.9.0 is currently in development and available for download; however, because it is still being developed, it is regarded as an experimental version.

Ruby Is Simple Yet Powerful

As an interpreted scripting language, Ruby is simple to use. Just open your favorite text or code editor, key in a little Ruby code, and then save your script file and it is ready to execute. If all goes well, your script will do whatever it is supposed to do. If, on the other hand, you made a typo when keying in a script statement or failed to follow Ruby's syntactical requirements when formulating your script statements, an error will occur when you attempt to run your script.

Ruby can be used to develop complete applications that involve network and database access. Tight integration with the operating systems also provides Ruby with access to a wealth of system resources. Its devotion to object-oriented programming and its extensive set of classes and libraries give it capabilities that rival or surpass most other scripting languages. In this sense, Ruby is quite easy to learn but at the same time difficult to master.

Ruby Is Interpreted

As an interpreted scripting language, Ruby scripts are not converted into executable code until you run them using a Ruby interpreter. An *interpreter* is an application that converts source code into a format that the operating system can actually execute. This makes Ruby a lot easier to work with than other compiled programming languages, which require you to go through a formal compile process after creating or making a change to your Ruby scripts before you can then run them. Thus if an error occurs in your Ruby script, you can open your script using your editor, find and fix the error, and then save and re-execute your script without a lot of fuss.

As an interpreted scripting language, it is especially easy to create small scripts and get them executing very quickly, perhaps in just a fraction of the time required to create a similar program using a compiled programming language like C++. However, in exchange for this simplicity and ease of use, your Ruby scripts run slower than their compiled counterparts, because each time you run a Ruby script, the script must be reinterpreted before it can execute, whereas a compiled program can begin executing immediately.

Ruby Supports a Natural English-Like Programming Style

Another feature of Ruby that makes it easy to use is its straightforward syntax, which makes learning how to work with the programming language easier to do than is the case with many other programming languages. Ruby is generally regarded as a natural, English-like scripting language. Unlike other programming languages such as Perl and Python, you can often tell exactly what a Ruby statement is doing just by looking at it, even if you are not familiar with the specific commands that make up the statement. For example, consider the following statement.

```
3.times do print "What's up doc? " end
```

Without knowing anything yet about programming using Ruby, I'll bet you can figure out in general terms what this statement will do when executed. Specifically, it will print out the string "What's up doc? " three times in a row.

Ruby Has Light Syntax Requirements

Another feature of Ruby programming that sets it apart from many other programming languages is its light syntax. Ruby does not force programmers to load up programming statements with brackets and parentheses characters, nor does is require every statement end with a semicolon. Statements tend to be less wordy than other scripting languages. As a result, there is less opportunity for you to make mistakes when writing script code. As an example of Ruby's simplistic syntax, consider variable declaration. For starters, Ruby does not require you to formally declare a variable prior to its use. This greatly facilitates the development of small one- and two-line scripts.

 A *variable* is a reference or a pointer to a location in memory where a piece of data is stored.

Despite its simplicities, Ruby is every bit as powerful and complex as any other modern programming language. Many programmers use Ruby to develop scripts that tie together other applications, providing the programmatic glue needed to take disparate applications and get them to work together to be more efficient.

Ruby Is Object Oriented

Unlike many other modern scripting languages, which include varying degrees of support for object-oriented programming, Ruby is as close to 100 percent object-oriented as it gets. In Ruby, everything is viewed as an object. Things that describe or characterize an object, such as size or type, are referred to as object *properties*, which are stored as variables. By accessing the contents of these variables, you can access information about objects. Similarly, by modifying values assigned to object properties, you can make changes that affect the object.

Actions that can be taken against the object or which the object can be directed to perform are stored as part of the object in *methods*. By creating objects and assigning program code to object methods, you are able to create Ruby scripts whose objects are able to perform any number of actions, such as collecting user input, performing complex mathematical calculations, accessing databases, etc.

> Like many scripting languages, Ruby allows programmers to work with it in a procedural manner, without defining any objects and instead using variables and custom functions to control script execution. However, under the covers, Ruby still enforces an object-oriented programming mode in that all variables and functions are automatically defined as properties and methods belonging to their script's default *main* or parent class. As such, Ruby is sometimes referred to as a multi-paradigm programming language.

Unlike many object-oriented programming languages, Ruby implements the principle of object-oriented programming to the nth degree. For example, consider the following statement.

```
3.times do print "What's up doc? " end
```

Unlike most object-oriented programming languages, Ruby treats numbers (as well as other primitive data types) as objects. As objects, numbers are associated with specific collections of properties and methods. In the preceding statement, the `times` method is executed. `times` is just one of many methods that belong to Ruby's integer class. To use it you must first specify an integer followed by a dot (.) character and the method name.

> The syntax used to specify the integer class's `times` method shown above is referred to as *dot notation*. Dot notation is also used when specifying object properties.

> A *class* is a definition or template used to define the properties and methods that represent objects.

Ruby Is Extremely Flexible

Using Ruby, programmers can create scripts that can automate any number of tasks. You can develop Ruby scripts that automate complex processes, thus eliminating the possibility of human error. Alternatively, Ruby scripts can be used to automate repetitive tasks, freeing you up to perform other tasks. In truth, Ruby can be used to perform just about any task you can think of. Today, programmers all around the world are using Ruby to develop scripts to perform tasks that include:

- **Processing Text Files.** Ruby has built-in classes that support file administration and provide the ability to parse file and string contents using regular expressions.
- **Network Programming.** Ruby supports the development of sockets-based applications capable of performing a range of networking tasks.
- **Application Prototyping.** Ruby can be used to quickly develop scripts that demonstrate a proof of concept before creating a final version of an application using a more complicated programming language such as C++.
- **System Administration.** Ruby can be used to automate the execution of complex tasks and repetitive system administration tasks, freeing up system administrators to perform other work.
- **Web Development.** In addition to using the Ruby on Rails framework, programmers can also use Ruby to support traditional CGI programming.

Ruby Exists in Many Different Environments

As you know, Ruby can run directly on Microsoft Windows, Mac OS X, and multiple versions of UNIX and Linux, as well as many other types of operating systems. Using the Ruby on Rails framework, Ruby also facilitates the development and execution of web applications. In addition, Ruby also runs within different virtual machine environments.

One such virtual machine environment is JRuby, which is a Java-based Ruby environment developed by Sun Microsystems. Using *JRuby*, programmers can develop Ruby scripts that can run on any Java-supported platform, including the Internet. Another virtual machine being developed for Ruby is Microsoft's IronRuby. *IronRuby* will support the development and execution of Ruby scripts that can interact with the Microsoft .NET Framework. Although not available as of the writing of this book, IronRuby promises to make available to Ruby programmers all of the resources currently available to other .NET-enabled programming languages.

    The .NET Framework is a Microsoft-developed framework that supports the development of desktop, network, and Internet-based applications and scripts.

In addition to JRuby and IronRuby, another Ruby-based virtual machine is currently in the works. This virtual machine evolved out of the YARV project. *YARV*, which stands for *Yet Another Ruby VM*, is designed to replace the current Ruby interpreter and has been designed to address one specific area of concern, speed. Compared with other scripting languages like Perl and Python, Ruby scripts generally run slower than Perl and Python scripts. Among other goals, the YARV virtual machine is designed to remedy this situation. It has been reported that under different benchmark tests, Ruby scripts processed by YARV have run between 2 and 10 times faster. YARV is currently being integrated into Ruby and will serve as the Ruby interpreter when version 1.9.1 is released, making it Ruby's official interpreter.

GETTING READY TO WORK WITH RUBY

By default, you will not find Ruby installed on a new computer running any version of Microsoft Windows. However, if you are running Mac OS X, version 10.3 or higher, Ruby should already be installed. If you are running one of the many versions of UNIX or Linux operating systems available today, there is a pretty good chance that Ruby may already be installed on your computer.

If Ruby is not installed on your computer, then you will need to download and install it, as explained in the sections that follow. If you are running a version of Ruby older than Ruby 1.8.2, you'll need to upgrade to a new version, which you can do by simply installing a new version of the language.

As of the writing of this book, the current version of Ruby is 1.8.6. Any example Ruby scripts that you see in this book were developed and tested using this version of Ruby. However, they should all work just fine on any version of Ruby, from Ruby 1.8.2 on.

Determining Whether Ruby Is Already Installed

Depending on your operating system, there are a number of ways to check and see if Ruby is installed on your computer. The following sections outline a number of these options.

Looking for Ruby on Microsoft Windows

If you are running Microsoft Windows, the easiest way to see if Ruby is installed is to look for the Ruby program group by clicking on Start and then All Programs and looking for a program group named something like Ruby-186-25. If it is there, click on the group to open it and look for an executable file named fxri – interactive Ruby Help & Console. If it's there, then Ruby is installed on your computer and should be ready for use.

Another way to determine if Ruby is installed on your computer and to ascertain its version number, if it is installed, is to click on Start > All Programs > Accessories > Command Prompt. This will display a Windows Console and provide you with access to the Windows command prompt. Type the following command at the Windows command prompt and press Enter.

```
ruby -v
```

If Ruby is installed, you should see output similar to that shown in Figure 1.7.

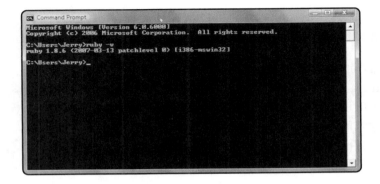

FIGURE 1.7

Retrieving
information about
the version of
Ruby installed on
the computer.

Looking for Ruby on Mac OS X

Unless it has been removed, Ruby should already be installed on any computer running Mac OS X 10.3 or later. To determine if Ruby is installed on a Mac computer, you need to open the Terminal application. To find the Terminal application, open your computer's startup disk and then find and open the Applications folder. Scroll to the bottom of the Applications folder and find and open the Utilities folder. Inside this folder you will find the Terminal application.

 Ruby programmers who develop scripts for Mac OS X will need to work with the Terminal application a lot. You may want to drag and drop the Terminal application icon onto the dock to have it nearby.

To start the Terminal application, just double-click on its icon. Once started, the terminal application will display a UNIX shell command prompt (Mac OS X is a UNIX-based operating system). To find out if Ruby is installed, type the following command at the command prompt and press Enter.

```
ruby -v
```

If Ruby is installed, a message will display indicating the version number. Assuming that the preceding command worked without any issues, type the following command.

```
irb
```

 irb stands for interactive Ruby. irb is used to interactively submit Ruby statements for processing and is commonly used by Ruby programmers as a means of tinkering with Ruby and testing different language features to see how they work. You will learn more about the irb later in this chapter.

This command starts a new interactive Ruby session. As a result, you should see the irb command prompt displayed as demonstrated here:

```
irb
irb(main):001:0>
```

If everything worked as described, Ruby is installed and ready for use on your computer.

Looking for Ruby on UNIX and Linux

Ruby is often automatically installed as part of many UNIX and Linux operating systems. To determine if Ruby is installed on a UNIX or Linux computer, you need to start a new command shell session using whatever terminal shell program has been supplied with your operating system. Once at the command prompt, type the following command.

```
irb
```

This command starts a new interactive Ruby session. As a result, you should see the irb command prompt displayed, as demonstrated here:

```
irb
irb(main):001:0>
```

If everything worked as described, Ruby is installed and ready for use on your computer.

Installing or Upgrading Ruby

When you install Ruby, the Ruby interpreter is installed. You also get a collection of Ruby libraries that support the execution of Ruby on the particular platform on which it has been installed.

Depending on which operating system you are using, there are a number of different options available to you for installing Ruby. When available, the easiest option is to install an already packaged copy of Ruby. In the absence of a pre-built installation package, you can always download the appropriate Ruby source code and perform a manual installation.

Installing Ruby on Microsoft Windows

By default, Microsoft Windows does not come with Ruby installed. So, unless someone else has already installed it on the computer you are using, you will need to install it yourself. The easiest way to install a new copy of Ruby is to download the one-click installer package made available at http://www.ruby-lang.org/en/downloads/. To install it, you must first download a copy of the installation package to your desktop, which you can do by clicking on the One-Click Installer link located on the Ruby on Windows section of the web page, as shown in Figure 1.8, and then saving the file to your desktop when prompted.

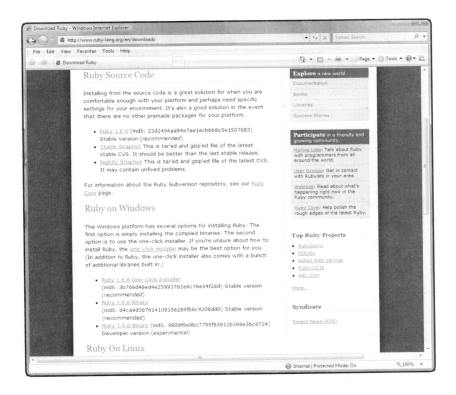

FIGURE 1.8

Searching for Ruby source code and installation packages.

Once the download is complete, you can install Ruby on your computer by executing the steps outlined in the following procedure.

1. Double-click on the installer program.
2. If Microsoft Windows displays a popup window with a security message, click on the Run button to allow the installation process to continue.
3. When prompted by the install program, click on Next to begin the install process.
4. Continue to click on Next when prompted to perform a standard installation of Ruby.
5. Once installation is complete, you will be prompted to click on Next one last time and then on the Finish button. At this point Ruby's installation is complete.

You can also use the preceding procedure to install a newer version of Ruby on your Windows computer.

Now that Ruby is installed, click on Start and then on All Programs. You should see a new program group named Ruby-XXX-XX (where XXX-XX identifies the specific version of Ruby that has been installed). Within this group you will find a number of items, including:

- **fxri - Interactive Ruby Help & Console.** An interactive graphical application that provides access to Ruby help files and Ruby's interactive environment.
- **SciTE.** A general code editor that can be used to create Ruby scripts.
- **Uninstall Ruby-XXX-XX.** An uninstall program for removing Ruby from your computer.
- **Ruby Documentation.** Contains links to online web pages and to Ruby's help files.
- **RubyGems.** A package manager that provides a standard format for distributing Ruby scripts.

Finding a Ruby Installation for Mac OS X

By default, Ruby comes preinstalled on all versions of Mac OS X starting with version 10.3. As such, unless it has been removed or you want to install a more current version of Ruby, you can simply begin working with it. If you visit http://www.ruby-lang.org/en/downloads, you will find several links in the Ruby on OS X section of the web page. Each of these links provides you with a different option for installing Ruby on Mac OS X. The names of these links and their respective URLs are listed here:

- **Locomotive**—http://locomotive.raaum.org/
- **MacPorts**—http://www.macports.org/
- **Fink**—http://www.finkproject.org/

You will find instructions for working with each of these installation options available on their respective websites.

Installing Ruby on UNIX and Linux

Many UNIX and Linux systems come with Ruby preinstalled. If this is not the case, the best approach is to see if your particular version of UNIX or Linux includes a package management utility that provides you with the ability to install Ruby by selecting it from a list of available applications.

Of course, you can always elect to install Ruby manually. To do so, go to http://www.ruby-lang.org/en/downloads/ and click on the Ruby X.X.X link located in the Ruby Source Code section of the web page and then click on Save when prompted to download the installation files to your computer. This downloads a compressed tar.gz file containing Ruby's installation files. This file is named ruby-X.X.X.tar.gz, where X.X.X represents the current stable versions of Ruby. For example, as of the wiring of this book the current version of Ruby is 1.8.6; therefore, the tar fail would be named ruby-1.8.6.tar.gz.

Using the contents of the tar.gz file, you can install Ruby on your UNIX or Linux system using the following steps, which you will need to perform while logged on with root access.

1. Start up a new shell session and navigate to the folder where you saved the tar.gz file.
2. Uncompress the file by typing **tar xzvf ruby-x-x-x.tar.gz** and pressing Enter.
3. From the command line, open the folder created during the decompress process.
4. Type **./configure** and press Enter. This will generate a makefile file and config.h file for Ruby.
5. Compile Ruby by typing **run** and pressing Enter.
6. Type **make install** and press Enter.

WORKING WITH RUBY INTERACTIVELY

There are a couple different ways of working interactively with Ruby. For starters, you can interact with Ruby from the operating system's command prompt, starting a temporary Ruby session to which you can submit individual Ruby statements for processing. Alternatively, you can start irb to set up an ongoing interactive Ruby session. The *irb* is a Ruby shell. The Ruby shell is an interface that facilitates interaction between you and Ruby, allowing you to interact with Ruby and execute as many statements as you want.

Working at the Command Prompt

One way to interact with Ruby is from the operating system command prompt. This option permits you to enter single line Ruby statements and execute them immediately.

 To access the command prompt on Mac OS X, open the Terminal application. To access the command prompt on UNIX or Linux, you must start a new shell session using whatever command console application has been supplied with your operating system. To access the command prompt on Microsoft Windows, click Start > All Programs > Accessories > Command Prompt.

Working with Ruby from the command prompt is relatively straightforward. For starters, you need to type the command **ruby** and press Enter. This starts up a new working session with Ruby, allowing you to enter any valid Ruby statement that you would like for Ruby to execute. Once you have finished typing in your statement, you need to inform Ruby that you are done. This is accomplished by pressing Control+D and subsequently pressing Enter. Once this is done, Ruby will execute the statement that you entered.

To see how all this works, consider the pair of examples shown next. In the example on the left, a Ruby session is started at the Microsoft Windows command prompt and then the statement `puts "Hello World!"` is keyed in after which the end of file character (Control+D) is executed. In response, Ruby displays the text string `Hello World!` on the console window. At this point the Ruby session is closed and the Windows command prompt is redisplayed.

```
Microsoft Windows          Unix\Linux
C:> ruby                   $ ruby
puts "Hello World!"        puts "Hello World!"
^d                         ^d
Hello World!               Hello World!
C:>                        $
```

Similarly, the example on the right shows the execution of the exact same process of this example on a computer running UNIX or Linux.

IRB—Interactive Ruby

To start the irb, type **irb** at the operating system command prompt and press Enter. The irb is available on Windows, Mac OS X, UNIX, and Linux. When you start the irb, an irb shell is opened. This shell provides a number of helpful features. For starters, the shell maintains a history of all commands that are entered during the current working session. This allows you to use the up and down arrows to move backward and forward in this history, retrieving and re-executing previous commands without having to type them again.

HINT You can also access the irb on Microsoft Windows through the fxri application, which is discussed in the next section.

Using the irb you can type in small code snippets, press the Enter key, and get immediate feedback on the results. When started, the irb command prompt displays, as shown here:

```
irb(main):001:0>
```

As you can see, the irb command prompt consists of several parts, each of which is separated by a colon, as outlined here:

- **(main).** The word listed inside the parentheses identifies the current class object (in this case it's the main object).
- **001.** This three-digit number represents a history showing the number of commands that have been entered for the current working session. A value of 001 indicates that that irb is waiting for the first command to be entered.
- **0.** The last number that makes up the irb command prompt represents the current queue depth when working with a class. (You'll learn what this means in Chapter 2, "Interacting with Ruby.")
- **>.** Identifies the end of the command prompt.

To see an example of how to start and interact with the irb, look at the following example.

```
C:\>irb
irb(main):001:0> "Hello World!"
=> "Hello World!"
irb(main):002:0>
```

Here, a new irb session has been started by entering irb at the command prompt. Next, a text string of "Hello World!" has been entered and then the Enter key pressed. In response, Ruby displays a line that reports on the result of the last expression that was executed. Finally, another irb command prompt is displayed, indicating that Ruby is now ready for another command.

HINT
You can stop the current irb session at any time and return to the operating system's command prompt by typing the word exit at the irb command prompt and pressing the Enter key.

Before moving on, let's look at another example of how to work with the irb.

```
irb(main):002:0> puts "Hello World!"
Hello World!
=> nil
irb(main):003:0>
```

This time the puts command, which displays a line of text on the console, is used. The line of text to be displayed is passed to the puts command as an argument. The irb responds by displaying Hello World!. Next, the irb displays a value of nil, indicating the result of the last expression that it processed.

HINT
nil is a Ruby value that indicates a value of nothing. Unlike most Ruby commands, the puts command always returns a value of nil.

As a new Ruby programmer, you are going to want to spend a lot of time working with the irb prompt to experiment with various language elements. You'll learn more about how to work with the irb in Chapter 2.

FXRI—Interactive Ruby Help and Console

Although you can use irb when working on a computer using Microsoft Windows, a second option known as fxri - Interactive Ruby Help and Console is also available to Windows users. *fxri* is a graphical interface that consists of three parts, as shown in Figure 1.9. On the left-hand side of the window is a list of language elements from which you can select to learn about them. The top-right portion of the window displays syntactical information about the selected item.

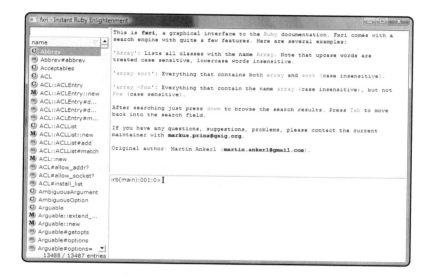

FIGURE 1.9

In addition to providing access to help information, fxri also provides access to the irb.

The lower-right side of the window provides access to the irb command prompt, which you can work with exactly as if you have accessed the irb via the Windows command prompt.

DEVELOPING RUBY SCRIPTS

While working with Ruby, using the command prompt or irb has certain advantages; to really take advantage of the programming language, you must of course learn how to create and execute Ruby scripts. By creating Ruby script files, you can develop programs that can be executed over and over again. Ruby script files have the suffix .rb.

Creating Ruby Scripts on Microsoft Windows

To create and save Ruby script files, you need access to a good text or script editor. If you are working on Microsoft Windows, you can use the Notepad text editor to create your scripts files. Alternatively, you can use the SciTE editor that is installed along with Ruby on Windows. SciTE is a generic code editor, designed to facilitate the development of scripts for a number of different programming languages.

Creating Ruby Scripts on Mac OS X

Mac OS X users can use the TextEdit application to create and save Ruby scripts. Alternatively, Mac users can download and install any of a number of third-party editors like TextMate (http://www.macromates.com) or Komodo IDE (http://www.activestate.com). Komondo IDE also runs on Windows and Linux.

In order to work correctly, Ruby scripts must be saved as plain text files. However, the Mac OS X TextEdit application is much more than a simple text editor, providing a number of advanced word processing features. To use it to save a Ruby script, you can enable the Make Plain Text option located under TextEdit's Format menu before saving your script file. Alternatively, you can change TextEdit's default file settings so that it automatically saves all files as plain text files by clicking on the TextEdit menu, selecting Preferences, and then selecting the Plain text radio button on the Preferences window.

Creating Ruby Scripts on Linux and UNIX

Linux and UNIX programmers can always use the vi editor to create and save Ruby scripts. However, unless you already have experience with vi and have a personal affinity for it, odds are you are going to want to look for an alternative. One alternative is KATE (KDE Advanced Text Editor). KATE is a free text editor available at http://kate-editor.org/.

Using a Cross-Platform Ruby Editor

If you are going to be developing Ruby scripts for execution on more than one type of operating system, then you might want to look into FreeRIDE, which you can download at http://rubyforge.org/projects/freeride/. FreeRIDE, shown in Figure 1.10, is a Ruby-specific code editor that you can download for free. FreeRIDE supports a number of advanced features, including statement color-coding and the ability to execute Ruby scripts without having to leave the editor and switch over to the command prompt. To learn more about FreeRIDE, check out http://freeride.rubyforge.org/wiki/wiki.pl.

Creating Your First Ruby Script

The process involved in creating a Ruby script is really not very different from that of creating a text file or spreadsheet. For starters, you must open your preferred text or code editor and create a new file. You are then ready to enter the code statements that will make up your Ruby script. Ruby scripts may be many hundreds of lines long or they may consist of a single statement.

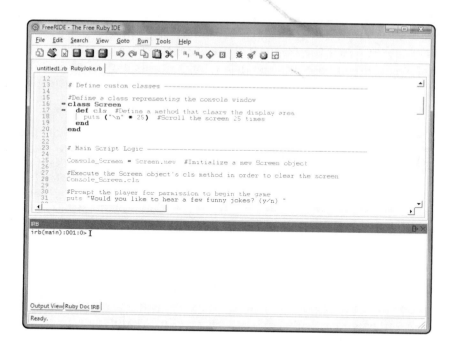

FIGURE 1.10

FreeRIDE is a Ruby script editor that works on Windows, Mac OS X, UNIX, and Linux.

For now, let's keep things simple by creating a Ruby script comprised of the following individual code statement.

```
puts "Hello World!"
```

This statement uses the `puts` command to display a text string. Now, save this file with a filename of HelloWorld.rb.

HINT

.rb is the file extension used to represent a Ruby script.

That's all there is to it. Your new Ruby script is ready for execution as explained in the next section.

HINT

I recommend that you create a folder where you can store all of your Ruby scripts. This will make them easy to find and manage.

Running Your Ruby Script

Once your new Ruby script has been saved, you can run it from the command prompt. So, to run it on Microsoft Windows, click on Start > All Programs > Accessories > Command Prompt. This will open a Windows console, providing access to the command prompt. Once at the command prompt, navigate to the folder where you stored your new Ruby script file and type in the following command.

```
ruby HelloWorld.rb
```

As you can see, the command that you are executing passes the name of the script to be run as an argument to the ruby command. Alternatively, you could execute the Ruby script by specifying its complete name and path. For example, the following command could be used to run the HelloWorld.rb script if it were stored in a folder named Ruby_Scripts located off of the root of the startup drive on a Windows computer.

```
ruby c:\Ruby_Scripts\HelloWorld.rb
```

Note that on Microsoft Windows, the .rb file extension is automatically registered with the operating system when Ruby is installed. As such, you can run your Ruby scripts from the Windows desktop by double-clicking on them and Windows will recognize the file as a Ruby script and run it automatically.

Ruby scripts on Mac OS X, UNIX, and Linux are run from the command prompt. As with Microsoft Windows, you can run them by specifying the ruby command followed by the name and path of the script, as demonstrated here:

```
ruby /Ruby_Scripts/HelloWorld.rb
```

Here a script named HelloWorld.rb, which is stored in the Ruby_Scripts folder, is executed. As an alternative to running your Ruby scripts this way on UNIX or Linux, you can include the following command as the first statement in your Ruby scripts.

```
#!/usr/local/bin/ruby -w
```

On Mac OS X, you'd rewrite this statement as shown here:

```
#!/usr/bin/ruby -w
```

These commands tell the operating system where to look to find Ruby and to use it to execute the contents of the script file. Note that if the default location of Ruby was changed during its installation, you will need to alter these commands accordingly. In addition to adding one of the above commands to your Ruby scripts, you must also mark your Ruby script file as being an executable file. This is accomplished using the chmod command, as demonstrated here:

```
chmod +x HelloWorld.rb
```

Once you have completed both of the preceding steps, you can then execute your Ruby script by navigating to the directory where it is stored and then entering the following command at the command prompt.

```
% ./HelloWorld.rb
```

 HINT   In the preceding statement, the . character was used to instruct the operating system to look in the current working directory for a file named HelloWorld.rb.

 TRICK   If you elect to use FreeRIDE as your code editor when creating your Ruby scripts, you can configure the editor to initiate the execution of your scripts from directly within the editor by clicking on the Edit menu and then selecting Preferences. This opens the FreeRIDE Configuration window. Next, select the Debugger/Run item located in the navigation pane. This displays a list of Debugger/Run Settings. Enable the Run Process in Terminal option located at the bottom of the window and click on the OK button. Once you have completed the above steps, all you have to do to run your script while still within FreeRIDE is click on the Run button located on the FreeRIDE toolbar.

BACK TO THE RUBY JOKE GAME

All right, that's enough background information on Ruby programming for now. It is time to turn your attention back to this chapter's game project, the Ruby Joke game. As you follow the steps required to create and execute this game, try not to get too hung up on the program code that you'll be asked to enter. For now, you should focus on the overall steps involved in creating and executing Ruby scripts and wait to learn the ins and outs of Ruby programming in later chapters.

Designing the Game

The development of the Ruby Joke game will follow a specific series of steps as outlined next. As you advance from step to step, be sure to follow along carefully. Do not skip any steps and make sure that you precisely follow the instructions provided in each step. This applies doubly when keying in the script's code statements. This will help you to avoid errors and will make things go a lot smoother.

1. Open your text or script editor and create a new file.
2. Add comment statements to the beginning of the script file to document the script and its purpose.
3. Define classes used in the script to instantiate objects.
4. Instantiate new objects used in the script.

5. Add the code statements that prompt the player for permission to continue.
6. Add the code statements that outline the script's high-level conditional logic.
7. Call upon the code statements that clear the display area.
8. Add the code statements that tell the game's first joke.
9. Add the code statements that tell the rest of the game's jokes.
10. Add the code statements that thank the player for playing.

Each of these steps is covered in detail in the sections that follow.

Step 1: Creating a New Ruby File

The first step in creating the Ruby Joke game is to open your text or code editor and create a new file. Once created, save your file with a name of RubyJoke.rb. If you have created a folder to store all of your Ruby scripts, make sure that you store your new game script there.

Step 2: Documenting the Script and Its Purpose

Okay, now you are ready to begin adding the code statements that will make up your script file. Let's begin by adding the following statements to the beginning of the script file. These statements are comments, which provide a little information about the script and its purpose.

```
#- - - - - - - - - - - - - - - - - - - - - - - - - - - - - - - - - - - - - - - - - - - - - - - -
#
# Script Name: RubyJoke.rb
# Version: 1.0
# Author: Jerry Lee Ford, Jr.
# Date: October 2007
#
# Description: This Ruby script tells a series of 5 humorous jokes
#
#- - - - - - - - - - - - - - - - - - - - - - - - - - - - - - - - - - - - - - - - - - - - - - - -
```

 A *comment* is a line of text that is preceded by the # character. Comments are ignored by the Ruby interpreter and have no effect on the execution of the script. Adding comments to Ruby scripts helps to make them easier to understand and maintain and is considered a good programming practice. As such, you can expect to find comments included in all of this book's game scripts.

Step 3: Defining a Class Representing the Computer Screen

Now that your script file's opening documentation has been added, it's time to get busy writing the code statements that will make your new script do something. Begin by adding the following statements to the end of the script file.

```
class Screen
  def cls  #Define a method that clears the display area
    puts ("\n" * 25)  #Scroll the screen 25 times
  end
end
```

Without getting into things too deeply at this point in the book, what these statements do is define a class named Screen that represents the console window in which the game will execute. Within the class definition, a method name cls is defined that when executed will write 25 blank links to the console window, thus clearing the display to make it ready to display new text.

Step 4: Instantiating New Objects

The Screen class defined in the preceding step is only a template. Using it, the first statement shown next creates or *instantiates* a new object based on that class. The new object is assigned a name of Console_Screen. The second statement shown next executes the Screen class's cls method to clear out the display area.

```
Console_Screen = Screen.new
Console_Screen.cls
```

Add these two statements to the end of your script file.

Remember, you have not learned anything about Ruby syntax or how to formulate Ruby statements yet, so do not be discouraged if the programming statements you are typing seem a little confusing. This understanding will be developed in later chapters. For now, focus your attention on the overall process you are going through to create your first Ruby script game.

Step 5: Prompting the Player for Permission to Continue

Before telling the game's first joke, the game prompts the player for permission to continue. This is accomplished by adding the following statements to the end of the script file.

```
puts "Would you like to hear a few funny jokes? (y/n) "
answer = STDIN.gets
answer.chop!
```

The first statement displays a text message asking for permission to tell some jokes, instructing the player to respond by typing either a y or n, representing answers of yes or no. The next two statements collect and format the input provided by the player.

Step 6: Outlining the Script's High-Level Conditional Logic

Once the player's input has been collected, it must be analyzed. If the player entered a value of n, the game should invite the player to return and play again later. If, on the other hand, the player enters a value of y, the game should start telling its jokes. In order to set up a high-level structure for managing this overall process, add the following statements to the end of your script file.

```
if answer == "n"

else

end
```

In the next several steps, you will be asked to return and key in script statements into this block of code.

Step 7: Clearing the Screen

The next two statements are responsible for inviting the player to return and play the game again another time. They should be executed in the event the player entered a value of n when prompted to play the game. Therefore, you will need to embed these statements into the preceding code block, between the first and second statements.

```
Console_Screen.cls
puts "Sorry to hear that. Please return and play again soon."
```

When executed, these two statements will call on the Screen class's cls method to clear the screen and then display a text message, encouraging the player to return and play again another time.

Step 8: Telling the First Joke

Now it is time to tell the game's first joke. This is accomplished by embedding the following statements between the second and third statements in the previously defined code block (e.g., after the else keyword and before the end keyword).

```
Console_Screen.cls

puts "What is black and white and red all over? (Press Enter) "
pause = STDIN.gets

puts "A messy penguin eating cherry pie! (Press Enter) "
pause = STDIN.gets
```

These statements are responsible for clearing the display area, and then displaying the first joke's opening line. The script is then paused to give the player the chance to read the setup line. The script resumes execution as soon as the player presses the Enter key, at which time the joke's punch line is displayed, and the script is halted again to give the player the chance to read it. Game play resumes again when the player presses the Enter key.

Step 9: Telling the Remaining Jokes

Now it is time to tell the rest of the script's jokes. This is accomplished by embedding the following statement between the second and third statements in the previously defined code block, just after the statements that are responsible for telling the game's first joke.

```
Console_Screen.cls

puts "What is black and white and red all over? (Press Enter) "
pause = STDIN.gets

puts "A sunburned penguin! (Press Enter) "
pause = STDIN.gets

Console_Screen.cls

puts "What is black and white and red all over? (Press Enter) "
pause = STDIN.gets

puts "An embarrassed Dalmatian puppy!! (Press Enter) "
pause = STDIN.gets

Console_Screen.cls

puts "What is black and white and red all over? (Press Enter) "
pause = STDIN.gets
puts "A zebra with a scratched knee! (Press Enter) "
pause = STDIN.gets

Console_Screen.cls

puts "What is black and white and red all over? (Press Enter) "
pause = STDIN.gets
```

```
puts "A skunk with diaper rash! (Press Enter) "
pause = STDIN.gets
```

In total, there are four additional jokes included in this group of code statements. If you look closely, you will see that the statements that tell each joke are nearly identical to the statements that tell the game's first joke, the only difference being that the text strings representing each joke's text have been rewritten to tell a different joke.

Step 10: Thanking the Player

You are almost done. All that remains at this point is to clear the screen one last time and thank the player for taking the time to play the game. This is accomplished by adding the following statement to the very end of the script file.

```
Console_Screen.cls
```

```
puts "Thanks for playing the Ruby Joke game!"
```

Running Your New Ruby Script Game

Well, that's it. Go ahead and save your Ruby script. At this point you have everything you need to build the Ruby Joke game. Because the development of this game involved numerous steps, there is plenty of opportunity to get confused and make mistakes when typing in the required script statements. To help clarify things a bit and to help ensure that your copy of the Ruby script is properly written, I've provided a copy of the fully assembled game below. In addition, I have also added a number of additional comment statements to the script file for the purpose of further documenting everything that is going on at different points within the script file.

```
#----------------------------------------------------------------
#
# Script Name: RubyJoke.rb
# Version: 1.0
# Author: Jerry Lee Ford, Jr.
# Date: October 2007
#
# Description: This Ruby script tells a series of 5 humorous jokes
#
#----------------------------------------------------------------


# Define custom classes -----------------------------------------
```

```ruby
class Screen
  def cls
    puts ("\n" * 25)
  end
end


# Main Script Logic -------------------------------------------------------

Console_Screen = Screen.new  #Initialize a new Screen object

#Execute the Screen object's cls method to clear the screen
Console_Screen.cls

#Prompt the player for permission to begin the game
puts "Would you like to hear a few funny jokes? (y/n) "

#Collect the player's response
answer = STDIN.gets

#Remove any extra characters appended to the string
answer.chop!

#Analyze the player's response
if answer == "n"   #See if the player elected not to play

  Console_Screen.cls  #Clear the display area

  #Invite the player to return and play again
  puts "Sorry to hear that. Please return and play again soon."

else

  Console_Screen.cls  #Clear the display area

  #Display the beginning of the first joke
  puts "What is black and white and red all over? (Press Enter) "
```

```
pause = STDIN.gets  #Force the player to press Enter to continue

#Display the punch line
puts "A messy penguin eating cherry pie! (Press Enter) "


pause = STDIN.gets  #Force the player to press Enter to continue


Console_Screen.cls  #Clear the display area

#Display the beginning of the second joke
puts "What is black and white and red all over? (Press Enter) "

pause = STDIN.gets  #Force the player to press Enter to continue

#Display the punch line
puts "A sunburned penguin! (Press Enter) "


pause = STDIN.gets  #Force the player to press Enter to continue


Console_Screen.cls  #Clear the display area

#Display the beginning of the third joke
puts "What is black and white and red all over? (Press Enter) "

pause = STDIN.gets  #Force the player to press Enter to continue

#Display the punch line
puts "An embarrassed Dalmatian puppy! (Press Enter) "


pause = STDIN.gets  #Force the player to press Enter to continue


Console_Screen.cls  #Clear the display area
```

```ruby
#Display the beginning of the fourth joke
puts "What is black and white and red all over? (Press Enter) "

pause = STDIN.gets  #Force the player to press Enter to continue

#Display the punch line
puts "A zebra with a scratched knee! (Press Enter) "


pause = STDIN.gets  #Force the player to press Enter to continue


Console_Screen.cls  #Clear the display area

#Display the beginning of the fifth joke
puts "What is black and white and red all over? (Press Enter) "

pause = STDIN.gets  #Force the player to press Enter to continue

#Display the punch line
puts "A skunk with diaper rash! (Press Enter) "


pause = STDIN.gets  #Force the player to press Enter to continue


Console_Screen.cls  #Clear the display area

puts "Thanks for playing the Ruby Joke game!"
```

```ruby
end
```

Assuming that you have finished keying in and saving your copy of the Ruby Joke game, all that remains is to run it and see what happens. To do so, access the operating system command prompt and navigate to the folder where you saved your Ruby script. Now, enter the following command and press the Enter key.

```
ruby RubyJoke.rb
```

Assuming that you followed along carefully and did not make any typing mistakes, the game should run exactly as described at the beginning of the chapter. If, however, you made a typo somewhere along the way, you'll get an error message when you try to run your script. If this happens, review the error message carefully and see if it provides you with any clue as to what when wrong. If you are unable to figure out what went wrong based on the text of the error message, go back and review your script file and look for mistyped or missing scripts statements. Once you think that you have identified and corrected all your typing errors, try running your Ruby script again.

Summary

In this chapter, you learned a little about Ruby's history and its influences. You also learned about many of the things that make Ruby a popular scripting language, including its object-oriented designed and support for cross-platform development on operating systems like Microsoft Windows, Mac OS X, UNIX, and Linux. This chapter provided you with instruction for installing Ruby on different operating systems and explained how to verify Ruby's operation. In addition, you learned how to create and execute Ruby scripts and created your first Ruby script, the Ruby Joke game.

Now, before you move on to Chapter 2, I suggest you take a few extra minutes to see if you can improve the Ruby Joke game by implementing the following list of challenges.

CHALLENGES

1. The jokes told by the Ruby Joke game are admittedly somewhat bland. Consider spicing things up a bit by replacing the game's joke with some of your own to personalize the game and make it suit your own sense of humor.

2. As currently written, the Ruby Joke game does not take long for the player to complete, telling only five jokes. See if you can add a few jokes to make things last a little longer. You should be able to do this by copying and pasting and then modifying the code statements that tell one of the game's other jokes.

INTERACTING WITH RUBY

uby is a robust programming language that programmers all over the world use to perform a whole range of tasks. Learning Ruby takes time. You are off to a good start by reading this book. One of the best ways to learn more about Ruby is to experiment with the language using the irb, also referred to as interactive Ruby. Using irb, you can formulate Ruby statements and expressions and execute them to see what happens. In doing so, you will gain insight into the operation of Ruby keywords, operators, commands, and object-oriented programming methodology. This chapter will provide you with an overview of the irb. In addition, you will learn how to access Ruby's documentation. On top of all this, you will learn how to create a new Ruby script, the Ruby Tall Tale game.

Specifically, you will learn how to:

- Start an irb session
- Use the irb to execute single and multi-line Ruby statements
- Access Ruby documentation

PROJECT PREVIEW: THE RUBY TALL TALE GAME

In this chapter, you will learn how to create your second computer game, the Ruby Tall Tale game. This Ruby script demonstrates how to collect and process player input through the development of an interactive mad-lib-style storytelling game. Player input is collected without telling the player in advance the context in which the input will be used. Once collected, the player's input is then plugged into the story plot. As a result, the story that is ultimately told has unpredictable elements that will result in different variations every time the game is played.

The game begins, as shown in Figure 2.1, by prompting the player for permission to begin the game.

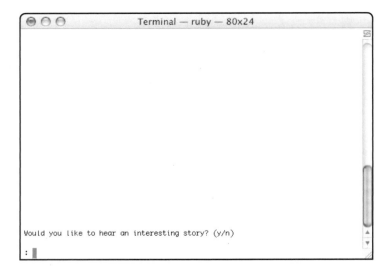

FIGURE 2.1

An example of the Ruby Tall Tale game running on Mac OS X.

If the player decides not to play, the game displays the window shown in Figure 2.2, encouraging the player to consider returning to play another time.

If, on the other hand, the player decides to play the game, the window shown in Figure 2.3 displays, prompting the player to answer the first of five questions.

Once all questions have been answered, the game plugs the input provided by the player into the story's plot and then begins to tell its story, a paragraph at a time. Figure 2.4 shows an example of how the story's first paragraph might read.

The second paragraph of the story introduces the story's antagonist, as shown in Figure 2.5.

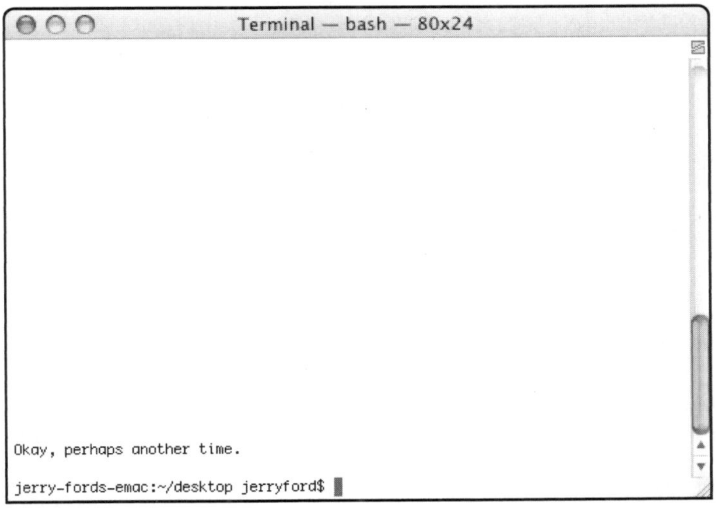

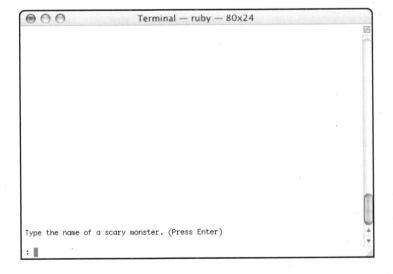

```
  ○ ○ ○              Terminal — bash — 80x24


















 Okay, perhaps another time.

 jerry-fords-emac:~/desktop jerryford$ ▌
```

FIGURE 2.2

The game politely encourages the player to play again some other time.

```
  ○ ○ ○              Terminal — ruby — 80x24


















 Type the name of a scary monster. (Press Enter)

 : ▌
```

FIGURE 2.3

The player is asked to answer five questions without being told the context in which the answers will be used.

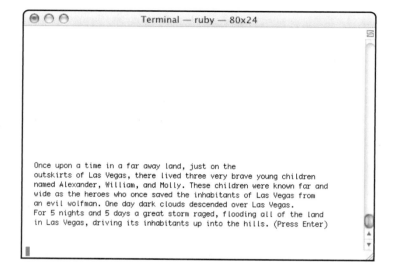

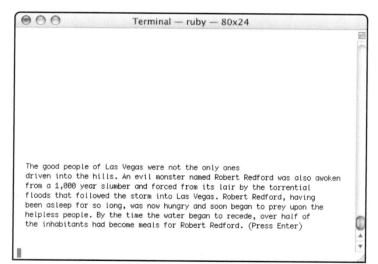

In the third paragraph, the story's heroes arrive on the scene just in time to save the day, as shown in Figure 2.6.

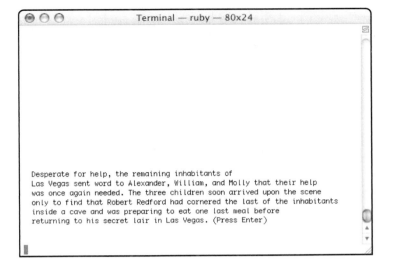

FIGURE 2.6

The third paragraph draws a picture of desperation and identifies the challenge facing its heroes.

Finally, the fourth paragraph displays, bringing the story to a happy ending, as shown in Figure 2.7.

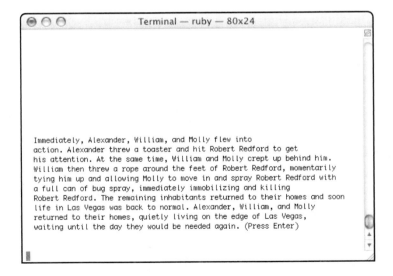

FIGURE 2.7

In the end the people are saved and the story's heroes quietly retire into obscurity.

With the story now told, the game pauses to thank the player for taking the time to play before terminating, as shown in Figure 2.8.

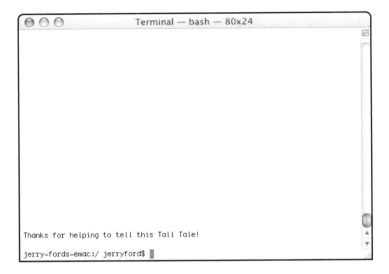

FIGURE 2.8

The game ends after thanking the player.

Inside terminal:
```
Thanks for helping to tell this Tall Tale!

jerry-fords-emac:/ jerryford$
```
(Terminal — bash — 80x24)

GETTING TO KNOW THE IRB

Whether you are trying to learn auto mechanics or a new programming language, sometimes the best way to get started is to look under the hood and just start tinkering. In programming terms, this means formulating and testing the execution of different programming statements to see what happens. While auto mechanics may find it difficult to find a fully operational automobile on which they can tinker at will, Ruby programmers do not have this problem. Every Ruby installation comes with a wonderfully convenient and powerful tool called the irb, which stands for interactive Ruby.

The irb provides Ruby programmers with command line access to a Ruby parser, allowing programmers to write and test different parts of a computer program on the fly. Many programmers use irb to experiment with and get a particular piece of code working like they want it to before adding that code to a Ruby script. New Ruby programmers tend to spend many hours working at the irb command prompt, learning Ruby programming basics.

Starting an irb Session

As you have already seen, the irb is started from the operating system command prompt by simply entering irb and pressing Enter, as demonstrated here:

```
C:\>irb
irb(main):001:0>
```

Here, a new irb session has been started on a computer running Microsoft Windows. When started this way, the irb displays a command prompt and waits for you to enter commands.

The irb command is actually quite flexible, allowing you to start it by specifying a number of different options using the syntax shown here:

`irb [Options] [Script] [Arguments]`

Options is a placeholder representing any number of optional argument supports by the irb, as outlined in Table 2.1. *Script* is the complete name and path of a Ruby script that you want the irb to run when it starts. *Arguments* is a list of one or more arguments that may need to be passed to the script in order for it to execute.

You have the option of passing the irb a number of different arguments when starting it, as well as the name of any Ruby script that you might want it to run, along with any argument that may need to be passed to the script.

TABLE 2.1 irb COMMAND LINE OPTIONS	
Option	**Description**
-d	Sets $DEBUG equal to true
-f	Prevents the processing of ~/.irbrc
-I path	Sets the $LOAD_PATH directory
-m	Enables Math mode
-r *module*	Loads module/s
-v	Displays irb version information
--back-trace-limit *x*	Displays backtrace data using the last x number of entries
-inf-ruby-mode	Configures the irb to run under Emacs
--inspect	Formats output using Object#inspect
--irb_debug *n*	Specifies the debug level
--noinspect	Disables the default --inspect option
--noprompt	Suppresses the display of the irb command prompt
--noreadline	Disables execution of the readline module
--prompt *type*	Configures the irb command prompt to one of the following: classic, null, xmp, simple, default, inf-ruby
--readline	Loads the readline module
--simple-prompt	Sets the irb command prompt to simple
--tracer	Configures the irb to display trace information
--version	Displays irb version information

To start the irb using the options specified in Table 2.1, let's look at a couple of examples. The first example, shown next, executes the -v option to display irb version information.

```
C:\>irb -v
irb 0.9.5(05/04/13)
```

Similarly, the following example demonstrates how to start the irb and specify the type of prompt the irb should display.

```
C:\>irb --prompt simple
>>
```

Working with Multiple irb Sessions

Each irb session exists within its own context. If you open up two separate irb sessions, each exists completely independently of the other. Each separate irb session maintains its own separate memory space. Therefore any classes, methods, or variables that you define in one irb session will not be visible or accessible in another session.

Additional irb sessions can be started by opening another terminal or command-line session. A new irb session can also be started from within another irb session by typing the irb command. Doing so begins a new irb session, with an entirely new context as demonstrated here:

```
irb(main):001:0> irb
irb#1(main):001:0> irb
```

Here, a new irb session has been started as designated by the presence of irb#1 at the beginning of the command prompt. Any objects created within this new context are available only within the context of the new session. Typing in exit will close the new (child) irb session and restore the parent irb session as demonstrated here:

```
irb#1(main):001:0> exit
=> #<IRB::Irb: @context=#<IRB::Context:0x36c6c60>, @signal_status=:IN_EVAL,
@scanner=#<RubyLex:0x36c6904>>
irb(main):002:0>
```

When restored, any objects previously defined within the parent session will still be accessible. However, any objects that were defined within the child session are not accessible.

HINT   In addition to closing an irb session using the exit command, you may also enter quit, irb_exit, or irb_quit to close an irb session. You can also close an irb session by pressing Ctrl+D.

ACCESSING THE irb ONLINE

If you do not have immediate access to the irb, perhaps because you are working from a computer where Ruby has not been installed, but you feel a pressing need to try to experiment with Ruby a bit, all is not lost. You can go online to http://tryruby.hobix.com/ and access a special web-enabled version of the irb made available on the Try Ruby! web page. Here you will be greeted by your friendly irb command prompt just waiting to process your commands. For example, if you check out Figure 2.9, you will see an example of the online irb session in action.

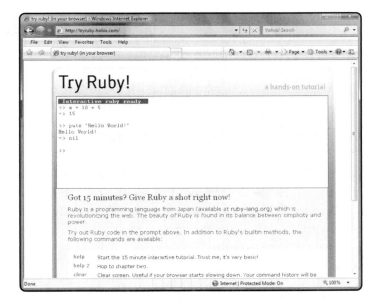

FIGURE 2.9

The Try Ruby! web page provides you with access to the irb no matter where you are.

As Figure 2.9 demonstrates, you can enter Ruby expressions and statements and the online irb will process them in exactly the same way that they are processed when executed by the irb running on your computer.

WORKING WITH THE irb

Using the irb, you can experiment with Ruby and learn how things work. Each time you start up a new Ruby session, the irb keeps track of any classes, objects, or variables that you define. Therefore, as you execute new script statements, you can create an environment very much like that of scripts in which you can refer to and interact with previously defined objects. Access to previously defined classes, objects, and variables is maintained for as long as the current irb session remains active.

In the sections that follow, you will learn the fundamentals of how to work with the irb.

Executing Ruby Statements

Let's begin by executing a print statement, as demonstrated in the following example.

```
irb(main):002:0> print "Welcome to Ruby"
Welcome to Ruby=> nil
irb(main):003:0>
```

Here, the print command, which displays a line of text to the screen, has been executed. The test string to be displayed is passed to the print command as an argument wrapped inside matching double quotation marks. The next line shows the result returned by the print command when executed. *nil* is a value that represents Ruby's interpretation of nothing. Unlike the print command, most commands that you execute at the irb formulate expressions that return a specific result.

An *expression* is a series of language keywords, operators, and variables that, when processed, return a result.

When executed within a Ruby script, the print command displays a text string but does not advance the cursor to the next line. As a result, back-to-back print commands will display the two text strings as if they were a single contiguous string. Most of the time, you are probably going to want to display individual text strings on separate lines. You can do this using the puts command, as demonstrated here:

```
irb(main):001:0> puts "Welcome to Ruby"
Welcome to Ruby
=> nil
irb(main):002:0>
```

As you can see, the puts command displays a line of text passed to it as an argument and then returns a nil value after execution. This next example shows an expression that returns a result.

```
irb(main):002:0> puts 5 + 1
6
    => nil
```

Here, the puts command passes an expression of 5 + 1. The irb processes the expression, adding the numbers together. The result is then passed to the puts command as an argument. The puts command displays the resulting value, after which a value of nil is displayed.

Following Ruby's Syntactical Rules

As you learn to work with different Ruby commands, keywords, and operators, you will have to learn to follow specific syntactical rules. Failure to follow these rules when formulating script statements will result in errors that prevent your scripts from executing. Look at the following.

```
irb(main):005:0* put "Welcome to Ruby"
NoMethodError: undefined method `put' for main:Object
        from (irb):5
irb(main):006:0>
```

Here, an error was made when keying in the puts command. If you look carefully, you will see that the command was misspelled. In response, an error message was generated that reports an undefined method named put. As another example of a syntactical error, look at the following.

```
irb(main):006:0> print 5 + "5"
TypeError: String can't be coerced into Fixnum
        from (irb):6:in `+'
        from (irb):6
irb(main):007:0>
```

Here, the print command is passed the results of an expression of 5 + "5". However, there is an error in the expression. Specifically, although strings can be added to strings, and numbers can be added to numbers, a numeric value cannot be added to a string value.

As you work your way through this book, you will see hundreds of examples of Ruby statements that demonstrate the proper way to formulate script statements. When you are not sure about the specific rules required to work with a specific Ruby method, it is best to check Ruby's documentation as described later in this chapter.

Executing Multiline Statements

The irb includes a Ruby parser. As a result, it can tell when the statements you enter are complete. If you press the Enter key without keying in a complete statement, the irb displays a modified version of the command prompt that includes an asterisk character. This character serves as a visual indicator that the irb is waiting on you to finish keying in the current statement, as demonstrated here:

```
irb(main):003:0> 5 - 1 +
irb(main):004:0*
```

Once a complete statement has been entered, irb processes the statement and redisplays its regular command prompt, as demonstrated here:

```
irb(main):001:0> 5 - 1 +
irb(main):002:0* 4
=> 8
irb(main):003:0>
```

Using irb to Test Ruby Scripts

Another handy use for the irb is to run and experiment with Ruby scripts or portions of Ruby scripts that you have already written. For example, suppose you had downloaded a Ruby script from the Internet that contained a set of code statements that performed a particular task and you were interested in understanding how they worked. You could quickly do this by copying and pasting the code statements into their own script and then executing them using the load command, as demonstrated here:

```
load 'c:\Ruby_Scripts\RubyJoke.rb'
```

As you can see, all you have to do is pass a string containing the complete path and filename of the Ruby script that you want to run and the irb will run the script, displaying the value returned by each statement as it executes, allowing you to develop a better understanding of how things work.

If copying and pasting the script statements into a new script file is too much work, you can just copy and paste the script statements that you want executed directly to the irb command prompt and the irb will immediately execute them. For example, suppose you wanted to test the execution of the Screen class that was created as part of the Ruby Joke script back in Chapter 1, "Ruby Basics." One way of doing so is to copy and paste the following statements to the irb command prompt.

```
class Screen
  def cls  #Define a method that clears the display area
    puts ("\n" * 25)  #Scroll the screen 25 times
  end
end
```

In response, the irb will load the class definition into the current irb session and return a nil value, as shown here:

```
irb(main):001:0> class Screen
irb(main):002:1>   def cls  #Define a method that clears the display area
irb(main):003:2>     puts ("\n" * 25)  #Scroll the screen 25 times
```

```
irb(main):004:2>    end
irb(main):005:1> end
=> nil
irb(main):006:0>
```

Because a class is just a definition or template, it does not do anything by itself. Its statements only execute when called upon to create a new Screen object. This is accomplished using the syntax outlined here:

```
variableName = ClassName.new
```

variableName is a placeholder representing any valid variable name you want to use to refer to the object being instantiated. *ClassName* represents the name of the class being used as the basis for instantiating the object, and new is the name of the method that, when executed, creates the actual object.

Instantiation is a term that describes the process used to create a new object. The object that is created is based on a predefined class definition. The object inherits all of the features of the class on which it is based. Therefore, if you were to create two different objects based on the same class definition, those two objects would be identical.

At this point, you can tell the irb to run the cls method defined inside the Screen class, as demonstrated here.

```
Console_Screen = Screen.new
```

A *method* is a collection of statements defined within a class that can be used to interact with and control the operation of objects created based on that class.

Once instantiated, you can interact with the new object using the syntax demonstrated here:

```
Console_Screen.cls
```

Here, the Screen class's cls method has been called upon to execute. When executed, this method writes 25 blank lines to the console screen, effectively clearing it and readying it for the display of new text.

USING THE IRB TO PERFORM MATHEMATICAL CALCULATIONS

As you have already seen, Ruby is proficient in working with numbers. As such, you can use the irb to experiment with various calculations to determine how Ruby will handle them.

You can also use the irb as a quick command-line calculator. Table 2.2 outlines the various mathematical operators that Ruby provides for performing basic calculations.

 HINT Actually, each of the operators listed in Table 2.2 is implemented in Ruby as a method, reflecting Ruby's dedication to the principles of object-oriented programming.

TABLE 2.2	RUBY MATH OPERATORS	
Operator	**Name**	**Description**
+	Addition	Adds two numbers together
–	Subtraction	Subtracts one number from another
*	Multiplication	Multiplies two numbers together
/	Division	Divides one number from another number
**	Exponentiation	Multiplies a number by itself a specified number of times
%	Modulus	Returns the remainder portion of a division operation

Using the irb as a Calculator

Using the math operators listed in Table 2.2, you can formulate mathematical expressions of any level of complexity when writing Ruby statements. For example, the following statements demonstrate how to add two numbers.

```
irb(main):001:0> 1 + 1
=> 5
irb(main):002:0>
```

Here, the irb has been used to add 1 + 1. After evaluating and executing this expression, the irb displays the result and then redisplays its command prompt. The following set of examples demonstrates how to work with each of the remaining operators shown in Table 2.2.

```
irb(main):002:0> 10 - 5
=> 5
irb(main):003:0> 3 + 2
=> 5
irb(main):005:0> 3 * 2
=> 6
irb(main):006:0> 8 / 2
=> 4
```

```
irb(main):007:0> 2**3
8
irb(main):008:0> 7 % 2
=> 1
irb(main):009:0>
```

In addition to the rather simple examples shown above, you can create mathematical expressions of great complexity, as demonstrated here:

```
irb(main):010:0* 7 * 4 / 3 - 4 % 3 + 8
=> 16
irb(main):011:0>
```

Accessing Methods Stored in the Math Module

In addition to the standard set of mathematical operator methods previously discussed, Ruby also provides you with access to a collection of mathematical methods stored in its Math module. A *module* is a structure used to store collections of classes, methods, and constants. The Math module includes a number of methods that support advanced mathematical operations. For example, the Math module includes a sqrt method that you can call upon to determine the square root of any number, as demonstrated here:

```
irb(main):005:0> Math.sqrt(16)
=> 4.0
```

Here, the square root of 16 has been calculated.

 TRAP Make sure you spell method names correctly; otherwise, you'll run into errors. For example, in order to call upon Math module methods, you must spell Math with an initial capital. If, instead, you spell the word Math in all lowercase letters (math), you will get the following error.

```
irb(main):006:0> math.sqrt(16)
NameError: undefined local variable or method `math' for main:Object
        from (irb):6
```

Ruby's Math module provides you with access to numerous mathematical methods. Examples of these methods include acos(), which computes the arc cosine for a specified value, and cos(), which computes the cosine for a specified value. To learn more about the methods contained in Ruby's Math module, visit http://www.ruby-doc.org/core/classes/Math.html.

Operator Precedence

Like all programming languages, arithmetic operations are performed in a predetermined order or precedence in Ruby scripts. Specifically, exponentiation is performed first followed by multiplication, division, and modulus division. Finally, addition and subtraction are performed. Operators with the same level or precedence are performed from left to right.

The best way to understand how Ruby's predefined order of precedence works is to see how it is applied in an example.

```
10 + 5 * 2 - 8 / 4 + 5**2
```

First, exponentiation is performed, so the value of 5**2 is calculated, resulting in a value of 25. Next, multiplication and division are performed from left to right, so 5 is multiplied by 2 resulting in a value of 10. Next 8 is divided by 4 resulting in a value of 2. At this point the expression logically could be rewritten as shown here:

```
10 + 10 - 2 + 25.
```

Next, addition and division are performed from left to right. Therefore, 10 is added to 10, resulting in a value of 20. Next, 2 is subtracted from 20 yielding a value of 18 to which a value of 25 is added. The end result is 43, as demonstrated here.

```
irb(main):001:0> 10 + 5 * 2 - 8 / 4 + 5**2
=> 43
irb(main):002:0>
```

Overriding Operator Precedence

Just like you learned in high school geometry and algebra, parentheses can be used to override Ruby's default order of precedence. Specifically, Ruby evaluates mathematical expressions by first evaluating anything inside parentheses and then following the order of precedence to process the expression.

First I will show you an example without parentheses and then I will show you the same example using parentheses.

```
irb(main):001:0> 4 + 7 * 3 - 7 / 2 + 5 ** 2
=> 47
```

Here, an expression has been processed by the irb that results in a value of 47. This expression is processed as follows. First, exponentiation occurs, so 5 is multiplied times itself, yielding a value of 25. At this point the expression looks like the example shown here:

```
4 + 7 * 3 - 7 / 2 + 25
```

Next, multiplication and division are performed from left to right. Therefore, 3 is multiplied by 7, yielding a value of 21, and 7 is divided by 2, yielding a value of 3. At this point the expression looks like the example shown here:

```
4 + 21 - 3 + 25
```

 HINT   By default, any time two integer numbers are divided in Ruby, the value that is returned is always an integer. As such, any remainder is automatically dropped. You will learn how to instruct Ruby to return a floating-point result in the next section.

All that remains to finish processing the expression is to perform all remaining addition and subtraction operations, which result in a final value of 47. Now, let's use parentheses to alter the way in which the expression is evaluated, as demonstrated here:

```
irb(main):002:0> (4 + 7) * 3 - 7 / (2 + 5) ** 2
=> 33
```

Here, an expression has been processed by the irb that results in a value of 33. This expression is processed as follows. First, anything inside parentheses is processed. At this point, the expression looks like this:

```
11 * 3 - 7 / 7 ** 2
```

Next, exponentiation occurs, so 7 is multiplied 2 times resulting in the following logical expression.

```
11* 3 - 7 / 49
```

Multiplication and division are then performed, so 11 is multiplied by 3 and 7 is divided by 49, resulting the following logical expression.

```
33 - 0
```

 NOTE   Dividing 7 by 49 results in a value of .142857142857143. However, since Ruby always returns an integer value when dividing two integers, a value of 0 is returned.

Finally, 33 is added to 0, resulting in a final result of 33.

```
33
```

Integers Versus Floating-point Numbers

Any time you work with whole numbers, Ruby treats the numbers in the resulting expression as integers. In Ruby, any operation performed using integers results in an integer value. In the preceding division example, the integers were carefully chosen to ensure that the precision of the results was not an issue. However, the following example provides a good demonstration of the effects of division using integers.

```
irb(main):001:0> 10 / 4
=> 2
irb(main):002:0>
```

As you can see, instead of returning a value of 2.5, a value of 2 was returned. The missing .5 is just thrown way. This is just how Ruby deals with integers. If you require a greater level of mathematical precision, you will need to use floating-point numbers (numbers that including a decimal point), as demonstrated here:

```
irb(main):003:0> 10.0 / 4.0
=> 2.5
irb(main):004:0>
```

Now that floating-point numbers have been specified, a value of 2.5 has been returned. You do not have to make both numbers floating-point numbers to ensure that Ruby performs floating-point division. All that Ruby requires is that you include a decimal point in one of the numbers being calculated, as demonstrated here:

```
irb(main):007:0> 10.0 / 4
=> 2.5
irb(main):008:0>
```

ACCESSING RUBY DOCUMENTATION

Thousands of methods are supported along with Ruby when Ruby is installed on your computer. There are too many of these methods to consider trying to cover them all in this book or any other book for that matter. Instead, easy access to documentation for most of these methods is provided via a system referred to as RDoc.

You can access the contents of RDoc online from a number of websites, most notably at http://www.ruby-doc.org/, as shown in Figure 2.10.

FIGURE 2.10

Accessing ruby documentation at www.ruby-doc.org.

You can also access Ruby documentation locally on your computer using ri. *ri* is a command line Ruby documentation viewer. For example, to use ri to display information about a Ruby class, all you have to do is access the operating system's command prompt and type ri followed by the name of the class, as demonstrated in Figure 2.11.

FIGURE 2.11

Using ri to view documentation about Ruby's Numeric class.

 TRAP Watch out for case sensitivity when working with ri. For example, when using ri to look up documentation for a class, you must spell the name of the class with an opening capital letter. Specifying ri Numeric returns documentation for the Numeric class. However, specifying ri numeric returns an error.

As you can see, the documentation presented typically includes a description and a list of other related language components. In the case of Ruby classes, this may include any number of methods. You can also use ri to retrieve documentation for Ruby methods. For example, you might try typing `ri Numeric.round` to display information about the `Numeric` class's `round` method, as demonstrated in Figure 2.12.

FIGURE 2.12

Using ri to view documentation about the `Numeric` class's round method.

Sometimes you can omit the inclusion of the owning class when displaying a method. As long as the method has only one owning class, you can view its documentation by simply typing `ri` followed by the name of the method. However, if the method being looked up is associated with more than one class, you will see a message similar to the following.

```
C:\>ri round
More than one method matched your request. You can refine
your search by asking for information on one of:

    Float#round, Integer#round, Numeric#round, REXML::Functions::round,
    Fox::FXGLViewer#getBackgroundColor,
    Fox::FXGLViewer#setBackgroundColor,
    Fox::FXTableItem#drawBackground,
    Windows::Window#GetForegroundWindow
```

As this example demonstrates, the `round` method is associated with many classes, including `Float`, `Integer`, `Numeric`, and `REXML`.

ri is a convenient and powerful tool. To learn more about it, type `ri` at the operating system command prompt and press Enter, as demonstrated in Figure 2.13.

```
Command Prompt - ri
ri v1.0.1 - 20041108

Usage:

  ri.bat [options] [names...]

Display information on Ruby classes, modules, and methods.
Give the names of classes or methods to see their documentation.
Partial names may be given: if the names match more than
one entity, a list will be shown, otherwise details on
that entity will be displayed.

Nested classes and modules can be specified using the normal
Name::Name notation, and instance methods can be distinguished
from class methods using "." (or "#") instead of "::".

For example:

  ri  File
  ri  File.new
  ri  F.n
  ri  zip

--- More ---
```

FIGURE 2.13

Viewing help
documentation
for ri.

BACK TO THE RUBY TALL TALE GAME

All right, it is time to turn your attention from the irb and RDoc and refocus on the development of the Ruby Tall Tale game. In this game, the player is prompted to answer a series of questions without being told how the answers that are given will be used. Once the player has answered every question, the game incorporates the player's input into the plot of the game's story, which is then displayed a paragraph at a time.

 HINT Don't worry if you do not yet understand the exact meaning of each of the script statements used to develop the Ruby Tall Tale game. You are still just at the beginning of this book. Much of what you need to know to really understand what is going on is provided in Chapters 3–6. For now, try to limit your focus to the overall big picture.

Designing the Ruby Tall Tale Game

As was done in the development of Chapter 1's Ruby Joke game, the development of the Ruby Tall Tale game will be constructed following a series of steps, as outlined next. As you move along from one step to the next, be sure to follow the instructions exactly as they are outlined.

1. Open your text or script editor and create a new file.
2. Add comment statements to the beginning of the script file to document the script and its purpose.
3. Define custom classes required by the game.
4. Prepare the game for play.
5. Add the code statements that outline the script's high-level conditional logic.
6. Terminate the game when the user decides not to play.
7. Prompt the player to provide story input for key story elements.
8. Assemble the game's story using the player's input.

9. Tell the game's story.

10. Thank the player for playing the game.

Each of these steps is covered in detail in the sections that follow.

Step 1: Creating a New Ruby File

The first step in developing the Ruby Tall Tale game is to start up your favorite text or code editor and create a new Ruby script file. Once created, save your script file in whatever location you've chosen to store your Ruby script files with a name of TallTale.rb.

Step 2: Documenting the Script and Its Purpose

The next step in the development of the Ruby Tall Tale game is to add the following statements to the beginning of the script file. These comment statements provide information about the script and its purpose.

```
#-------------------------------------------------------------------------
#
# Script Name: TallTale.rb
# Version:     1.0
# Author:      Jerry Lee Ford, Jr.
# Date:        October 2007
#
# Description: This Ruby script demonstrates how to collect and process
#              user input through the development of an interactive story
#              telling game.
#
#-------------------------------------------------------------------------
```

Step 3: Defining Custom Classes

The Ruby Tall Tale game includes two custom classes. The script statements that make up these two statements are shown next and should be added to the end of the script file.

```
class Screen

  def cls
    puts ("\n" * 25)
    puts "\a"
  end

end
```

```
class Tale

  attr_accessor :monster, :villain, :object, :place, :location

  attr_accessor :P1, :P2, :P3, :P4

  def tell_Story(paragraph)
    puts paragraph
  end

end
```

The first class is named Screen and it contains a method named cls that when called will clear the terminal window. In addition, the cls method includes a statement that uses the puts method. This puts method is passed a string that contains the \a escape character sequence. The \a character sequence does not display any visible text. Instead, it plays an audible beep sound, whose purpose in this method is to notify the player each time the terminal screen is cleared.

An *escape character* is a pair of characters that begin with the \ character followed by a letter. When Ruby comes across the \a escape character inside a text string, it plays a beep sound. You will learn more about escape characters in Chapter 3, "Working with Objects, Strings, and Variables."

The second class is named Tale and it defines properties representing key components of the game's story plot. The :monster, :villain, :object, :place, and :location properties represent pieces of input that will be collected from the player when the game executes and :P1, :P2, :P3, and :P4 will be used to store the paragraphs that make up the game's story line. The Tale class also includes a method named tell_Story, which displays any text that is passed to it as an argument.

Note the use of indentation in the previous class definition as well as throughout the rest of this Ruby script. Indenting programming statements in this manner helps to visually organize script statements and make them easier to read and understand. While indentation is not required, it is considered a good programming practice and I strongly recommend you use it.

Step 4: Preparing the Game for Execution

The next step in the development of the Ruby Tall Tale game is to clear the screen by instantiating a Screen object and then executing the Screen class's cls method. This is accomplished by adding the following statements to the end of the script file.

```
Console_Screen = Screen.new

Console_Screen.cls

print "Would you like to hear an interesting story? (y/n)\n\n: "

answer = STDIN.gets
answer.chop!
```

Once the cls method has been executed, the player is then prompted to confirm the decision to play the game. As you can see, the player is instructed to reply with a y or n response. The player's response is retrieved using the STDIN class's gets method and assigned to a variable named answer. The chop! method is then executed in order to remove the end of line character from the end of the value stored in answer.

Step 5: Outlining the Script's High-Level Conditional Logic

With the player's responses now in hand, the next set of statements to be added to the script file, shown next, are responsible for analyzing the player's input.

```
if answer == "n"

else

end
```

These statements should be added to the end of the script file. The rest of the statements in the script will be embedded within these statements. These statements control the high-level conditional logic for the script. The statements that you embed between the first two statements will execute when the player responds with a reply of n when asked for permission to play the game. The statements that you embed between the last two statements will execute when the player responds with a reply that is anything other than n when prompted for confirmation to play the game.

HINT   As written, the game only recognizes responses of y or n. If the player responds by entering anything other than one of these two letters, the game will treat the response as if a y was entered.

You will learn the ins and outs of applying conditional logic in Ruby later in Chapter 4, "Implementing Conditional Logic."

Step 6: Prematurely Terminating Game Execution

The following pair of statements clears the console screen and then displays a text string that encourages the player to return and play the game another time. These statements are to be executed when the player tells the game that she does not want to play. The statements should therefore be placed between the opening if statement and the else statement that you added to the script file in the preceding step.

```
Console_Screen.cls
```

```
puts "Okay, perhaps another time.\n\n"
```

Step 7: Collecting Player Input

The rest of the statements that you will add to the script file need to be placed between the else and the end statements that are responsible for outlining the script's overall controlling logic. For starters, add the following statements.

```
Story = Tale.new

Console_Screen.cls

print %Q{Type the name of a scary monster. (Press Enter)\n\n: }
monster = STDIN.gets
monster.chomp!

Console_Screen.cls

print %Q{Who is your favorite movie star? (Press Enter)\n\n: }
villain = STDIN.gets
villain.chomp!

Console_Screen.cls

print %Q{Type in the name of a thing. (Press Enter)\n\n: }
object = STDIN.gets
object.chomp!
```

```
Console_Screen.cls

print %Q{Enter the name of a good hiding place. (Press Enter)\n\n: }
place = STDIN.gets
place.chomp!

Console_Screen.cls

print %Q{Enter the name of a popular vacation site. (Press Enter)\n\n: }
location = STDIN.gets
location.chomp!
```

The first statement instantiates an object based on the Tale class. The terminal window is then cleared and a text string displays that presents the player with a question. The player's input is stored in a variable named monster. Four additional questions display and the player's responses are recorded in separate variables.

Step 8: Building the Game's Story

The next set of statements is responsible for assigning each of the game's four paragraphs to different properties belonging to the Story object. Each paragraph is written as a large text string. Variables have been embedded inside the text string and will be replaced by their assigned values.

```
Story.P1 = %Q{  Once upon a time in a far away land, just on the
outskirts of #{location}, there lived three very brave young children
named Alexander, William, and Molly. These children were known far and
wide as the heroes who once saved the inhabitants of #{location} from
an evil #{monster}. One day dark clouds descended over #{location}.
For 5 nights and 5 days a great storm raged, flooding all of the land
in #{location}, driving its inhabitants up into the hills. (Press Enter)

}

Story.P2 = %Q{  The good people of #{location} were not the only ones
driven into the hills. An evil monster named #{villain} was also awoken
from a 1,000 year slumber and forced from its lair by the torrential
floods that followed the storm into #{location}. #{villain}, having
been asleep for so long, was now hungry and soon began to prey upon the
```

helpless people. By the time the water began to recede, over half of
the inhabitants had become meals for #{villain}. (Press Enter)

}

Story.P3 = %Q{ Desperate for help, the remaining inhabitants of
#{location} sent word to Alexander, William, and Molly that their help
was once again needed. The three children soon arrived on the scene
only to find that #{villain} had cornered the last of the inhabitants
inside a #{place} and was preparing to eat one last meal before
returning to his secret lair in #{location}. (Press Enter)

}

Story.P4 = %Q{ Immediately, Alexander, William, and Molly flew into
action. Alexander threw a #{object} and hit #{villain} to get
his attention. At the same time, William and Molly crept up behind him.
William then threw a rope around the feet of #{villain}, momentarily
tying him up and allowing Molly to move in and spray #{villain} with
a full can of bug spray, immediately immobilizing and killing
#{villain}. The remaining inhabitants returned to their homes and soon
life in #{location} was back to normal. Alexander, William, and Molly
returned to their homes, quietly living on the edge of #{location},
waiting until the day they would be needed again. (Press Enter)

}

 HINT The trick to understanding how these code statements work is to understand
that in addition to enclosing text strings inside double quotations marks as you
have seen done many times already in this book, you can also create string statements by embedding them inside %Q{ and } characters. In addition, variable
substitution is performed within the strings by placing the variable name inside
#{ and } characters. You will learn the specifics of how this works in Chapter 3,
"Working with Objects, Strings, and Variables."

Step 9: Telling the Game's Story

Now that the story's plot has been mapped out, it is time to begin telling the story to the
player. This is accomplished by adding the following set of statements immediately after the

preceding set of statements (inside the else and end statements that are part of the script's controlling logic).

```
Console_Screen.cls
Story.tell_Story Story.P1
STDIN.gets

Console_Screen.cls
Story.tell_Story Story.P2
STDIN.gets

Console_Screen.cls
Story.tell_Story Story.P3
STDIN.gets

Console_Screen.cls
Story.tell_Story Story.P4
STDIN.gets
```

These statements are grouped into five nearly identical sets. Each set begins by calling on the Screen class's cls method to clear the console window. Next, the Tale class's tell_Story method is called and passed a paragraph to display. The STDIN class's gets method is then run in order to pause the execution of the script until the player presses the Enter key.

Step 10: Thanking the Player

The last statements to be added to the Ruby Tall Tale game are shown next and should be appended to the previous set of statements (placed inside the else and end statements that are part of the script's controlling logic).

```
Console_Screen.cls
puts "Thanks for helping to tell this Tall Tale!\n\n"
```

These two statements clear the console window and display a closing message thanking the player for taking time to play the game.

Running Your New Ruby Script Game

Well, that's it. You are ready to save and then execute your Ruby script. To help clarify things a bit and to help ensure that your copy of the Ruby script is properly written, I've provided a copy of the fully assembled game next. In addition, I have added a number of comment statements to the script file for the purpose of further documenting everything that is going on at different points within the script file.

```
#-------------------------------------------------------------------
#
# Script Name: TallTale.rb
# Version:     1.0
# Author:      Jerry Lee Ford, Jr.
# Date:        October 2007
#
# Description: This Ruby script demonstrates how to collect and process
#              user input through the development of an interactive story
#              telling game.
#
#-------------------------------------------------------------------


# Define custom classes ---------------------------------------------

#Define a class representing the console window
class Screen

  def cls  #Define a method that clears the display area
    puts ("\n" * 25)  #Scroll the screen 25 times
    puts "\a"  #Make a little noise to get the player's attention
  end

end

#Define a class representing the game's story
class Tale

  #Define class properties representing story elements
  attr_accessor :monster, :villain, :object, :place, :location

  #Define class properties representing story paragraphs
  attr_accessor :P1, :P2, :P3, :P4
```

```ruby
    #Define a method to be used to display story paragraphs
    def tell_Story(paragraph)
      puts paragraph
    end

end


# Main Script Logic ------------------------------------------------------

Console_Screen = Screen.new  #Initialize a new Screen object

#Execute the Screen object's cls method in order to clear the screen
Console_Screen.cls

#Prompt the player for permission to begin the game
print "Would you like to hear an interesting story? (y/n)\n\n: "

answer = STDIN.gets  #Collect the player's response
answer.chop!  #Remove any extra characters appended to the string


#Analyze the player's response
if answer == "n"  #See if the player elected not to play

  Console_Screen.cls  #Clear the display area

  #Invite the player to return and play again
  puts "Okay, perhaps another time.\n\n"

else

  Story = Tale.new  #Instantiate a new story object

  ##################################################
  # It is time to start collecting player input #
  ##################################################
```

```
Console_Screen.cls  #Clear the display area

#Prompt the player to provide some input
print %Q{Type the name of a scary monster. (Press Enter)\n\n: }
monster = STDIN.gets  #Force the player to press Enter to continue
monster.chomp!  #Remove any extra characters appended to the string

Console_Screen.cls  #Clear the display area

#Prompt the player to provide some input
print %Q{Who is your favorite movie star? (Press Enter)\n\n: }
villain = STDIN.gets  #Force the player to press Enter to continue
villain.chomp!  #Remove any extra characters appended to the string

Console_Screen.cls  #Clear the display area

#Prompt the player to provide some input
print %Q{Type in the name of a thing. (Press Enter)\n\n: }
object = STDIN.gets  #Force the player to press Enter to continue
object.chomp!  #Remove any extra characters appended to the string

Console_Screen.cls  #Clear the display area

#Prompt the player to provide some input
print %Q{Enter the name of a good hiding place. (Press Enter)\n\n: }
place = STDIN.gets  #Force the player to press Enter to continue
place.chomp!  #Remove any extra characters appended to the string

Console_Screen.cls  #Clear the display area

#Prompt the player to provide some input
print %Q{Enter the name of a popular vacation site. (Press Enter)\n\n: }
location = STDIN.gets  #Force the player to press Enter to continue
location.chomp!  #Remove any extra characters appended to the string


#############################################
# It is time to start telling the story     #
#############################################
```

```
#Display the first paragraph of the story
Story.P1 = %Q{  Once upon a time in a far away land, just on the
outskirts of #{location}, there lived three very brave young children
named Alexander, William, and Molly. These children were known far and
wide as the heroes who once saved the inhabitants of #{location} from
an evil #{monster}. One day dark clouds descended over #{location}.
For 5 nights and 5 days a great storm raged, flooding all of the land
in #{location}, driving its inhabitants up into the hills. (Press Enter)

}


#Display the second paragraph of the story
Story.P2 = %Q{  The good people of #{location} were not the only ones
driven into the hills. An evil monster named #{villain} was also awoken
from a 1,000 year slumber and forced from its lair by the torrential
floods that followed the storm into #{location}. #{villain}, having
been asleep for so long, was now hungry and soon began to prey upon the
helpless people. By the time the water began to recede, over half of
the inhabitants had become meals for #{villain}. (Press Enter)

}


#Display the third paragraph of the story
Story.P3 = %Q{  Desperate for help, the remaining inhabitants of
#{location} sent word to Alexander, William, and Molly that their help
was once again needed. The three children soon arrived on the scene
only to find that #{villain} had cornered the last of the inhabitants
inside a #{place} and was preparing to eat one last meal before
returning to his secret lair in #{location}. (Press Enter)

}


#Display the fourth paragraph of the story
Story.P4 = %Q{  Immediately, Alexander, William, and Molly flew into
action. Alexander threw a #{object} and hit #{villain} to get
his attention. At the same time, William and Molly crept up behind him.
William then threw a rope around the feet of #{villain}, momentarily
tying him up and allowing Molly to move in and spray #{villain} with
```

a full can of bug spray, immediately immobilizing and killing
#{villain}. The remaining inhabitants returned to their homes and soon
life in #{location} was back to normal. Alexander, William, and Molly
returned to their homes, quietly living on the edge of #{location},
waiting until the day they would be needed again. (Press Enter)

```
  }

  Console_Screen.cls  #Clear the display area
  Story.tell_Story Story.P1  #Tell the story's first paragraph
  STDIN.gets  #Force the player to press Enter to continue

  Console_Screen.cls  #Clear the display area
  Story.tell_Story Story.P2  #Tell the story's second paragraph
  STDIN.gets  #Force the player to press Enter to continue

  Console_Screen.cls  #Clear the display area
  Story.tell_Story Story.P3  #Tell the story's third paragraph
  STDIN.gets  #Force the player to press Enter to continue

  Console_Screen.cls  #Clear the display area
  Story.tell_Story Story.P4  #Tell the story's fourth paragraph
  STDIN.gets  #Force the player to press Enter to continue

  Console_Screen.cls  #Clear the display area
  puts "Thanks for helping to tell this Tall Tale!\n\n"

end
```

Assuming that you followed along exactly as explained and that you did not make any typing mistakes when keying in the script's code statements, everything should run exactly as expected. When you are ready, start up a new operating system shell session and navigate to the folder where you have stored your Ruby scripts. Next, type **Ruby TallTale.rb** and press the Enter key.

At this point your new Ruby script should start running. However, if you made any typos along the way, you will get an error message instead. If this is the case, take a look at the error message and see if it provides any information that you can use to identify what went wrong. If you cannot determine what has happened based on the error message, you will need to review your script file and track down your mistake. Once you think you have located and fixed all your errors, rerun your Ruby script.

SUMMARY

In this chapter, you learned how to formulate and execute different Ruby expressions and statements using interactive Ruby, otherwise known as the irb. This chapter showed you how to start up irb sessions and demonstrated how to execute single and multiline Ruby statements. Using the irb, you can tinker around with and learn much about how things work in Ruby. This chapter also showed you how to access Ruby's documentation via RDoc.

Now, before you move on to Chapter 3, why don't you set aside a little extra time to work on the Ruby Tall Tale game by implementing the following list of challenges.

CHALLENGES

1. The Ruby Tall Tale game tells a story that is just a few paragraphs long. Consider making the story more interesting by expanding upon its lengths and improving its plot.

2. As currently written, the Ruby Tall Tale game collects only five pieces of information from the player. As a result, there is a limit to how dynamic the story can be. Review the story and look for opportunities to replace other keywords with user input.

3. As a programmer, it is important to take credit for your hard work. Consider adding one more paragraph at the end of the story and using it as an opportunity to tell the player a little information about the game and its author. If you have a website, you might want to display your URL as well.

Part

II

Learning How to Write Ruby Scripts

WORKING WITH OBJECTS, STRINGS, AND VARIABLES

I n the first two chapters of this book, you focused on learning about Ruby's overall capabilities, how to experiment with Ruby using the irb, and how to create and execute Ruby scripts. Now it is time to begin digging into the language and seeing how things work. In this chapter, you will learn a number of fundamental object-oriented programming techniques, including how to define custom classes, which you can use as a template for instantiating new objects. You will also learn how to create and work with strings and to store and retrieve object data using variables. On top of all this, you will learn how to create a new Ruby script, the Ruby Virtual Crazy 8 Ball game.

Specifically, you will learn how to:

- Create and work with text strings
- Assign and retrieve object data using variables
- Define custom classes and use them to instantiate objects
- Define class properties and methods

PROJECT PREVIEW: THE RUBY VIRTUAL CRAZY 8 BALL GAME

In this chapter, you will learn how to create a new computer game called the Ruby Virtual Crazy 8 Ball game. In developing this Ruby script, you will learn how to work with text strings, objects, and variables. You will also learn how to generate random numbers, which will be used as the basis for creating a virtual crazy 8 ball game that provides randomly selected answers to player questions.

The game begins by displaying a welcome screen as shown in Figure 3.1. To begin the game, the player must press the Enter key.

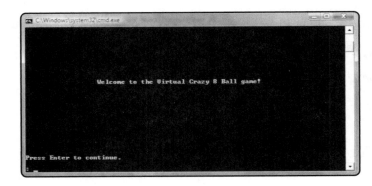

FIGURE 3.1

The welcome screen for the Virtual Crazy 8 Ball game.

Next, the game prompts the player for permission to play the game, instructing the player to respond with a y or an n, as shown in Figure 3.2.

FIGURE 3.2

The game requires that the player provide confirmation before play begins.

If the player responds with anything other than y or n, the game will redisplay the screen shown in Figure 3.2. If the player responds by typing n, the game responds by displaying the screen shown in Figure 3.3.

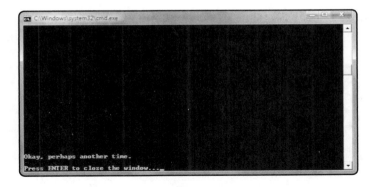

If, on the other hand, the player responds with a y, the game prompts the player to ask it a question and then press the Enter key (see Figure 3.4).

The game then answers the player's questions by displaying one of six randomly selected answers, as demonstrated in Figure 3.5.

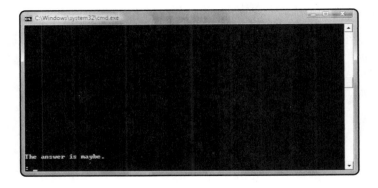

Once the player dismisses the game's answer by pressing the Enter key, the game responds by asking the player if she would like to ask a new question, as demonstrated in Figure 3.6.

FIGURE 3.6

The player can quit playing at any time by typing q and pressing the Enter key.

The last screen displayed thanks the player for taking time to play the game, as shown in Figure 3.7.

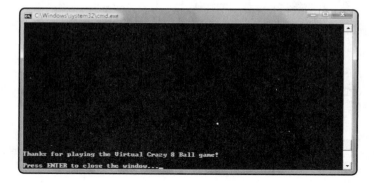

FIGURE 3.7

The Virtual Crazy 8 Ball game has ended.

WORKING WITH TEXT STRINGS

As you are no doubt aware by this point in the book, text plays a big role in most Ruby scripts, especially when communicating with users. Text can consist of letters, numbers, special characters, or even blank spaces. So far, all of the text strings that you have worked with in this book have been enclosed inside matching pairs of double quotation marks, as demonstrated here:

```
"Sample text string"
```

However, there are other ways of creating text strings within Ruby scripts. Strings can be created by enclosing them within matching single quotation marks, as demonstrated here:

```
'Sample test string'
```

Deciding whether to use matching double or single-quoted strings is more than a matter of personal preference. Ruby allows you to do things to text strings enclosed inside matching double quotes that it does not allow within matching single quotes. For example, when working with double-quoted strings, Ruby is able to perform escaping and variable substitution operations using #{}. Single-quoted strings do not support either of these operations.

Formatting Text Strings

When working with double-quoted strings, Ruby recognizes a number of escape characters that, when found, are automatically replaced with the appropriate corresponding operation. For example, Ruby supports escape characters that execute tab and new line operations. By embedding these escape characters within double-quoted strings, you can exercise detailed control over the manner in which Ruby renders the strings when it displays them. Table 3.1 provides a list of escape characters that you can use to exercise control over text formatting within strings.

TABLE 3.1 STRING ESCAPE SUBSTITUTION CHARACTERS	
Option	Description
\b	Backspace
\f	Formfeed
\n	New line
\r	Return
\s	Space
\t	Tab

To get a good understanding of how to work with escape characters, it helps to see a few examples.

```
puts "1 2 3 4 5"
```

When executed, this statement results in the following output.

```
1 2 3 4 5
```

Now, let's reformat this example by embedding a series of \t escape characters.

```
puts "\t1 \t2 \t3 \t4 \t5"
```

This time when you execute the statement, the following output is displayed.

```
     1     2     3     4     5
```

As you can see, by embedding the \t escape character, you can perform tab operations that affect how the string is displayed. Now, look at this next example.

```
puts "\n1 \n2 \n3 \n4 \n5"
```

This time the \n escape character has been placed before each number in the text string. Since this escape character is the equivalent of a new line operation, when executed this statement produces the following output.

```
1
2
3
4
5
```

HINT You will get the chance to work with escape characters again when you work on this chapter's game project, the Ruby Virtual Crazy 8 Ball game.

Variable Interpolation

String interpolation, also referred to as variable substitution, is performed by embedding a text string inside other strings using the #{} characters. Interpolation is the process of substituting the value of an expression or variable inside a string. To see how this works, look at the following statements.

```
totalScore = 100
puts "Game over. Your score is #{totalScore}."
```

When executed, these two statements produce the following output.

```
Game over. Your score is 100.
```

As you can see, the value stored in the totalScore variable has been substituted into a pre-specified location in the text string. As has been stated, interpolation also works with expressions.

```
totalScore = 100
bonusPoints = 50
puts "Game over. Your score is #{totalScore + bonusPoints}."
```

When executed, these statements generate the following output.

```
Game over. Your score is 150.
```

As you can see, Ruby added together the values of totalScore and bonusPoints and then substituted the resulting value into the text string in place of the specified expression.

 You will get the chance to work with variable substitution again when you work on this chapter's game project, the Ruby Virtual Crazy 8 Ball game.

OTHER OPTIONS FOR MANIPULATING STRINGS

Ruby provides you with many different ways of working with strings. For starters, you can compare two different strings to see if they are the same, concatenate them together to create new strings, and multiply them together. You can also compare one string to another to see if they match or spread text strings out over multiple lines. In addition, you can use Ruby's support for regular expressions to perform a host of other string-manipulation techniques.

 Regular expressions are covered in Chapter 7, "Working with Regular Expressions."

Concatenating Text Strings

Earlier in the chapter, you learned how to perform string interpolation. As an alternative to string interpolation, you could achieve the same results using string concatenation. Concatenation is the process of joining two strings together to form a new string. Concatenation is performed using the + string method. To see how concatenation works, consider the following example.

```
totalScore = 100
puts "Game over. Your score is " + totalScore.to_s + "."
```

Here, three strings have been concatenated together. The first string is "Game over. Your score is ". The second string was created by converting the numeric value of totalScore to a string using the to_s method, and the third string is ".". When executed, this statement generates the following output:

```
Game over. Your score is 100.
```

Here is another example of how to concatenate strings together. This time, in addition to concatenating the two strings, the \n escape character has been included to control the format of the resulting new string.

```
story = "Welcome to Ruby Programming for the Absolute Beginner"
author = "by Jerry Lee Ford, Jr."
puts story + "\n\n" + author
```

When executed, these statements generate the following output.

```
Welcome to Ruby Programming for the Absolute Beginner

by Jerry Lee Ford, Jr.
```

Multiplying Text Strings

In addition to creating new strings by concatenating existing strings together, you can also create new strings by multiplying existing strings. This is accomplished using the String class's * method.

```
x = "Happy birthday to you. " * 3
puts x
```

Here, the text string "Happy birthday to you. " is repeated three times as shown here:

```
Happy birthday to you. Happy birthday to you. Happy birthday to you.
```

Comparing Text Strings

Another commonly performed string operation is to compare two strings to see whether they are equal. This is accomplished using the equality operator (= =). You have already seen examples of string comparisons numerous times in this book. For example, look at the following statements.

```
puts "Would you like to hear a few funny jokes? (y/n) "
answer = STDIN.gets
answer.chop!

if answer = = "n"   #See if the player elected not to play
```

Here, the user is prompted to enter a value of y or n. The user's input is then captured as answer, which is then used in the last statement to determine whether the value of answer is equal to the value of "n".

TRAP

String comparisons are performed using the == operator and not the = operator. Because they are similar, it is easy to get them mixed up. To see what I mean, start up a new irb session, and execute the statements shown here:

```
irb(main):001:0> x = 1
=> 1
irb(main):002:0> y = 2
=> 2
```

```
irb(main):003:0> puts "x and y are equal" if x = y
x and y are equal
=> nil
```

Here, x has been set equal to 1 and y has been set equal to 2. The puts statement displays a text string message only in the event that the values of x and y are equal. Therefore, when the puts statement is executed, it would seem to make sense that nothing would be displayed. However, this is not the case. Instead, the test string "x and y are equal" is displayed. To find out why, execute the commands shown here:

```
irb(main):004:0> x
=> 2
irb(main):005:0> y
=> 2
```

As you can see, the value of x is set equal to 2 as expected. However, the value of y has also been set to 2 and not to 1. The reason is because there is an error in the puts statement that was previously executed. It used the equals assignment operator (=) and not the equals comparison operator (==). As a result, instead of comparing x and y, the puts statements assigned the value of y to x.

Now, to prove that the above explanation is accurate, execute the following statements using the irb.

```
irb(main):001:0> x = 1
 => 1
irb(main):002:0> y = 2
=> 2
irb(main):003:0> puts "x and y are equal" if x == y
=> nil
```

This time, things went as expected and the test string was not displayed because the values of x and y were different.

Creating Multiline Text Strings

In addition to creating text strings by embedding them inside matching quotation marks, you can also create text strings by embedding text inside the %q{ and } characters or the %Q { and } characters. Embedding characters inside the %q{ and } characters creates a string that is equivalent to a single-quoted string. Embedding characters inside the %Q{ and } characters creates a string that is equivalent to a double-quoted string.

The advantage of using the %q{ and } and %Q{ and } characters in place of quotation marks is that these characters allow you to create strings that span multiple lines, as demonstrated here:

```
story = %Q{Once upon a time there were
three children named Alexander, William,
and Molly.}
```

Using the %q{ and } and %Q{ and } characters to define strings, there is no practical limit as to the length of your text strings. In addition, strings created using the %Q{ and } characters provide the same support for escape characters and interpolation as do double-quoted strings.

 TRICK

When creating multiline text strings, you can replace the opening and closing brackets with any matching set of characters you want. For example, the following example uses the %q[and] characters to define a string.

```
story = %q[Once upon a time there were
three children named Alexander, William,
and Molly.]
```

The important thing to remember when deciding which characters you want to substitute when creating a string is to make sure that those characters do not also appear inside the string text; otherwise, Ruby will get confused and things will not work correctly.

WORKING WITH STRING CLASS METHODS

In addition to the previously discussed options for manipulating text strings, Ruby's String class provides you with access to a number of additional string manipulation methods, as shown in Table 3.2.

Let's look at a few examples that demonstrate how to work with these String class methods. For starters, look at the following example.

```
irb(main):028:0> story = "Once upon a time"
=> "Once upon a time"
irb(main):029:0> puts story.length
16
=> nil
irb(main):030:0>
```

TABLE 3.2	A LISTING OF SOME OF THE METHODS BELONGING TO THE STRING CLASS

Method	Description
capitalize	Capitalizes the first letter of a string
downcase	Converts a string to all lowercase letters
chop	Removes the last character from a string
length	Returns an integer representing the number of characters in a string
next	Replaces the next letter in a string with the next letter in the alphabet
reverse	Reverses the spelling of a string
swapcase	Reverses the case of each letter in a string
upcase	Converts a string to all uppercase letters

Here, the String class's length method was used to display the number of characters that make up the string stored in the story variable. In this next example, the upcase method is used to convert the content of the string to all uppercase characters.

```
The irb(main):030:0> story = "Once upon a time"
=> "Once upon a time"
irb(main):031:0> puts story.upcase
ONCE UPON A TIME
=> nil
irb(main):032:0>
```

As this last example demonstrates, Ruby allows you to combine different string methods.

```
irb(main):001:0> story = "Once upon a time"
=> "Once upon a time"
irb(main):002:0> puts story.reverse.upcase
EMIT A NOPU ECNO
=> nil
irb(main):003:0>
```

Here, the reverse and upcase methods were chained together and executed. The reverse method reversed the order of all the characters in the string and the upcase method converted them to all uppercase.

 Refer to RDoc to learn more about the methods associated with the String class.

OBJECT-ORIENTED PROGRAMMING

Ruby is an *object-oriented* programming language. It sees everything that it interacts with, including data, as an object. *Objects* are self-contained entities, meaning that they include information about themselves in the form of properties and provide program code stored as methods for interacting with and manipulating themselves.

Objects are defined in what is referred to as a *class*. Using the information defined within a given class, you can create or instantiate new object instances based on that class. So for an `automobile` class, you could create specific object instances, each of which would represent an individual automobile. You could then assign each automobile instance a different color by assigning a color to the appropriate object property and controlling the operation of the object by executing its methods.

In addition to its name, an object may be assigned any number of properties. *Object properties* are implemented as named variables. An object representing an automobile might have properties representing the model and color of the vehicle. To store data for each of these properties, object properties are stored in *variables*, which are pointers to locations in memory where data is stored. The code defined within an object definition that you use in your Ruby scripts to interact with and control an object is referred to as object methods. Returning to the automobile example, you might define methods for starting and stopping the car and for turning on and off different features like headlights.

Defining a New Class

Ruby scripts use this object-orientedness to define real-world concepts like files, folders, and network resources, or perhaps things like people, automobiles, and animals. Once they're defined, you can interact with and control objects and define relationships between objects.

Objects are defined as classes using the syntax outlined here:

```
class ClassName
    statements
end
```

`class` is a keyword that tells Ruby that a new class is being defined. `ClassName` is the name that is being assigned to the new class. You must assign a capital letter as the first character of every class definition. `statements` is a placeholder for one or more script statements that define class attributes (properties) and methods. `end` is a keyword that identifies the end of the class definition. For example, the following statements begin the outline of a class named `Automobile`.

```
class Automobile

end
```

A *Class* definition represents a template that can be used to create or *instantiate* individual objects. In the case of the preceding example, the class represents the logical definition of an automobile. The `end` keyword marks the end of the class definition.

Defining Class Properties

Within the class definition, you can define one or more attributes that describe characteristics associated with the class. For example, you might want to define class attributes such as model and color to the `Automobile` class. Class attributes, also referred to as *properties*, are defined inside the class using the *attr_accessor* keyword using the syntax outlined here:

```
attr_accessor :attribute1, :attribute2, …
```

attr_accessor is a keyword that identifies a list of one or more object properties. Each property is preceded by the colon character. Successive properties are separated from each other with a comma. There is no limit to the number or properties that you can define. The following example demonstrates how to assign two properties to the `Automobile` class.

```
class Automobile
  attr_accessor :model, :color
end
```

The first property specifies the model or type of automobile being defined and the second property will be used to store the color of the automobile.

Instantiating and Interacting with New Objects

At this point, the `Automobile` class represents a functional class definition that is ready to be used as the basis for instantiating scripts objects, which is accomplished using the syntax outlined here:

```
variableName = ClassName.new
```

variableName is the name of a variable that will be used to store and refer to the object, and *ClassName* is the name of the class being used to create the new object. *new* is a method that initiates the creation of the new object. Using the above syntax, you can create a new object as shown here:

```
superCar = Automobile.new
```

When executed, this statement creates a new object named `superCar` using the `Automobile` class as its template. Once instantiated, you can assign values to the object's properties, as demonstrated here.

```
superCar.model = "Edsel"
superCar.color = "Red"
```

Once defined, you can reference object property values as shown here.

```
puts "Super car is the car of tomorrow. It is based on the " +
"original #{superCar.model} design."
```

When executed, this statement displays the text string shown here:

```
Super car is the car of tomorrow. It is based on the original Edsel design.
```

If you want, you can modify the value assigned to a property by reassigning another value as demonstrated here.

```
superCar.model = "Mustang"
```

Defining Class Methods

In order to control your objects, you need to define class methods. You can then use the methods to programmatically interact with any object you instantiate. Ruby methods are defined using the following syntax.

```
def methodname(arguments)
    Statements
end
```

methodname is the name to be assigned to the new method. *arguments* is a comma-separated list of parameters passed to the method for processing. Within the method, the parameters are treated as local variables. *Statements* is a placeholder representing one or more statements that will be executed whenever the method is called. To get a better feel for how to define a custom method, take a look at the following example.

```
class Automobile

  attr_accessor :model, :color

  def honk
    puts "Honk!!!"
  end
end
```

As with properties, you can interact with object methods by specifying the name of the class, followed by a period and then the name of the method.

The following statements demonstrate how to create a new object based on the `Automobile` class and how to execute the class's `honk` method.

```
myCar = Automobile.new
myCar.honk
```

Inheritance

One of the primary benefits of object-oriented programming is its ability to allow programmers to model the creation of classes (and therefore objects) based on real-life concepts like automobiles, tools, people, or anything else you can imagine. In real life, objects often have relationships with one another. For example, you have a father from whom you inherited certain qualities. You may have children to whom you will pass on certain attributes. In addition, you may have brothers or sisters with whom you share common attributes.

By supporting an object-oriented process known as inheritance, Ruby allows you to use one class definition as the basis for creating another class definition. In this case, the new or child class is created as a copy of the original or parent class. You can create as many child instances as you want. If necessary, you can modify the characteristics of the child class to suit your particular needs.

Thanks to inheritance, you can define classes that model real-life concepts. For example, you might define a generic automobile class that defines all of the basic properties associated with a car and which includes all of the methods required to control the car. And then you can use this class as a template for creating a whole series of child subclasses, each of which might represent an individual make and model of a car. For example, the class definition for a simple car is outlined here:

```
class Automobile

  attr_accessor :model, :color

    def honk
        puts "Honk!!!"
    end
end
```

Here, an `Automobile` class has been defined that contains two property definitions, `model` and `color`, and a method named `honk`. If you want, you can use the `Automobile` class as the basis for defining a new class. Once way of doing this would be to copy and paste the Automobile class and then to rename it as shown here:

```
class Edsel

  attr_accessor :model, :color

  def honk
    puts "Honk!!!"
  end
end
```

Creating a new class in this manner is highly inefficient because it results in two nearly identical sets of code that must be maintained. Should you later want to make a change in the class by adding another property, you have to make the modification twice, once for the Automobile class and again for the Edsel class. Instead of doing things this way, a much better way of creating another, related class of cars would be to base the new Edsel class on the Automobile class, taking advantage of object inheritance as demonstrated here:

```
class Edsel < Automobile

end
```

Here the superclass operator was used to create a new class named Edsel, which is modeled on the Automobile class. The Edsel class inherits all of the properties and methods in the Automobile class. Not only does this require less code, but this approach also reduces the chance of making typing errors since there is less to type in. In addition, if you should later decide to make a fundamental change that would affect all the car-related classes, all you have to do is make that change in the Automobile class and any child classes (or subclasses) will automatically inherit the change as well. There is no limit to the number of child classes that you can create from a parent class. Therefore, if you need to expand your product line to include a second type of car, you could easily do so as demonstrated here:

```
class Mustang < Automobile

end
```

Here, a new Mustang class has been created. It automatically inherits all the properties and methods of the Automobile class. Ruby allows you to modify child classes as necessary to customize them to match up to whatever changes need to be made to differentiate the child class from it parent class. For example, take a look at the following statements.

```
class Explorer < Automobile

 attr_accessor :transmission

 def breaks
    puts "... screech!"
  end

end
```

Here, a new `Explorer` class has been defined based on the `Automobile` class. In addition to inheriting all of the `Automobile`'s properties and methods, the `Explorer` class has been modified to include a new property and a new method that is unique unto itself.

HINT

This book has shown you how to use a number of different methods. In most cases, you've been told which class the method is associated with. However, for methods like `puts`, `chop!`, and `print`, you've simply been shown how to use them without any explanation of where they come from. These methods are just a few of the methods stored in the `Kernel` module. A *module* is a container used to group classes, methods, and constants. This module is a component of the `Object` class. Methods belonging to the `Object` class are made available to every Ruby object.

Normally when you work with a method, you do so by specifying the name of the class where the method resides followed by a period and then the method name, as demonstrated here:

```
pause = STDIN.gets
```

When working with methods belonging to the `Kernel` module, you can simply specify the method's name, as demonstrated here:

```
puts "Well, hello there."
```

Alternatively, if you want to be specific, you could rewrite the preceding statement as shown here:

```
Kernel.puts "Well, hello there."
```

CONVERTING FROM ONE CLASS TO ANOTHER

As has already been stated, in Ruby, numbers and strings are really just different types of objects. Ruby supports a number of different types of numeric classes, including `Fixnum`, `Integer`, `Bignum`, and `float`. Ruby automatically handles numeric class assignments. For the most part, you do not need to concern yourself with the class that Ruby has assigned to a given number. However, you may come across situations where you need to convert an object from one type to another. In some situations, Ruby will implicitly handle object conversion for you. Consider the following example:

```
irb(main):001:0> x = 10
```

Here, a variable named x has been assigned a value of 10. In response, Ruby will create a new object based on the Fixnum class. To verify this, you can execute the class method as demonstrated here:

```
irb(main):002:0> x.class
=> Fixnum
```

Implicit Class Conversion

As you can see, x is assigned to the Fixnum class. However, if you reassign a value too large to fit into that class, Ruby will automatically, or implicitly, convert x to Bignum, as demonstrated here:

```
irb(main):007:0> x = 1000000000000000
=> 1000000000000000
irb(main):008:0> x.class
=> Bignum
```

If you then assign a string as the value of x, Ruby will again change the object's class, as demonstrated here:

```
irb(main):009:0> x = "Hello"
=> "Hello"
irb(main):010:0> x.class
=> String
```

Explicit Class Conversion

In addition to *implicitly* changing or coercing an object from one class to another, Ruby also provides you with the ability to *explicitly* coerce objects from one class to another. You might need to do this if you have written a script that collects and processes user input. By default, any input provided by the user will be treated by Ruby as a string, even if the input that was provided was a number. For example, consider the following example.

```
irb(main):001:0> answer = STDIN.gets
10
=> "10\n"
```

HINT The previous example collects user input by executing the STDIN class's gets method. This method pauses the console session and waits for the user to provide input, which is then assigned the specified variable.

As you can see, the value entered by the user was the number 10. Ruby appended the \n characters to the end of the user's input when the Enter key was pressed. Executing the following command, remove the trailing /n characters, ensuring that the value assigned to answer is exactly what the user entered.

```
irb(main):002:0> answer.chop!
=> "10"
```

TRICK When the user presses the Enter key to submit her input, Ruby automatically appends an end of line marker to the end of the input. In this example, the presence of the end of line marker has no impact on the example.

The end of line marker can easily be removed from the answer variable using the chop! method. When executed, this method removes the last character from a specified string. If the string ends with the \n characters, the chop! method will remove both characters.

Using this method, you can easily remove the /n characters from any input provided by the user, as demonstrated here:

```
answer = STDIN.gets
answer.chop
```

If you now try to perform addition using the input, you will run into an error because Ruby is unable to explicitly convert a value of "10" to 10.

```
irb(main):003:0> x = 5 + answer
TypeError: String can't be coerced into Fixnum
        from (irb):3:in '+'
        from (irb):3
irb(main):004:0>
```

To prevent this type of error from occurring and to get the results you expect, you can explicitly force the conversion of an object's type using different conversion methods. For example, you could use the to_i method to return the value stored in answer to an integer.

```
irb(main):005:0> x = 5 + answer.to_i
=> 15
irb(main):006:0>
```

As you can see, once explicitly converted, the error no longer occurs and the expected result is attached. If you prefer, you can use the tp_f method to convert a string to a floating point number. Going in the opposite direction, you can use the to_s method to convert any numeric value to a string, as demonstrated here:

```
irb(main):001:0> x = 5
=> 5
irb(main):002:0> y = 4
=> 4
irb(main):003:0> z = x + y
=> 9
```

In this example, two variables are defined and assigned values of 5 and 4, which are then added together and assigned to a variable named z. Using the to_s method, you can instruct Ruby to treat the values assigned to x and y as strings instead of numeric values, as demonstrated here:

```
irb(main):004:0> z = x.to_s + y.to_s
=> "54"
irb(main):005:0>
```

This time, instead of adding two numeric values together, Ruby coerces x and y into strings and concatenates both strings together to form a new string that is then assigned to a variable named z. If you use the class method to check on the z variable's class type assignment, you will see that it has been set to String.

```
irb(main):006:0> z.class
=> String
irb(main):007:0>
```

STORING AND RETRIEVING DATA

When working with numbers, strings, and other types of objects, it often helps to be able to store their values in order to later be able to reference and modify them. This is accomplished through the use of variables. A *variable* is a pointer to a location in memory where the objects that are created in your scripts are stored. These objects may include numbers, text, or any custom objects that you have defined. For example, the following statement defines a variable named x and assigns it an integer value of 10.

```
x = 10
```

Likewise, the following statement assigns a text string to a variable named y.

```
y = "Well, hello there."
```

Variables are an essential part of any Ruby script, which is why you have already seen them used many times in this book. Now it is time to learn more about how to create and work with them.

Naming Variables

In Ruby, variable names are case sensitive. This means that to Ruby, `totalcount` and `TotalCount` are two separate variables. Ruby has a few rules that you need to be familiar with regarding the naming of variables. These rules are listed here:

- Variable names must begin with a letter or an underscore character
- Variable names can only contain letters, numbers, and underscore characters
- Variable names cannot include blank spaces

Following these rules, each of the following variable names would be regarded by Ruby as valid.

- `Totalscore`
- `totalScore`
- `total_score`
- `Total_Score`
- `x`
- `TotalTimes2`

The variable names shown in Table 3.3, on the other hand, are not considered by Ruby to be valid.

TABLE 3.3   INVALID VARIABLE NAMES

Option	Description
total score	Variable names cannot include blank spaces
@totalScore	Special characters are not allowed
total-score	Only letters, numbers, and the underscore characters are permitted
2TimesLucky	Variable names cannot begin with a number

Variable Assignments

As you have already seen many times, variable value assignments in Ruby are made using the equals assignment operator (=), as demonstrated here:

```
x = 10
```

Here an integer value of 10 has been assigned to a variable named x. Use the equals assignment operator to also modify a variable's value by assigning it the results of an expression, as demonstrated here:

```
x = 1
x = x + 1
```

Here, a variable named x is assigned an initial value of 1. Then the value assigned to x is modified by assigning the values returned from the expression x + 1 to x. As a result the value of x was incremented by 1.

Incrementing a variable's value is a common task. To help make it easier to perform, you can use the += operator, as demonstrated here:

```
x += 1
```

The += operator provides a shorthand way of incrementing a variable's value of a specified amount. In the case of the previous example, the value of x is incremented by 1.

Variable Scope

In Ruby, variable access depends on the scope that has been set for that variable. Scope is a term that describes the areas within a script where a variable can be seen and accessed. Ruby supports three different scopes, as outlined in Table 3.4.

TABLE 3.4	VARIABLE SCOPES	
Type	Opening Character(s)	Description
Local	a–z and _	Scope is limited to each iteration loop, module, class, and method in which it is defined or to the entire script if the variable is defined outside of one of the structures.
Instance	@	Scope is limited to the scope associated with the object itself.
Class	@@	Scope is limited to objects of class.
Global	$	Scope has no limit, allowing the variable to be accessed throughout the script.

In Ruby, variable scope is indicated by the characters you use at the beginning of the variable name. As Table 3.4 shows, a variable whose name begins with the $ character is a global variable, and a variable that begins with a lowercase letter or the underscore character is a local variable. For this book, you will only need to worry about working with local and global variables.

Local variables are variables that have a limited scope. For example, as Table 3.4 shows, any variable whose name begins with a lowercase letter and that is defined inside a method is accessible only within that method. For example, the following statements show a method named Add_Stuff. This method accepts two arguments, x and y, which are local variables within the method and thus not accessible outside of the method.

```
def Add_Stuff(x, y)
    puts x + y
end
```

If you key this example into the irb and then execute it by passing the method arguments of 3 and 4, a result of 7 will be displayed.

```
irb(main):004:0> Add_Stuff(3, 4)
7
```

However, if you attempt to access either the x or the y variable from outside of the method, as demonstrated next, an error will occur.

```
irb(main):005:0> puts x
NameError: undefined local variable or method 'x' for main:Object
        from (irb):5
```

Global variables can be accessed from anywhere within a Ruby script and are created by making the first character of the variable name a $, as demonstrated here:

```
$x = 1000
```

The $x variable will be accessible from anywhere within the Ruby script that it is defined in. You will see an example of how to use global variables later in this chapter's game project, the Ruby Virtual Crazy 8 Ball game.

STORING DATA THAT DOES NOT CHANGE

Any time you are creating a Ruby script that will use a value that is known at design time and not subject to change, you should define that value as a constant. A *constant* is very much like a variable, the differences being that constant names begin with a capital letter and will generate warning messages in the event you change their values during script execution.

TRAP   If you change a constant's value, Ruby will complain, displaying a warning message, allowing the scripts to continue running. This makes Ruby different from most other programming languages that generate an error message and halt script and program execution.

The following expression demonstrates how to define a constant and assign it a value.

```
irb(main):001:0> Pi = 3.14
=> 3.14
```

Once defined, you can reference the value assigned to the constant as needed. If you forget that you are working with a constant and change the value that is assigned to it, Ruby will generate a working message while allowing the script to continue running.

```
irb(main):002:0> Pi = 3.1415
(irb):2: warning: already initialized constant Pi
=> 3.1415
```

BACK TO THE RUBY VIRTUAL CRAZY 8 BALL GAME

Okay, now it is time to turn your attention back to the development of this chapter's game project, the Ruby Virtual Crazy 8 Ball game. As you follow along with the development of this script file, be sure to focus on the usage of text strings, variables, classes, and objects. In particular, pay close attention to the manner in which the script interacts with and controls objects once they have been instantiated.

Designing the Game

The development of the Ruby Virtual Crazy 8 Ball game will be completed in 10 steps, as outlined here:

1. Open your text or script editor and create a new file.
2. Add comment statements to the beginning of the script file to document the script and its purpose.
3. Define a class representing the terminal window.
4. Define a class representing the game's virtual 8 ball window.
5. Instantiate custom script objects.
6. Display a greeting message.
7. Get confirmation before continuing game play.
8. Analyze the player's reply.
9. Manage early game termination.
10. Process and respond to player questions.

Remember to follow along carefully and not to skip any steps or parts of steps as you work your way through this exercise. Specifically, look out for typos and make sure that you do things in the correct order.

Step 1: Creating a New Ruby File

The first step in creating the Ruby Virtual Crazy 8 Ball game is to start up your preferred text or code editor and then to create a new Ruby script file. Save this file with a file name of Crazy8Ball.rb and store it in whatever folder you have decided to keep your Ruby scripts.

Step 2: Documenting the Script and Its Purpose

Once you have created your new script file, the next step is to add the following comment statements to it. These statements provide a high-level description of the game and its purpose.

```
#--------------------------------------------------------------
#
# Script Name: Crazy8Ball.rb
# Version:     1.0
# Author:      Jerry Lee Ford, Jr.
# Date:        October 2007
#
# Description: This Ruby script demonstrates how to work with variables
#              and to generate random numbers in order to create a fortune
#              telling game that provides randomly selected answers to
#              player questions.
#
#--------------------------------------------------------------
```

HINT   To get as much value as possible out of the script's opening documentation statements, modify them to suit your own needs. For example, you might want to consider including a place for your URL if you have a website. In addition, you might want to add a space for recording changes, game instructions, or anything else that you think would be useful.

Step 3: Defining a Screen Class

Now it is time to define the first of two custom classes used by the script. The first class is named Screen. It closely resembles the Screen class used in Chapter 2. However, this version of the Screen class includes a new method definition.

```
# Define custom classes ---------------------------------------------------

#Define a class representing the console window
class Screen

  def cls  #Define a method that clears the display area
    puts ("\n" * 25)  #Scroll the screen 25 times
    puts "\a"  #Make a little noise to get the player's attention
  end

  def pause  #Define a method that pauses the display area
    STDIN.gets  #Execute the STDIN class's gets method to pause script
                #execution until the player presses the Enter key
  end

end
```

The first method defined within this class is the `cls` method. It contains two statements. The first statement writes 25 blank lines to the console window, clearing the screen. The second statement processes a string containing the \a escape character sequence, which makes an audible beep sound, thus notifying the player each time the terminal screen is cleared.

Step 4: Defining a Ball Class

The script's second class is named `Ball`. It serves as a template that the script will use to instantiate an object that represents a virtual 8 ball. As such, the class defines a number of properties and methods required to operate and interact with the 8 ball.

```
#Define a class representing the 8 ball
class Ball

  #Define class properties for the 8 ball
  attr_accessor :randomNo, :greeting, :question, :goodbye

  #Define a method to be used to generate random answers
  def get_fortune
    randomNo = 1 + rand(6)

    #Assign an answer based on the randomly generated number
    case randomNo
```

```ruby
      when 1
        $prediction = "yes"
      when 2
        $prediction = "no"
      when 3
        $prediction = "maybe"
      when 4
        $prediction = "hard to tell. Try again"
      when 5
        $prediction = "unlikely"
      when 6
        $prediction = "unknown"
    end

  end

#This method displays the 8 ball greeting message
def say_greeting
    greeting = "\t\t  Welcome to the Virtual Crazy 8 Ball game!" +
    "\n\n\n\n\n\n\n\n\n\n\n\nPress Enter to " +
             "continue. \n\n: "
  print greeting
 end

#This method displays the 8 ball's primary query
def get_question
    question = "Type your question and press the Enter key. \n\n: "
  print question
 end

#This method displays the 8 ball answers
def tell_fortune(randomAnswer)
  print "The answer is " + randomAnswer + ". \n\n: "
 end

#This method displays the 8 ball's closing message
def say_goodbye
    goodbye = "Thanks for playing the Virtual Crazy 8 Ball game!\n\n"
```

```
    puts goodbye
  end

end
```

The `class` definition begins by specifying four class properties. The `randomNo` property will be used to store a random number between 1 and 6. The `greeting` property will be used to store a text string containing the game's welcome message. The `question` property will be used to store a text string that will be used to notify the player when it is time to ask a question. The `goodbye` property will be used to store a text string that holds the game's closing message.

In addition to the four class properties, the class also defines five methods. The first method is named `get_fortune` and is responsible for randomly selecting one of six possible answers to the player's questions. It accomplishes this task using the `rand` method, which retrieves a random number in the form of an integer.

 The `rand` method returns a random number between 1 and the specified upper limit. Therefore `rand(6)` returns a number that is greater than 0 and less than 6. Adding 1 to this number results in a range of number from 1 to 6.

The randomly generated number, stored in `randomNo`, is used in a case code block that assigns a text string representing one of six 8 ball answers to the `$prediction` global variable.

 A *case* code block is a structure for implementing conditional logic. It compares a single value, in this case `randomNo`, to a series of possible matching values, as specified by one or more `when` statements. You will learn more about how to work with the case code block in Chapter 4, "Implementing Conditional Logic."

The next method defined is the `say_greeting` method, which assigns a text string to the class's `greeting` property and then uses the `print` method to display that string. The `get_question` method comes next. It assigns a text string to the class's `question` property and then uses the `print` method to display that string. The `tell_fortune` method is then defined. It accepts a single argument, which is assigned to a local variable named `randomAnswer`. This variable is then used to formulate a text statement that is displayed using the `print` method. The last method that is defined is the `say_goodbye` method, which assigns a text string to the class's `goodbye` property and then uses the `print` method to display that string.

Step 5: Instantiating New Objects

The next step in creating the Ruby Virtual Crazy 8 Ball game is to instantiate both of the custom classes that you just defined by adding the following statements to the end of the script file.

```
# Main Script Logic -------------------------------------------------

Console_Screen = Screen.new  #Initialize a new Screen object
Eight_Ball = Ball.new  #Initialize a new Ball object
```

As you can see, a single object is being instantiated based on each class using the new method. A variable named Console_Screen is used to represent the Screen object and a variable named Eight_Ball is used to represent the Ball object.

Step 6: Greeting the Player

Now that the scripts' objects have been instantiated, it is time to begin working with them to interact with and control both the screen and 8 ball. To begin, add the following statements to the end of the script file.

```
Console_Screen.cls  #Clear the display area

Eight_Ball.say_greeting  #Call method responsible for greeting the player

Console_Screen.pause  #Pause the game
```

The first statement executes the Screen class's cls method to clear the display area. The second statement executes the Ball class's say_greeting method to display a greeting message. The last statement uses the Screen class's pause method to pause the game and give the player a chance to review the greeting message.

Step 7: Prompting for Confirmation to Continue

Once the player dismisses the 8 ball's greeting message, the game sets up a loop that requires the player to provide confirmation of her intention to play. This will provide the player the chance to cancel game play in the event the game was started by accident. The script statements responsible for performing this task are shown next and should be added to the end of the script file.

```
answer = ""  #Initialize variable that is used to control the game's first
             #loop

#Loop until the player enters y or n and do not accept any other input.
```

```
until answer == "y" || answer == "n"

  Console_Screen.cls  #Clear the display area

  #Prompt the player for permission to begin the game
  print "Would you like to have your fortune predicted? (y/n)\n\n: "

  answer = STDIN.gets  #Collect the player's response
  answer.chop!  #Remove any extra characters appended to the string

end
```

The first statement initializes a variable that will be used to control the execution of the loop that follows, in which a series of script statements have been embedded. The loop has been set up to execute until the player enters a value of y or n when prompted for confirmation. By using a loop to control the execution of the embedded statements, you are able to validate the player's input. If the player responds by keying in anything other than a y or n, the loop will execute again, re-prompting the player to provide valid input.

 A *loop* is a structure that permits a set of statements to be executed repeatedly a preset number of times or until a specified condition occurs. You will learn all about Ruby's support for loops in Chapter 5, "Working with Loops."

Step 8: Analyzing the Player's Response

The next step in the development of the game is to further analyze the input that the player has provided. This is accomplished by adding the following conditional logic statements to the end of the script file.

```
#Analyze the player's response
if answer == "n"  #See if the player elected not to play

else  #The player has elected to play the game

end
```

 The rest of the statements in the script will either be embedded within these statements or placed immediately after them. These statements control the high-level conditional logic for the script. The statements that you embed between the first two statements will execute when the player responds with a reply of n when asked for permission to play the game. The statements that you embed between the last two statements will execute when the player responds with a reply of y.

Step 9: Managing Early Termination of the Game

This next script statements are to be executed when the player responds with a value of n when prompted for confirmation to play the game and therefore should be placed between the opening if statement and the else statement that you added to the script file in the previous step.

```
Console_Screen.cls  #Clear the display area

#Invite the player to return and play again
puts "Okay, perhaps another time. \n\n"
```

As you can see, these statements clear the scripts and then display a text message that encourages the player to return and play again later.

Step 10: Responding to Player Questions

The rest of the statements that you will add to the script file need to be placed between the else and the end statements that are responsible for outlining the script's overall controlling logic.

```
#Initialize variable that is used to control the game's primary loop
gameOver = "No"

#Loop until the player decides to quit
until gameOver == "Yes"

  Console_Screen.cls  #Clear the display area

  #Call upon the method responsible for prompting the player to ask a
  #question
  Eight_Ball.get_question

  #Call upon the method responsible for generating an answer
  Eight_Ball.get_fortune

  Console_Screen.pause  #Pause the game
```

```
Console_Screen.cls  #Clear the display area

#Call upon the method responsible for telling the player the 8 ball's
#answer
Eight_Ball.tell_fortune $prediction

Console_Screen.pause  #Pause the game

Console_Screen.cls  #Clear the display area
#Find out if the player wants to ask another question
print "Press Enter to ask another question or type q to quit. \n\n: "

answer = STDIN.gets  #Collect the player's response
answer.chop!  #Remove any extra characters appended to the string

#Analyze the player's response
if answer == "q"  #See if the player elected not to play
  gameOver = "Yes"  #The player wants to quit
end

end

Console_Screen.cls  #Clear the display area

#call upon the method responsible for saying goodbye to the player
Eight_Ball.say_goodbye
```

This final set of statements is responsible for managing the overall play of the game. For starters, a variable named gameOver is defined and assigned an initial value of "No". This variable is used to control the execution of the loop that follows. This loop contains the script statements that prompt the player to ask the 8 ball a question and then call upon the various object methods as required to execute Screen and Ball methods that control Screen and Ball interaction.

Upon each execution of the loop, the Ball class's get_question method is executed. This method displays a message that is used to prompt the player to enter a question. Next, the get_fortune method is called. This method is responsible for randomly selecting the 8 ball's answer. The 8 ball's answer is then displayed by calling on the tell_fortune method. Finally, a message is displayed that instructs the player to either press the Enter key to ask another question or to type q and press Enter to end the game. The player's response is then collected and assigned to the answer variable. The String class's chop! method is executed to remove the end of line character from the end of the variable's value, after which the value is analyzed to determine whether it is equal to q. If it is, the value of gameOver is set equal to "Yes", resulting in the end of the loop. Otherwise the value of gameOver remains unchanged and the loop executes again.

Once the loop finishes executing, it is time to bring the game to a close. This is accomplished with the last three statements shown above—which clear the screen and display the 8 ball closing message, thanking the player for taking time to play.

Running Your New Ruby Script Game

Okay, that's it. Go ahead and save your Ruby script. Assuming that you have followed along carefully and that you did not make any typing mistakes when keying in the code statements that make up the script file, everything should work as expected. If you run into any errors, read the resulting error messages carefully to ascertain what went wrong. If necessary, go back and review the script and look for mistyped or missing scripts statements.

 If you really run into trouble when creating your version of the Ruby Virtual Crazy 8 Ball game, you can go to this book's companion website at www.courseptr.com/downloads and download the source code for this game and then compare it to your script file to see where things went wrong.

SUMMARY

In this chapter, you learned how to create and work with text strings. This includes learning different ways of formulating strings as well as how to manipulate strings using different string methods. You learned how to define custom classes and then to instantiate new objects based on these classes. You learned how to define object properties and methods and to reference these properties and methods. You also learned how to store and retrieve object data using variables and the rules for formulating variables names.

Now, before you move on to Chapter 4, "Implementing Conditional Logic," I suggest you set aside a few more minutes to work on the Ruby Virtual Crazy 8 Ball game by implementing the following list of challenges.

CHALLENGES

1. As currently written, the Ruby Virtual Crazy 8 Ball game is a little sparse when it comes to communicating effectively with the player. Consider spicing things up a bit to make it more descriptive and interesting.

2. Currently, the game responds to player questions by retrieving one of six randomly selected answers. Consider making the game more unpredictable by expanding the list of possible choices from six to ten or more.

IMPLEMENTING CONDITIONAL LOGIC

A
s has already been demonstrated in each of the game scripts that you have worked on in this book, it is virtually impossible to create Ruby scripts of any level of complexity without performing some degree of conditional analysis. This analysis might involve examining things like player input or the value of a randomly generated number. To perform this analysis, Ruby provides you with access to a number of conditional expressions, modifiers, and logical operators that you can use to compare different values and control the logical execution of different script statements. This will allow you to create Ruby scripts that are capable of altering their execution based on the data that they are presented with and will result in scripts that are adaptive and handle many different types of situations. In addition to showing you how to apply conditional logic within your Ruby scripts, this chapter will show you how to create your next computer game, the Ruby Typing Challenge game.

Specifically, you will learn how to:

- Work with if expressions and modifiers
- Work with unless expressions and modifiers
- Use the case block to compare one condition against a range of values
- Use different logical operators to perform different types of comparisons
- Use the ternary operator to perform conditional analysis

PROJECT PREVIEW: THE RUBY TYPING CHALLENGE GAME

In this chapter, you will learn how to create a new computer game called the Ruby Typing Challenge game. This Ruby script will demonstrate how to apply conditional logic to analyze user input through the development of a computer typing test that evaluates the player's typing skills.

The Ruby Typing Challenge game begins displaying a welcome screen as shown in Figure 4.1.

FIGURE 4.1

The welcome screen for the Ruby Typing Challenge game.

Next, the game prompts the player for permission to begin the test as demonstrated in Figure 4.2. The player is instructed to respond with a y/n answer.

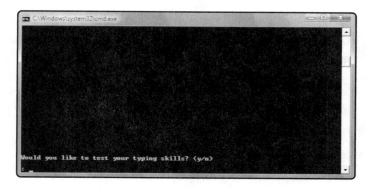

FIGURE 4.2

Player confirmation is required to begin taking the test.

If the player decides not to take the typing test, the screen shown in Figure 4.3 displays and the game will end once the player presses the Enter key.

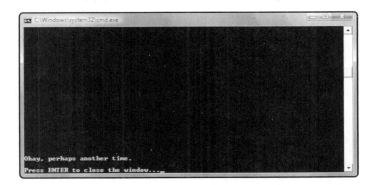

FIGURE 4.3

The player has elected not to take the test.

If, on the other hand, the player elects to take the typing test, the instructions shown in Figure 4.4 display.

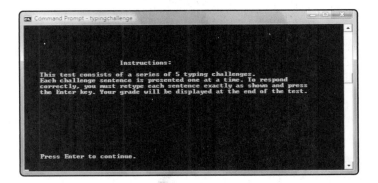

FIGURE 4.4

Instructions provide the player with information needed to understand how to take the test.

Next, the first of a series of five sentences is presented as demonstrated in Figure 4.5. In response, the player must type the sentence exactly as shown and then press the Enter key.

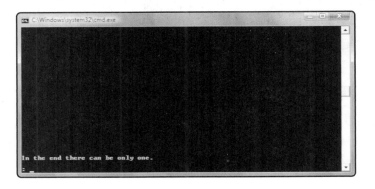

FIGURE 4.5

An example of one of the Ruby Typing Test game's typing challenges.

As soon as the player presses the Enter key, the game analyzes the player's input to determine whether it exactly matches the game's sentence. If the player's input is identical to the game's sentence, the screen shown in Figure 4.6 displays. If the player makes one or more typing mistakes, a different message displays notifying the player that she has failed to correctly type the sentence.

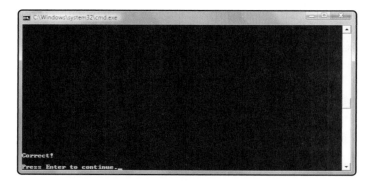

FIGURE 4.6

The player has correctly typed the challenge sentence.

The game's sentences grow longer as the test progresses. Once the player has typed in all five sentences, the game analyzes the player's score and displays a message indicating whether or not the player has passed the test as demonstrated in Figure 4.7.

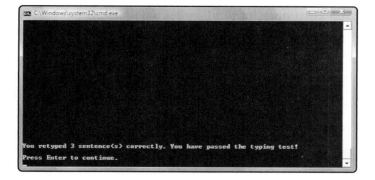

FIGURE 4.7

To pass the test the player must correctly type at least three sentences.

Once the player presses the Enter key, the screen showing the score is dismissed. Finally, a message displays thanking the player for taking the time to take the typing test as shown in Figure 4.8.

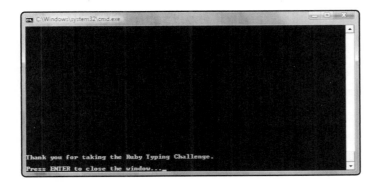

FIGURE 4.8

The game ends after thanking the player for taking the time to play.

USING CONDITIONAL LOGIC TO CREATE ADAPTIVE SCRIPTS

Using Ruby, you can create scripts that consist of a series of statements that are executed in sequential order, one after the other, without any alteration in the logical flow of the scripts. However, while this approach may work well with small scripts that perform simple tasks, scripts that process sequentially are not well suited to tasks that involve any level of complexity. For example, as you have already seen in all the game scripts that you have worked on in this book, some level of conditional execution is almost always required. This execution might involve prompting the player for permission to play a game and then either ending or continuing the game based on an analysis of the player's response.

People use conditional logic all the time. Therefore, from a programming standpoint, it is a relatively easy concept to understand. For example, every morning people around the globe awake and must make a decision as to whether or not to go to work. Based on that decision, different courses of action must be taken. For example, take a look at Figure 4.9, which visually outlines the conditional logic involved in selecting from two alternatives.

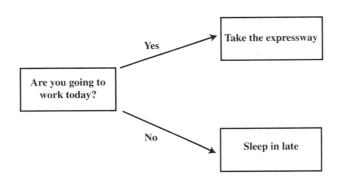

FIGURE 4.9

Choosing between different courses of action.

This same basic logic can easily be applied to the development of a computer program or script. For example, take a look at Figure 4.10.

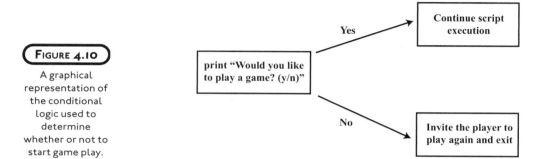

FIGURE 4.10

A graphical representation of the conditional logic used to determine whether or not to start game play.

HINT

Figures 4.9 and 4.10 are both examples of simple flowcharts. A *flowchart* is a tool used to graphically represent some or all of a script's logical flow. Flowcharts are often created by programmers to outline the overall design of the logic involved in designing a computer program or script prior to beginning work on it. By first creating a flowchart, programmers provide themselves with a high-level outline of the overall logic involved. This gives programmers the ability to focus on the overall process required to create the program and helps to identify logical errors in the program's design before investing time in program development and testing.

Flowcharts are often used in large projects involving the combined efforts of many programmers. Once created, flowcharts can be used to identify different parts of a program or project, making the division of work easier while also helping to ensure that each programmer has a good understanding of how the part of the program or project he is assigned fits into the overall scheme of things.

As you can see, Figure 4.10 outlines two separate and distinct courses of action, of which only one will be followed, based on the user's response as to whether or not to begin game play. The logic outlined in the flowchart can be directly translated into script statements, as demonstrated here:

```ruby
puts "Would you like to play a game? (y/n) "
answer = STDIN.gets
answer.chop!

if answer == "n"
  puts "Sorry to hear that. Please return and play again soon."
```

```
else
  puts "OK, let's play!"
  .
  .
  .
end
```

Here, the `puts` method is executed and passed a text string that is used to display a message that prompts the player to respond with a value of y or n to indicate whether to continue game play. The player indicates her decision by keying in the appropriate response and pressing the Enter key.

The key point to understand regarding the application of conditional programming logic is that when it comes right down to it, all that is happening is an evaluation of whether a tested condition is true or false. Based on the result of the analysis, the appropriate set of program statements is then executed.

Ruby provides programmers with access to several ways of applying conditional logic, each of which is designed to address a specific type of situation. A list of available options for applying conditional logic is outlined here.

- **The `if` modifier.** A conditional evaluation appended to the end of Ruby statements to conditionally control the execution of the statement.
- **The `unless` modifier.** A conditional evaluation appended to the end of Ruby statements that performs the opposite type of evaluation as the `if` modifier.
- **The `if` expression.** Used to create complex conditional evaluations spread out over multiple lines.
- **The `unless` expression.** Used to create complex conditional evaluations spread out over multiple lines that perform the opposite type of evaluation as an `if` expression.
- **`Case`.** A conditional evaluation that performs a series of conditional tests, each of which is compared to a single value.
- **The Ternary Operator.** An operator that facilitates the inclusion of a conditional expression within another statement.

PERFORMING ALTERNATIVE TYPES OF COMPARISONS

Up to this point in the book, all the comparison operations that have been demonstrated have used the == comparison operator. Like other modern programming languages, Ruby provides programmers with access to a range of comparison operators. For example, instead of setting up a comparison test that evaluates whether one value is equal to another, you might want to know whether one value is greater than or less than another value. This type of analysis uses comparison operators. Table 4.1 provides a list of the comparison operators supported by Ruby.

TABLE 4.1	RUBY COMPARISON OPERATORS
Operator	**Description**
==	Equal
!=	Not equal
<	Less than
<=	Less than or equal to
>	Greater than
>=	Greater than or equal to

The rest of this chapter will provide you with examples of how to work with the comparison operators shown in Table 4.1.

CONDITIONAL LOGIC MODIFIERS

One quick and easy way that Ruby allows you to integrate conditional logic into your Ruby scripts is through the use of conditional logic modifiers. Using Ruby's modifiers, you can append a conditional check onto the end of other Ruby statements to control the conditional execution of the statement.

The if Modifier

Using the if modifier, you can attach a conditional test to the end of a Ruby statement to control the execution of that statement. This conditional test consists of the if keyword followed by an expression formulated using a comparison operator as demonstrated in the following example.

```
print "Enter your age and press Enter:  "
answer = STDIN.gets
answer.chop!

puts "You must be 18 or older to play this game!" if answer.to_i < 18
```

Here, the user is prompted to specify her age. The value of the number that is supplied by the user is then analyzed to determine whether it is less than 18. If it is, the puts statement to which the modifier has been appended is executed. However, if the number entered by the user is 18 or greater, the execution of the puts statement is skipped.

An advantage of appending conditional modifiers to the end of script statements is that it helps you to write compact script statements and thus to reduce the overall size of your script files. A disadvantage of this approach is that modifiers only work with individual statements. If you need to control the execution of multiple lines of code, you will be better off using conditional expressions as demonstrated later in this chapter.

The unless Modifier

As an alternative to the if modifier, you might want to use the unless modifier. The unless modifier is the logical opposite of the if modifier. As such, there is nothing that you can accomplish using the unless modifier that you cannot accomplish with the if modifier. Therefore, its use is really just a matter of preference.

To see the unless modifier in action, take a look at the following example.

```
print "Enter your age and press Enter:   "
answer = STDIN.gets
answer.chop!

puts "You must be 18 or older to play this game!" unless answer.to_i > 17
```

As you can see, this example is nearly identical to the previous example, except instead of using the if modifier, the unless modifier has been substituted. In addition, the less than comparison operator was replaced with the greater than operator and the number 18 has been replaced with the number 17. Both this and the preceding example produce the same result.

WORKING WITH IF AND UNLESS EXPRESSIONS

Using if and unless expressions, you can spread out conditional statements over multiple lines, making these forms of conditional tests even more powerful than their modifier equivalents. As such, you can use conditional expressions to group together and control the execution of large numbers of statements, making your scripts easier to read and maintain.

Building if Expressions

Unlike if modifiers, if expressions are capable of controlling the execution of more than one statement, making them even more powerful and useful. The if expression supports a very flexible syntax that provides the ability to use the expression in a number of different ways. A high-level outline of the if expression's syntax is provided here:

```
if condition then
  statements
elsif condition then
  statements
  .
  .
  .
else
  statements
end if
```

condition represents an expression that is to be tested. *statements* represents one or more script statements that are to be conditionally executed. *elsif* represents an option keyword that when used allows additional conditional tests to be performed. else is another optional keyword that when specified allows you to identify an alternate set of programming statements that are to be executed when none of the preceding conditions that have been tested evaluates as being true.

Replacing if Modifiers with if Expressions

To better understand how to work with this powerful and extremely useful expression, you need to see examples of it in action. Earlier in this chapter, the following example was presented to demonstrate the use of the if modifier.

```
print "Enter your age and press Enter:  "
answer = STDIN.gets
answer.chop!


puts "You must be 18 or older to play this game!" if answer.to_i < 18
```

Using the if expression, this example could be rewritten as shown here.

```
print "Enter your age and press Enter:  "
answer = STDIN.gets
answer.chop!


if answer.to_i < 18 then
  puts "You must be 18 or older to play this game!"
end
```

As you can see, this version of the example is more longwinded than the if modifier example. However, as demonstrated in the next code block, you can use the if expression to include any number of statements inside the opening `if` and closing `end` statements, allowing the conditional execution of any number of statements.

```
if answer.to_i < 18
  puts "You must be 18 or older to play this game!"
  puts "Goodbye."
  exit
end
```

 Note the use of the `exit` method in the previous example. The `exit` method is provided by the `kernel` class. This method forces the immediate termination of a Ruby script.

Creating Single-Line if Expressions

As has been stated, the syntax support of the `if` expression is very flexible, allowing for many formats. For example, the following example demonstrates how to format an `if` expression that fits on a single line.

```
x = 10
if x == 10 then puts "x is equal to 10" end
```

When used in this format, the `if` expression is very similar to the `if` modifier, except that in the case of the `if` modifier, the conditional logic that is executed is appended to the end of the statement instead of being defined at the beginning of the statement as demonstrated here.

```
x = 10
puts "x is equal to 10" if x == 10
```

Providing an Alternative Course of Action

In addition to executing one or more script statements when a test condition evaluates as being true, you can modify an `if` expression to execute one or more statements in the event the test condition evaluates as being false. To accomplish this, you need to add the optional `else` keyword to the expression as demonstrated here.

```
x = 10
if x == 10 then
  puts " x is equal to 10"
else
  puts " x does not equal 10"
end
```

Here, either of two `puts` statements executes depending on whether or not the value assigned to x is equal to 10.

Checking for Alternative Conditions

There will be times when you will need to examine a series of conditions to find out which one of them evaluates as being true. One way of accomplishing this is to define a series of statements as demonstrated here.

```
if x == 10 then puts "x is 10"  end
if x == 15 then puts "x is 15"  end
if x == 20 then puts "x is 20"  end
if x == 25 then puts "x is 25"  end
```

The objective of these statements is to find out which of four possible values has been assigned to x. If you prefer, you could use the `if` expression's optional `elsif` keyword to rewrite this example as shown here.

```
if x == 10 then puts "x is 10"
elsif x == 15 then puts "x is 15"
elsif x == 20 then puts "x is 20"
elsif x == 25 then puts "x is 25"
end
```

HINT

If you need to execute more than one statement when a matching condition is found, you would need to reformat the previous example as shown here.

```
if x == 10 then
  puts "x is 10"
elsif x == 15 then
  puts "x is 15"
elsif x == 20 then
  puts "x is 20"
elsif x == 25 then
  puts "x is 25"
end
```

You could also include the optional `else` keyword to provide an alternative course of action should none of the preceding tests evaluate as being true.

```
if x == 10 then puts "x is 10"
elsif x == 15 then puts "x is 15"
```

```
elsif x == 20 then puts "x is 20"
elsif x == 25 then puts "x is 25"
else puts "The value of x is unknown"
end
```

 TRICK   If you want to save a few keystrokes when keying in your script statements, Ruby allows you to replace the then keyword with the : character as demonstrated here.

```
if x == 10 : puts "x is 10"
elsif x == 15 : puts "x is 15"
elsif x == 20 : puts "x is 20"
elsif x == 25 : puts "x is 25"
end
```

Creating unless Expressions

Just like the if modifier and the unless modifier, the unless expression is the polar opposite of the if expression. As such, there is nothing that you can accomplish with an if expression that you cannot accomplish with an unless expression. For example, take a look at the following if expression.

```
print "Enter your age and press Enter:   "
answer = STDIN.gets
answer.chop!

if answer.to_i < 18
  puts "You must be 18 or older to play this game!"
end
```

To convert it to an unless expression, all you need to do is replace the if keyword with the unless keyword and then replace the < operator with the > operator as shown here. Also note that the number 18 has been replaced with the number 17.

```
print "Enter your age and press Enter:   "
answer = STDIN.gets
answer.chop!

unless answer.to_i > 17
  puts "You must be 18 or older to play this game!"
end
```

Obviously, when it comes right down to it, the decision whether to use an `if` expression or an `unless` expression is really just a matter of personal preference.

USING CASE BLOCKS TO ANALYZE DATA

In addition to the `if` and `unless` modifiers and expressions, Ruby also provides you with access to the `case` block as a means of comparing a series of expressions against a single expression to see whether any of the expressions being evaluated result in equivalent value. Although you can accomplish the same thing using an `if` expression that includes a series of `elsif` statements, the `case` block is better suited for situations where you need to compare a single condition to a whole range of possible matches. The syntax for the `case` block is outlined here:

```
case expression
  when value
    statements
      .
      .
      .
  when value
    statements
  else
    statements
end
```

As you can see, the `case` block includes one or more `when` statements. The *expression* that is evaluated is compared to the value associated with one or more `when` statements. If a match occurs with one of the `with` statements, any statements associated with that `when` statement are executed. If none of the `when` statements matches the value of the expression being evaluated, the statements belonging to the optional `else` statement (if present) are executed.

 TRICK   As is the case with the `if` expression, you can replace the `then` keyword with a colon (`:`).

As a quick example of how to set up a `case` block, take a look at the following statements.

```
x = 10

case x

  when 1
```

```
    puts "*"
  when 5
    puts "*****"
  when 10
    puts "**********"
  else
    puts "No stars"

end
```

Here, the value assigned to x is compared to a series of values specified in a case block. Since the value of x is 10, the `puts "**********"` will be executed. Had none of the when statements contained a matching value, the `puts` statement associated with the else keyword would have executed. In most cases, you will find that it takes fewer lines of code to set up a case block than an equivalent if expression using multiple elsif keywords.

If you want, you can omit the specification of an expression on the open case statement when setting up a case block as demonstrated here.

```
puts "\nWelcome to the vacation calculator!\n\n"

print "How many years have you worked for the company? \n\n: "
answer = STDIN.gets
answer.chop!
answer = answer.to_i

case
  when (answer.between?(1, 5))
    puts "You are entitled to 1 week of vacation per year."
  when (answer.between?(6, 10))
    puts "You are entitled to 2 weeks of vacation per year."
  when (answer.between?(11, 15))
    puts "You are entitled to 3 weeks of vacation per year."
  when (answer.between?(16, 20))
    puts "You are entitled to 4 weeks of vacation per year."
  else
    puts "You are entitled to 5 weeks of vacation per year."
End
```

Here, a series of unique expressions has been specified for each when statement. The statements belonging to the first expression that evaluates as true will be executed and the rest of the statements are skipped.

 TRICK   Note the use of the between? method in each of the expressions in the previous example. Each of Ruby's numeric classes supports this method, which returns a value of true or false depending on whether or not a number is within a specified range.

USING THE TERNARY OPERATOR

Ruby provides you with an additional option, known as the ternary operator (?:), available for setting up conditional logic. Using the ternary operator, you can evaluate the value of two different expressions and make variable assignments as a result of that comparison. The syntax required to work with the ternary operator is

```
variable = expression ? true_result : false_result
```

Here, *variable* is assigned the value returned by the statement. *expression* represents the expression that is evaluated. *true_result* is the value that is assigned if the expression evaluates as true and *false_result* is the value returned if the expression evaluates as being false. To get a better understanding of how to work with the ternary operator, take a look at the following example.

```
print "\n\nEnter your age and press Enter:   "
answer = STDIN.gets
answer.chop!
answer = answer.to_i

result = answer < 18 ? "denied!" : "approved!"

puts "\n\nYour access has been " + result + "\n\n"
```

Here, the user is prompted to enter her age. The statement that contains the ternary operator evaluates the expression answer < 18. If the user enters a value of 17 or less, the expression evaluates as true, and a value of "denied!" is assigned to a variable named result. On the other hand, if the user enters a value that is 18 or higher, the expression evaluates as being false and a value of "approved!" is assigned to result.

NESTING CONDITIONAL STATEMENTS

Some situations require more complicated analysis than can be accomplished using an individual conditional modifier expression. In these situations, you may need to perform one conditional evaluation based on the result of another evaluation. One way of addressing this type of challenge is to embed one conditional statement inside another through a process called *nesting*. To get a better understanding of how nesting works, take a look at the following example.

```
redStatus = "Go"
blueStatus = "Go"
greenStatus = "Go"

if redStatus == "Go" then
  if blueStatus == "Go" then
    if greenStatus == "Go" then
      puts "All systems are go. Prepare for launch!"
    end
  end
end
```

Here, a series of three `if` expressions has been set up. If the first expression evaluates as false, the remaining `if` expressions are skipped. Otherwise, the second `if` expression is executed. If the second `if` expression proves false, the third `if` expression is skipped. Otherwise, it is executed. Nesting also works just as effectively for `unless` expressions.

TRAP   Although there is no limitation on how deeply you can nest conditional statements within one another, going more than two or three deep will result in script code that is difficult to read and maintain.

COMBINING AND NEGATING LOGICAL COMPARISON OPERATIONS

Like most modern programming languages, Ruby also supports the use of a number of logical, or Boolean, operators. These operators are listed in Table 4.2.

As you can see, the and and && operators are essentially identical. The only difference between the two is that the and operator has a higher level of precedence than the && operator. Likewise, the or and || operators work identically, the only difference being precedence, with or having higher precedence than ||. The and and && operators evaluate the second operand only if the first operand is true. The or and || operators evaluate the second operand only if the first operand is false.

Operator	Type	Example
and	Evaluates as true if both comparisons evaluate as true	x > 1 and x < 10
&&	Evaluates as true if both comparisons evaluate as true	x > 1 && x < 10
or	Evaluates as true if either comparison evaluates as true	x I I or x I I0
||	Evaluates as true if either comparison evaluates as true	x I I yyx I I0
not	Reverses the value of a comparison	not (x > 5)
!	Reverses the value of a comparison	! (x > 5)

TABLE 4.2   RUBY BOOLEAN OPERATORS

To get a better understanding of how to work with these operators, let's look at a few examples. For starters, take a look at the following statements.

```
print "Enter your age and press Enter:   "
reply = STDIN.gets
reply.chop!
reply = reply.to_i


puts "You are eligible to play this game!" if reply >= 18 && reply <= 65
```

Here, the `if` modifier at the end of the last statement uses the `&&` operator to determine whether the value assigned to `reply` is both greater than or equal to 18 and less than or equal to 65. If both expressions evaluate as true, the `puts` statement executes. Otherwise, the `puts` statement is skipped.

HINT

If you want, you can enclose expressions within parentheses to make things easier to understand as demonstrated here:

```
puts "You are eligible to play this game" if (reply >= 18) && (reply <= 65)
```

Next, let's look at an example that uses the || operators.

```
print "What is your rank?: "
rank = STDIN.gets
rank.chop!
rank = rank.to_i


puts "Access is permitted." if rank == 1 || rank == 3
```

Here, the last statement shown above uses the || operator to determine if the value assigned to rank is equal to 1 or to 3. If either (or both) or these expressions proves true, the associated puts statement executes. If neither expression proves true, the puts statement is skipped.

This final example demonstrates how to work with the ! operator, which negates or reverses the value returned from a conditional expression.

```
randomNo = 1 + rand(10)

print "What number am I thinking of? \n\n:   "
answer = STDIN.gets
answer.chop!

puts "Wrong! My number was " + randomNo.to_s if ! (answer.to_i == randomNo)
```

Here, a random number between 1 and 10 is generated using the rand method and assigned to a variable named randomNo. The user is then prompted to try and guess the randomly generated number. The player's answer is then converted to an integer and compared to the value or randomNo. If these two values are not equal, the associated puts statement executes. Otherwise, it does not execute.

BACK TO THE RUBY TYPING CHALLENGE GAME

Okay, now it is time to turn your attention back to the development of this chapter's game project, the Ruby Typing Challenge game. As you work on creating this script, focus on the conditional expression to control the script's overall controlling logic and its use in evaluating the accuracy of the player's typing.

Designing the Game

The development of the Ruby Typing Challenge game will be completed in 13 steps as outlined here.

1. Open your text or script editor and create a new file.
2. Add comment statements to the beginning of the script file to document the script and its purpose.
3. Define a Screen class representing the console window.
4. Define a Test class representing the typing test.
5. Develop a method in the Test class that displays a greeting message.
6. Develop a method in the Test class that displays test instructions.
7. Develop a method in the Test class that presents typing challenge sentences.
8. Develop a method in the Test class that displays test results.

9. Initialize script objects.
10. Prompt the player for permission to start the typing test.
11. Develop the overall programming logic responsible for analyzing the player response.
12. Manage early game termination.
13. Execute methods required to deliver the typing test.

Remember to follow along carefully and not to skip any steps or parts of steps as you work your way through.

Step 1: Creating a New Ruby File

The first step in creating the Ruby Typing Challenge game is to open your text or code editor and create a new Ruby script file. Assign the script a filename of TypingChallenge.rb and save it in the folder where you have decided to store all your Ruby script files.

Step 2: Documenting the Script and Its Purpose

Now that you have created a new script file, the next step is to add the following comment statements to it. These statements document the name of the script and its purpose.

```
#-------------------------------------------------------------------
#
# Script Name: TypingChallenge.rb
# Version:     1.0
# Author:      Jerry Lee Ford, Jr.
# Date:        October 2007
#
# Description: This Ruby script demonstrates how to apply conditional logic
#              in order to analyze user input and control script execution
#              through the development of a computer typing test that
#              evaluates the player's typing skills.
#
#-------------------------------------------------------------------
```

Step 3: Defining a Class Representing the Console Window

Now it is time to define the first of two new classes. The first class is named Screen. This is accomplished by adding the following statements to the end of the script file.

```
# Define custom classes ------------------------------------------

#Define a class representing the console window
class Screen
```

```
def cls  #Define a method that clears the display area
  puts ("\n" * 25)  #Scroll the screen 25 times
  puts "\a"  #Make a little noise to get the player's attention
end

def pause    #Define a method that pauses the display area
  STDIN.gets  #Execute the STDIN class's gets method to pause script
             #execution until the player presses the Enter key
end

end
```

The first method defined in the class is the `cls` method. The method contains two statements. The first statement writes 25 blank lines to the console window to clear the screen. The second statement processes a string that contains the `\a` escape character, in order to play an audible beep sound, notifying the player each time the terminal screen is cleared.

Step 4: Defining a Class Representing the Typing Test

The next step in the development of the Ruby Typing Challenge game is to begin the definition of a new class that will represent the game's typing test. This is accomplished by adding the following statements to the end of the script file. This class will be named `Test` and will eventually be populated with four methods.

```
#Define a class representing the typing test
class Test

end
```

Step 5: Defining the display_greeting Method

Now it is time to begin developing the methods belonging to the `Test` class. The script statements that make up this class's first method are shown here and should be inserted in between the class's opening and closing statements.

```
#This method displays the 8-ball greeting message
def display_greeting

  Console_Screen.cls  #Clear the display area

  #Display a welcome screen
  print "\t\t  Welcome to the Ruby Typing Challenge game!" +
```

```
        "\n\n\n\n\n\n\n\n\n\n\n\nPress Enter to " +
                "continue. \n\n: "


Console_Screen.pause         #Pause the game

    end
```

This method, named `display_greeting`, is responsible for displaying the game's welcome screen.

Step 6: Defining the display_instructions Method

The script statements for the `Test` class's next method are shown here and should be added to the end of the class definition, immediately following the previously defined method.

```
#Define a method to be used to present test instructions
def display_instructions

    Console_Screen.cls       #Clear the display area
    puts "\t\t\tInstructions:\n\n"  #Display a heading

    #Display the game's instructions
    puts %Q{    This test consists of a series of 5 typing challenges.
    Each challenge sentence is presented one at a time. To respond
    correctly, you must retype each sentence exactly as shown and press
    the Enter key. Your grade will be displayed at the end of the test.
    \n\n\n\n\n\n\n\n\n
    Press Enter to continue.\n\n}

    Console_Screen.pause         #Pause the game

End
```

This method, named `display_instructions`, is responsible for displaying a text string containing instructions for playing the game.

Step 7: Defining the present_test Method

The script statements for the `Test` class's third method are shown here and should be added to the end of the class definition.

```
#Define a method to be used to present typing challenges
def present_test(challenge)

  Console_Screen.cls      #Clear the display area
  print challenge + "\n\n: "  #Display the challenge sentence
  result = STDIN.gets  #Collect the player's input
  result.chop!          #Remove the end of line marker

  #Analyze the player input and see if it is correct
  if challenge == result then

    #Keep track of the number of correctly retyped challenge sentences
    $noRight += 1
    Console_Screen.cls      #Clear the display area
    #Keep the player informed
    print "Correct!\n\nPress Enter to continue."
    Console_Screen.pause      #Pause the game

  else

    Console_Screen.cls      #Clear the display area
    #Keep the player informed
    print "Incorrect!\n\nPress Enter to continue."
    Console_Screen.pause      #Clear the game

  end

end
```

This method, named present_test, is responsible for displaying sentences passed to it as string arguments and for collecting and storing player input. Next, an if expression has been set up to analyze the player's input to see whether it matches the original sentence. If the player input matches the original sentence, the value of $noRight is incremented by one to keep track of the number of correctly typed sentences. In addition, a text string is displayed that notifies the player of the match.

If, on the other hand, the player makes a typing mistake when keying in the sentence, the value of $noRight is not incremented and a different text string is displayed, notifying the player of her mistake.

Step 8: Defining the determine_grade Method

The script statements for the Test class's final method are shown here and should be added to the end of the class definition.

```
#Define a method to be used to display test results
def determine_grade

  Console_Screen.cls        #Clear the display area

  #To pass the test the player must correctly retype 3 sentences
  if $noRight >= 3 then

    #Inform the player of the good news
    print "You retyped " + $noRight.to_s + " sentence(s) correctly. "
    puts "You have passed the typing test!\n\nPress Enter to continue."

  else  #The player has failed the test

    #Inform the player of the bad news
    print "You retyped " + $noRight.to_s + " sentence(s) correctly. "
    puts "You have failed the typing test!\n\nPress Enter to continue."

  end

end
```

This method, named determine_grade, is responsible for determining whether the player has passed the typing test. To pass, the player must correctly type in at least three sentences. To determine the player's score, an if expression has been set up to evaluate the value assigned to $noRight to see if it is greater than or equal to three. If it is, a text string is displayed notifying the player that she has passed.

If, on the other hand, the value of $noRight is not greater than or equal to three, the else portion of the if expression is executed, informing the player that she has failed the test.

Step 9: Initializing Script Objects

Now it is time to initialize instances of both the Screen and the Test classes. This is accomplished by adding the following statements to the end of the script file.

```
# Main Script Logic ------------------------------------------------------

#Initialize global variable that will be used to keep track of the number
#of correctly retyped sentences
$noRight = 0

Console_Screen = Screen.new  #Instantiate a new Screen object
Typing_Test = Test.new       #Instantiate a new Test object

#Execute the Test object's display_greeting method
Typing_Test.display_greeting
```

In addition to instantiating the `Console_Screen` and `Typing_Test` objects, these statements initialize a global variable named `$noRight`, which will be used to keep track of the number of correctly typed sentences and also execute the `Test` class's `display_greeting` method.

Step 10: Getting Permission to Begin the Test

The next step in the development of the Ruby Typing test game is to add programming logic that prompts the player for permission to start the test. This is accomplished by adding the following statements to the end of the script file.

```
#Execute the Screen object's cls method in order to clear the screen
 Console_Screen.cls

#Prompt the player for permission to begin the test
print "Would you like to test your typing skills? (y/n)\n\n: "

answer = STDIN.gets  #Collect the player's response
answer.chop!  #Remove any extra characters appended to the string

#Loop until the player enters y or n and do not accept any other input.
until answer == "y" || answer == "n"

  Console_Screen.cls  #Clear the display area

  #Prompt the player for permission to begin the test
  print "Would you like to test your typing skills? (y/n)\n\n: "

  answer = STDIN.gets  #Collect the player's response
```

```
answer.chop!  #Remove any extra characters appended to the string
```

```
end
```

Step 11: Developing the Controlling Logic Required to Administer the Test

At this point, all that remains to be done is to develop the controlling logic responsible for analyzing the player's response when prompted for permission to begin the test. This is accomplished by adding the following statements to the end of the script file.

```
#Analyze the player's response
if answer == "n"  #See if the player elected not to play


else  #The player wants to take the test


end
```

The code statements from the next step will need to be embedded into the first part of the above if expression and the statements from the last step will need to be embedded at the end of the if expression (between the else and end statements).

Step 12: Managing Early Game Termination

This next set of script statements is executed in the event the player responds with a value of n when prompted for permission to start the typing test and therefore should be placed in between the opening if statement and the else statement that you added to the script in the previous step.

```
Console_Screen.cls  #Clear the display area


#Invite the player to return and play again
puts "Okay, perhaps another time.\n\n"
```

These statements clear the screen and then display a text message encouraging the player to return and take the test at another time.

Step 13: Executing the Typing Test

This final set of script statements is responsible for administering the typing test and should be embedded into the bottom half of the if expression that you added to the script file in step 11.

```
#Execute the Test object's display_instructions method
Typing_Test.display_instructions
```

```
#Display typing challenges and grade each answer by calling on the
#Test object's present_test method
Typing_Test.present_test "In the end there can be only one."
Typing_Test.present_test "Once a great plague swept across the land."
Typing_Test.present_test "Welcome to Ruby Programming for the Absolute" +
" Beginner."
Typing_Test.present_test "There are very few problems in the world " +
"that enough M&Ms cannot fix."
Typing_Test.present_test "Perhaps today is a good day to die. Fight " +
"beside me and let us die together."

#Notify the player of the results by executing the Test object's
# determine_grade method
Typing_Test.determine_grade

Console_Screen.pause        #Pause the game

Console_Screen.cls  #Clear the display area
#Thank the player for taking the typing test
puts "Thank you for taking the Ruby Typing Challenge.\n\n"
```

As you can see, these statements consist of a series of calls to methods belonging to the `Typing_Test` and `Console_Screen` objects. The first method that is called is the `display_instructions` method. This is followed by five separate calls to the `present_test` method. Each of these calls passes a different text string to the method, which displays the sentence and then prompts the player to retype it. Next, the `determine_grade` method is called. This method determines whether the player passed or failed the test. Finally, the screen is cleared and a message is displayed thanking the player for taking time to play the Ruby Typing Challenge game.

Running Your New Ruby Script Game

All right! You now have everything that you need to build and execute the Ruby Typing Challenge game. Go ahead and save and then run your new Ruby script. As long as you have followed along carefully and have not mistyped anything or accidentally skipped the keying in of any statements, everything should work as advertised. In the event you run into any errors, carefully review them and look for clues regarding where things may have gone awry. If necessary, go back and review the entire script and look for mistyped or missing script statements.

SUMMARY

In this chapter you learned different ways of implementing conditional logic in your Ruby scripts. This included learning how to work with `if` and `unless` modifiers and expressions. This chapter showed you how to use the ternary operator to perform conditional analysis. You also learned how to use the `case` statement to match one value up against a range of possible options and to use different types of logical operations to perform different types of comparisons. Last, you learned how to combine and negate logical comparison operations using Ruby Boolean operators.

Now, before you move on to Chapter 5, "Working with Loops," I suggest you set aside a little extra time to make a few improvements to the Ruby Typing Challenge game by implementing the following list of challenges.

CHALLENGES

1. As currently provided, the game's instructions are limited. Consider revising them to provide more detailed information to the player, including an explanation of how the typing test is graded.

2. Consider modifying the game to make it a more meaningful experience. For example, consider increasing the number of typing challenges from 5 to 10. In addition, consider increasing the length and complexity of any additional sentences that you may add.

3. Rather than using a pass/fail grading systems, consider assigning grades like A, B, C, D, and F to the player. To do so, you will have to further analyze the player's grade using either a `case` statement or a series of `elsif` statements.

4. Consider modifying the game to display a list of all mistyped sentences at the end of the game to give the player the opportunity to determine where typing error(s) were made.

WORKING WITH LOOPS

Loops are an essential part of most Ruby scripts. Loops provide you with the ability to repeat a set of statements over and over again as many times as necessary to perform a particular task. Using a minimum amount of code, loops facilitate the development of scripts that can process huge amounts of data. Loops can also be used when interacting with users to create scripts capable of collecting any amount of input the user wants to supply. Ruby provides support for loops in a number of different ways, including built-in language constructs, statement modifiers, and object methods. Ruby also provides you with commands that you can use to alter and control the execution of loops. In addition to showing you how to develop programming logic, this chapter will also show you how to develop your next computer game, the Superman Movie Trivia Quiz.

Specifically, you will learn how to:

- Set up `while`, `until`, and `for…in` loops
- Work with `while` and `until` modifiers
- Work with `times`, `upto`, `downto`, and `step` loop methods
- Use the `break`, `redo`, `next`, and `retry` commands to alter loop execution

PROJECT PREVIEW: THE SUPERMAN MOVIE TRIVIA QUIZ

In this chapter, you will learn how to create a new computer game called the Superman Movie Trivia Quiz. This Ruby script demonstrates how to work with loops when collecting player input through the creation of an interactive quiz that evaluates the player's knowledge of the Superman movies series. The game begins by displaying a welcome screen, as shown in Figure 5.1.

FIGURE 5.1

The welcome screen for the Superman Movie Trivia Quiz.

After pressing the Enter key to dismiss the welcome screen, the player is prompted for permission to begin the quiz, as shown in Figure 5.2.

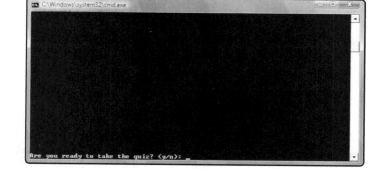

FIGURE 5.2

The player must provide confirmation before the quiz can begin.

If the player decides not to play and responds by entering a value of n, the message shown in Figure 5.3 displays, encouraging the player to return and take the quiz another day.

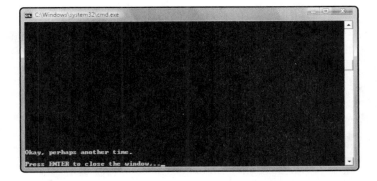

FIGURE 5.3

The player is
encouraged to
return and take
the quiz some
other time.

If the player elects to take the quiz, the instructions shown in Figure 5.4 are displayed, providing the player with an understanding of how the quiz will be administered.

FIGURE 5.4

Like any good
game, instructions
on how to play are
provided.

Next, the first of five questions is displayed and the player is prompted to specify a letter representing one of four possible answers, as demonstrated in Figure 5.5.

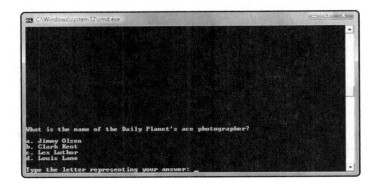

FIGURE 5.5

All quiz questions
are multiple
choice.

To advance to the next quiz question, the player must enter an a, b, c, or d and press the Enter key. Any other input is rejected. Once a valid answer has been provided, the game evaluates the player's input and then displays the next quiz question. Once all questions have been answered, the game displays a message indicating whether the player has passed or failed the quiz. If the player has passed, ranking is assigned as demonstrated in Figure 5.6.

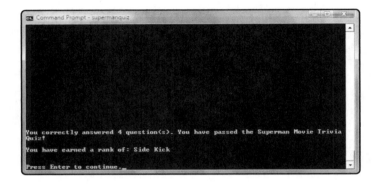

FIGURE 5.6

To pass the quiz, the player must correctly answer a minimum of three questions.

Finally, once the player presses the Enter key to dismiss the previous screen, the screen shown in Figure 5.7 displays.

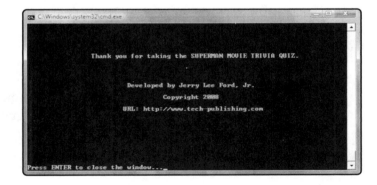

FIGURE 5.7

The Superman Movie Trivia Quiz's closing screen thanks the player for taking the quiz.

GETTING LOOPY

In order to effectively process large amounts of data, you need to learn how to work with loops. A *loop* is a collection of statements that execute repeatedly as a unit. Loops facilitate the processing of large text files or the collection of unlimited amounts of user input. Loops also provide you with the ability to develop scripts that can repeat the execution of any number of commands.

Using loops, you can develop computer games that can be replayed over and over again. Loops also provide the basis for developing program logic that helps to process and validate user input, allowing the script to continue only once valid data has been input. Loops let you develop powerful programming logic using a minimum number of lines of code that can be executed as many times as necessary to accomplish a particular task. This helps reduce the size of your Ruby scripts, making them easier to develop and maintain.

Ruby provides you with access to many different types of loops, which can be organized broadly using the following three categories.

- **Language constructs**. Language commands that are part of the core Ruby scripting language.
- **Modifiers**. A modifier appended to the end of a Ruby statement to repeat the statement until a specified condition is met.
- **Methods**. Loops provided as methods associated with specific objects.

Each of these three categories of loops will be examined in detail throughout the rest of this chapter.

REPEATING THINGS USING LOOPS

As has been stated, loops provide you with the ability to identify a collection of statements that need to be repeatedly executed. One way of adding loops to your Ruby script files is to work with the `while`, `until`, and `for` loops. These three loops are supported by Ruby as a part of the core programming language. These loops are sometimes thought to be a little "old school" by many Ruby programmers who prefer instead to work with loop methods provided by various object classes. Still, `while`, `until`, and `for` loops are still widely used and an understanding of how to work with them is fundamental to becoming a good Ruby programmer.

Working with while Loops

The `while` loop is a loop that executes as long as a tested condition is true. The syntax for this loop is outlined here:

```
while Expression [ do | : ]
  Statements
end
```

Expression is any valid Ruby expression that is tested at the beginning of each iteration of the loop. do or : are mutually exclusive and can be left off if you decide to spread the loop out over more than one line. *Statements* represents any number of statements that you want to execute each time the loop repeats.

To get a good feel for how to work with the `while` loop, take a look at the following example.

```
x = 1

while x <= 10 do
   puts x
   x += 1
end
```

Here, a variable named `x` has been defined and assigned a value of 1. Next, a `while` loop has been set up to run as long as the value of `x` is less than or equal to 10. The first statement in the loop prints the current value assigned to `x` and the second statement increments the value of `x` by 1. As a result, when executed, this loop will display a list of numbers from one to ten as shown here:

```
1
2
3
4
5
6
7
8
9
10
```

 TRAP One thing to be on the lookout for whenever you work with any type of loop is an endless loop. An *endless loop* is a loop that is set up in such as way that it never stops executing, unnecessarily using computer resources.

Working with until Loops

The `until` loop is pretty much the opposite of the `while` loop. Instead of looping while a tested expression remains true, the `until` loop executes until the tested condition becomes true. The syntax for the `until` loop is outlined here:

```
until Expression [ do | : ]
   Statements
end
```

Expression is any valid Ruby expression that is tested at the beginning of each iteration of the loop. `Do` or `:` are mutually exclusive and can be left off if you decide to spread the loop out over more than one line. *Statements* represents any number of statements that you want to execute each time the loop repeats.

As the following example demonstrates, the until loop works very much like the while loop.

```
x = 1

until x >= 10 do
  puts x
  x += 1
end
```

Here, a variable named x has been defined and assigned a value of 1. Next, an until loop has been set up to run until the value of x becomes greater than or equal to 10. The first statement in the loop prints the current value assigned to x and the second statement increments the value of x by 1. When executed, this example displays a list of numbers from one to nine, as shown here:

```
1
2
3
4
5
6
7
8
9
```

Working with for...in Loops

The for...in loop is provided as part of Ruby's core programming language. This loop is designed to process collections of data. The syntax of the for...in loop is outlined here:

```
for Variable in Expression [ do | : ]
  Statements
End
```

Variable represents a variable used by the loop to store the value of the current item in the collection that is being processed. *Expression* is any valid Ruby expression that specifies the collection to be processed. Do or : are mutually exclusive and should be left off if you decide to spread the loop out over more than one line. *Statements* represents any number of statements that you want to execute each time the loop repeats.

To get a good feel for how to work with the for...in loop, take a look at the following example.

```
MyList = ["Molly", "William", "Alexander", "Jerry", "Mary"]

for x in MyList
 print "Hi ", x, "!\n"
end
```

Here, an array named MyList has been created and assigned a list of five names. Next, a for...in loop has been set up that will repeat once for each element stored in the array. Each time the loop repeats, or iterates, it prints a text string that displays the value of the array item currently being processed.

An *array* is an indexed collection of items stored as a list. You will learn how to create and work with arrays in Chapter 6, "Working with Collections of Data."

When executed, the preceding example displays the following output.

```
Hi Molly!
Hi William!
Hi Alexander!
Hi Jerry!
Hi Mary!
```

The for...in loop can also be used to process a range of items, as demonstrated here:

```
for i in 1..5
   puts i
end
```

When executed, this example displays the following output.

```
1
2
3
4
5
```

Ruby range operator (..) provides you with the ability to display a range of consecutive letters or numbers. For example, (1..5) would create the following set of numbers: 1 2 3 4 5. Likewise, (a..z) would produce a set of all lowercase letters starting with the letter a going consecutively all the way to the letter z.

USING LOOP MODIFIERS

A loop modifier is an expression added to the end of another Ruby statement that executes that statement as a loop. Ruby supports both `while` and `until` loop modifiers. Loop modifiers are perfect for situations where you only need to repeat the execution of a single statement.

The while Modifier

The `while` modifier evaluates a Boolean expression and then conditionally executes the statement to which is has been appended as long as that condition remains true. The `while` modifier supports the following syntax.

```
Expression while Condition
```

Expression is any Ruby statement that you want to be conditionally executed. *Condition* is a Boolean expression that, once evaluated, determines whether the opening expression is executed. To better understand how to work with the `while` modifier, take a look at the following example.

```
counter = 1
counter += 1 while counter < 10
puts counter
```

Here, a variable named `counter` has been assigned a value of 1. Next, the value of `counter` is incremented by 1 if and only if the value assigned to `counter` is less than 10. The `while` modifier, attached to the second statement, repeats the statement over and over again, incrementing the value of `counter` repeatedly until `counter` becomes equal to 10, at which time the loop stops executing and the last statement executes, displaying the value of `counter`, which of course is 10.

The until Modifier

The `until` modifier is pretty much the opposite of the `while` modifier, executing the statement to which it has been appended repeatedly until a specified condition is evaluated as being true. The syntax used by the `until` modifier is shown here:

```
Expression while Condition
```

Expression is any Ruby expression that you want to be conditionally executed. *Condition* is a Boolean expression that, once evaluated, determines whether the opening expression is executed. To better understand how to work with the `until` modifier, take a look at the following example.

```
counter = 1
counter += 1 until counter >= 10
puts counter
```

Here, a variable named `counter` has been assigned a value of 1. Next, the value of `counter` is increment by 1 over and over again until the value of `counter` becomes equal to or greater than 10.

EXECUTING LOOPING METHODS

Ruby provides you with access to a number of different looping methods belonging to various classes. These methods simplify loop construction and help to eliminate the chance of errors that can otherwise sometimes occur if you work instead with Ruby's built-in language looping constructions (`while`, `until`, and `for...in`).

Working with the each Method

One very commonly used looping method is the `each` method. This method is supported by a number of different Ruby classes, including the `Array`, `Dir`, `Hash`, and `Range` classes.

The `each` method supports the following syntax.

Object`.each {  |i|  `*Statement*` }`

Object represents the object upon which the `each` loop will operate. *i* represents a variable used by the `each` loop to represent the current item being processed by the loop, and *Statement* represents a Ruby statement that you want to be repeatedly executed.

The previous syntax outlines the use of the `each` method when processing a single Ruby statement. If you want, you may use the following syntax when working with the `each` method to repeat the execution of one or more statements.

Object`.each do |i|`
    Statements
`end`

To better understand how to work with the `each` method, take a look at the following example.

```
MyList = ["Molly", "William", "Alexander", "Jerry", "Mary"]

MyList.each do |x|
 print "Hi ", x, "!\n"
end
```

Here, a loop made up of five items has been defined. Next, the Array class's each method is used to process and display each of the items stored in the array. The first time the loop executes, the value of the first array element ("Molly") is assigned to the x variable, which is then used inside the loop to display the element. The each method automatically iterates once for each item stored in the array, resulting in the display of the following output.

```
Hi Molly!
Hi William!
Hi Alexander!
Hi Jerry!
Hi Mary!
```

HINT

When compared to built-in language-based loop constructs like while and until, the elegance and sophistication of Ruby's method-based loops become quickly apparent. For example, you could use one of these types of loops to process the contents of an array as demonstrated here.

```
MyList = ["Molly", "William", "Alexander", "Jerry", "Mary"]
x = 0

while (x < MyList.length)
 print "Hi ", MyList[x], "!\n"
 x += 1
end
```

When executed, this example produces results that are identical to those produced by the previous example, which used the each method. However, unlike the each method, which automatically takes care of the processing of every element in the array for you, when you use the while or until loops, it is up to you to specify a variable that will be used to control how many times the loop iterates. In addition, it is also up to you to determine how many times the loop repeats. You must also provide an expression for tracking the last element processed in the array and also remember to increment the value of the controlling variable at the end of each execution of the loop.

Clearly, using the each method, and the other class methods outlined in the following sections, is not only easier and more straightforward, but it also removes the many opportunities for error that occur when you try working with more traditional loop constructs.

Working with the times Method

The times method is used to execute a code block a specific number of times. The times method is provided by the Integer class. The times method supports the following syntax.

Integer.times { |*i*| *Statement* }

Here, *Integer* represents a numeric integer value. *i* represents an iterator used by the times method to represent the current item being processed by the loop, and *Statement* represents a Ruby statement that you want to be repeatedly executed.

    An *iterator* is a variable used to process the contents of a list of items.

The previous syntax outlined the use of the times method when processing a single Ruby statement. If you want, you may use the following syntax when working with the times method to repeat the execution of one or more statements.

Integer.times do |*i*|
  Statements
end

To better understand how to work with the times method, take a look at the following example.

```
puts "Watch me count!"
10.times {|x| puts x}
```

Here, the times method has been used to set up an example that will iterate 10 times. Upon each iteration of the loop, the value x is assigned an integer value representing the number of iterations of the loop, which is then displayed on the screen using the puts method. The end result is the display of the following output.

```
Watch me count!
0
1
2
3
4
5
6
7
8
9
```

If you prefer, you could rewrite the example as shown next using the multiline version of the `times` method's syntax.

```
puts "Watch me count!"

10.times do
  |x| puts x
end
```

Working with the upto Method

Another time-saving looping method that merits discussion is the `upto` method, which is provided by the `Integer` class. This method results in a loop that iterates a predetermined number of times. The syntax for a single-line version of the `upto` method is outlined here:

```
Integer.upto(EndValue) { |i| Statement }
```

Integer represents a numeric integer value. *EndValue* is an integer that is passed to the `upto` method as an argument and which is used to tell the method how many times to iterate. *i* represents a variable used by the `upto` method to represent the current item being processed by the loop, and *Statement* represents a Ruby statement that you want to be repeatedly executed.

The multiline version of this method's syntax is shown here:

```
Integer.upto(endValue) do |i|
  Statements
end
```

To better understand how to work with the `upto` method, take a look at the following example.

```
1.upto(10) do |x|
  print x, ") Hello!\n"
end
```

Here, a loop has been set up that executes 10 times (starting at 1 and ending at 10) as specified by the value the integer and the argument (10) passed to the `upto` method. When executed, this example displays the following output.

```
1) Hello!
2) Hello!
3) Hello!
4) Hello!
5) Hello!
6) Hello!
```

```
7) Hello!
8) Hello!
9) Hello!
10) Hello!
```

Working with the downto Method

Another time-saving looping method that merits discussion is the downto method, which is provided by the Integer class. As its name implies, it allows you to set up a loop that iterates a predetermined number of times, starting at a specified integer value and counting down to whatever integer value that is passed to it.

The syntax for the single-line version of the downto method is outlined here:

```
Integer.downto(EndValue) { |i| Statement }
```

Integer represents a numeric integer value. *EndValue* is an integer that is passed to the downto method as an argument and is used to tell the method how many times to iterate. *i* represents a variable used by the downto loop to represent the current item being processed by the loop and *Statement* represents a Ruby statement that you want to be repeatedly executed.

The multiline version of this method's syntax is shown here:

```
Integer.downto(endValue) do |i|
   Statements
end
```

To better understand how to work with the downto method, take a look at the following example.

```
5.downto(1) do |x|
 print x, ") Hello!\n"
end

puts "That's all folks!"
```

Here, a loop has been set up that iterates five times. The first time that loop iterates, x is assigned a value of 5. Upon each subsequent iteration, the value of x is decremented. The loop repeats over and over again (from 5 down to 1). When executed, this example generates the output shown here:

```
5) Hello!
4) Hello!
3) Hello!
```

```
2) Hello!
1) Hello!
That's all folks!
```

Working with the step Method

The step method is used to set up loops that execute a predefined number of times. The step method works with the Float and Integer classes. The syntax for a single-line version of the step method is outlined here:

```
Number.step(EndNumber, Increment) { |i|  Statement }
```

Number represents an integer or floating point number. *EndNumber* specifies a value that when reached will terminate the loop's execution. *Increment* specifies the value used to increment the loop each time it iterates. *i* represents a variable used by the step method to represent the current item being processed by the loop and *Statement* represents a Ruby statement that you want to be repeatedly executed.

The multiline version of this method's syntax is shown here:

```
Number.step(EndNumber, Increment) do |i|
  Statements
end
```

To better understand how to work with the step method, take a look at the following example.

```
1.step(10,2) do |x|
 print x, ". Counting by 2\n"
end
```

Here, a loop has been set up that will execute five times. The first time the loop executes, the value of i is set to 1. The value of i is then incremented by two upon each subsequent iteration, resulting in the following output.

```
1. Counting by 2
3. Counting by 2
5. Counting by 2
7. Counting by 2
9. Counting by 2
```

The step method is quite flexible. You can set it up to decrement instead of increment, as demonstrated here:

```
50.step(10,-5) do |x|
  print x, ". I'm getting smaller!\n"
end
```

Here, the loop has been set up to start at 50, decrementing by 5 upon each iteration until a value of 10 is reached. As a result, the following output is displayed.

```
50. I'm getting smaller!
45. I'm getting smaller!
40. I'm getting smaller!
35. I'm getting smaller!
30. I'm getting smaller!
25. I'm getting smaller!
20. I'm getting smaller!
15. I'm getting smaller!
10. I'm getting smaller!
```

Working with the loop Method

Another useful loop method is the aptly named loop method. This method belongs to the Kernel module. Like all of the other looping methods, the loop method supports two forms of syntax. The single-line version of its syntax is outlined here:

```
loop { Statement }
```

Here, *Statement* represents a statement that is executed each time the loop iterates. The multiline version of its syntax is outlined here:

```
loop do
  Statements
end
```

Loops created using the loop method run forever unless you provide a way to terminate them. To better understand how to work with the loop method, take a look at the following example:

```
counter = 1

loop do

  print counter.to_s + " "
  counter += 1
```

```
  break if counter == 10

end
```

Here, a variable named `counter` is assigned a value of 1. Next, a loop has been set up using the `loop` method. Upon each iteration, the `print` method is used to display the current value assigned to `counter`. In addition, the value of `counter` is incremented by 1. At the end of each iteration of the loop, the last statement ensures that the loop has a way of terminating, executing the `break` command if the value of counter is equal to 10. When executed, this example generates the following output.

```
1 2 3 4 5 6 7 8 9
```

ALTERING LOOP EXECUTION

There may be times in which certain events occur that will make you want to prematurely halt the execution of a loop. For example, you might set up a loop that processes the elements stored in an array, looking for a particular item. Once found, you might want to stop executing the loop, rather than wasting unnecessary resources processing the rest of the elements in the array when you have no use for them. You could accomplish this by executing the `break` command, which is just one of a number of commands supplied by Ruby as a means of altering a loop's default execution. A list of these commands, as well as brief descriptions of each, is provided here:

- `break`. Terminates the execution of a loop.
- `redo`. Repeats the current execution of the loop without evaluating its condition and without iterating.
- `next`. Stops the current iteration of the loop and immediately begins a new iteration.
- `retry`. Restarts the loop from the beginning, resetting the value of the iterator.

Prematurely Terminating Loop Execution

The `break` command provides the ability to terminate the execution of a loop at any time. To see an example of how you might use this command, take a look at the following example.

```
loop do

  print "Type q to quit this script. "

  answer = STDIN.gets
  answer.chop!
```

```
  break if answer == "q"

end
```

Here, a loop has been set up that by default will repeat forever. Each time the loop executes, a message is displayed that prompts the user to type q to quit the script. The user's response is captured and stored in a variable named answer. The last statement in the loop has been set up to conditionally execute the break command based on whether the user provides the proper input.

Repeating the Current Execution of a Loop

The redo command forces a loop to repeat without evaluating its condition and without iterating. As such, it might be used to force a loop to execute again should something occur that you do not like. To see how this command works, take a look at the following example.

```
i = 1

loop do
  puts i
  redo if i == 3
  i += 1
end
```

Here, a loop has been set up that will execute forever. Each time the loop repeats, the value of a variable named i is incremented by 1. The second statement within the loop conditionally executes the redo command when the value of i becomes 3. As such, after the third iteration of the loop, once the value of i has become 3, the redo command is executed, preventing the last statement in the loop from executing again, as demonstrated here:

```
1
2
3
3
3
.
.
.
```

Skipping to the Next Iteration of a Loop

The next command stops the current iteration of the loop and immediately begins a new iteration. However, before the new iteration occurs, the loop condition is evaluated. Thus the loop only executes again if the analysis of the loop condition permits it. To see an example of how you might use the redo command, look at the following example.

```
for i in 1..5
  next if i == 3
  puts i
end
```

Here a for…in loop has been set up to execute over a range of numbers, starting at 1 and going through 5. Upon the third execution of the loop, when the value of i is equal to 3, the next command is executed. However, the loop continues executing two more times, ultimately resulting in the following output.

```
1
2
4
5
```

Restarting a Loop from the Beginning

The retry command restarts a loop from the beginning. As such, the value of the loop's iterator is reset, starting the loop over from the beginning, as demonstrated here:

```
for i in 1..5
  puts i
  retry if i == 3
end
```

Here, a for…in loop has been set up that repeats for a range of numbers from 1 to 5. Each time the loop runs, the value of i is displayed. When the value of i becomes equal to 3, the retry command is executed, starting the loop over again. As such, an endless loop has been created that repeatedly counts from 1 to 3 forever, as demonstrated here:

```
1
2
3
1
```

2
3
.
.
.

BACK TO THE SUPERMAN MOVIE TRIVIA QUIZ

Okay, now it is time to turn your attention back to the development of this chapter's game project, the Superman Movie Trivia Quiz. As you follow along with the development of this script, focus on the use of loops to manage the process of prompting the player for permission to start the quiz to ensure that only valid input is accepted.

Designing the Game

The development of the Superman Movie Trivia Quiz will be completed in 12 steps, as outlined here:

1. Open your text or script editor and create a new file.
2. Add comment statements to the beginning of the script file to document the script and its purpose.
3. Define a class representing the terminal window.
4. Define a class representing the game's quiz.
5. Add a `display_greeting` method to the `Quiz` class.
6. Add a `display_instructions` method to the `Quiz` class.
7. Add a `disp_q` method to the `Quiz` class.
8. Add a `determine_grade` method to the `Quiz` class.
9. Add a `display_credits` method to the `Quiz` class.
10. Instantiate script objects.
11. Prompt the player for permission to begin the quiz.
12. Administer the quiz.

As you work your way through each of the steps in the development of the Superman Trivia Quiz, remember to follow along carefully, not skip any steps, and to be on the lookout for typos.

Step 1: Creating a New Ruby File

The first step in developing the Superman Movie Trivia Quiz is to start up your text or script editor and then create a new Ruby script file. Once created, save this file with a file name of SupermanQuiz.rb.

Step 2: Documenting the Script and Its Purpose

The next step in the creation of the Superman Movie Trivia Quiz is to add the following statements to the script file. These statements provide a high-level description of the game and its purpose.

```
#------------------------------------------------------------------
#
# Script Name: SupermanQuiz.rb
# Version:     1.0
# Author:      Jerry Lee Ford, Jr.
# Date:        October 2007
#
# Description: This Ruby script demonstrates how to work with loops when
#              collecting user input through the creation of an
#              interactive quiz that evaluates the player's knowledge of
#              the Superman movie series.
#
#------------------------------------------------------------------
```

Step 3: Defining a Screen Class

The Superman Movie Trivia Quiz makes use of two custom classes, each of which contains numerous methods that control the overall interaction with the user and the execution of the game. The first of these classes is named screen. The script statements that make up this class are provided next and should be added to the end of the script file.

```
# Define custom classes ---------------------------------------------

#Define a class representing the console window
class Screen

  def cls  #Define a method that clears the display area
    puts ("\n" * 25)  #Scroll the screen 25 times
    puts "\a"  #Make a little noise to get the player's attention
  end

  def pause    #Define a method that pauses the display area
    STDIN.gets  #Execute the STDIN class's gets method to pause script
                #execution until the player presses the Enter key
```

```
   end

end
```

The first method defined within this class is the `cls` method. The method consists of two statements. The first statement writes 25 blank lines to the console window to clear the screen. The second statement contains a string that is made up of the `\a` escape character that when executed results in an audible beep, whose purpose is to notify the player that the terminal screen has been cleared.

Step 4: Defining a Class Representing the Quiz

The second class definition that you need to add to your new Ruby script is the `Quiz` class. This class will be used to represent the game's quiz and will contain methods used to administer and control the delivery of the quiz. Let's begin the creation of the `Quiz` class by adding the following statements to the end of the script file.

```
#Define a class representing the Superman Movie Trivia Quiz
class Quiz

end
```

Step 5: Defining the display_greeting Method

The `Quiz` class consists of five methods. The first of these methods is named `display_greeting` and is comprised of the statements outlined next and should be inserted between the class's opening and closing statements.

```
#This method displays the quiz's opening screen
def display_greeting

  Console_Screen.cls  #Clear the display area

  #Display welcome message
  print "\t\t  Welcome to the Superman Movie Trivia Quiz!" +
  "\n\n\n\n\n\n\n\n\n\n\n\n\nPress Enter to " +
          "continue."

  Console_Screen.pause      #Pause the game

end
```

This method is responsible for displaying the quiz's welcome screen and should be placed inside the Quiz class.

Step 6: Defining the display_instructions Method

The second method to be added to the Quiz class is the display_instructions method. The statements that make up this class are shown next and should be added to the end of the class definition, immediately following the previously defined method.

```
#Define a method to be used to present quiz instructions
def display_instructions

  Console_Screen.cls      #Clear the display area
  puts "INSTRUCTIONS:\n\n"  #Display a heading

  #Display the game's instructions
  puts "You will be presented with a series of multiple choice"
  puts "questions. To answer a question, type in the letter of"
  puts "the corresponding answer and press the Enter key. Your"
  puts "grade will be displayed at the end of the test.\n\n\n"
  puts "Good luck!\n\n\n\n\n\n\n\n\n"
  print "Press Enter to continue."

  Console_Screen.pause      #Pause the game

end
```

This method is responsible for displaying a text string containing instructions for taking the Superman Movie Trivia quiz.

Step 7: Defining the disp_q Method

The script statements for the Quiz class's third method are provided next and should be added to the end of the class. This method is responsible for presenting the player with quiz questions and processing the player's answers.

```
#Define a method to be used to present and process quiz questions
def disp_q(question, q_A, q_B, q_C, q_D, answer)

  #Loop until the player inputs a valid answer
  loop do
```

```
Console_Screen.cls        #Clear the display area

#Format the display of the quiz question
puts question + "\n\n"
puts q_A
puts q_B
puts q_C
puts q_D
print "\nType the letter representing your answer: "

reply = STDIN.gets  #Collect the player's answer
reply.chop!          #Remove the end of line marker

#Analyze the player's input to determine if it is correct
if answer == reply then

  #Keep track of the number of correctly answered questions
  $noRight += 1

end

#Analyze the answer to determine if it was valid
if reply == "a" or reply == "b" or reply == "c" or reply == "d" then

  break  #Terminate the execution of the loop

end

  end

end
```

This method consists of a loop that repeatedly executes until the player provides a valid answer to the currently presented quiz question. Quiz questions pass to the method a series of arguments. The first argument that is passed is a text string representing the quiz question. The next four arguments that are passed are mapped to variables named q_A, q_B, q_C, and q_D, which represent four different multiple-choice answers that will be presented along with the question. The last argument passed to the method is assigned to a variable named answer, which is assigned the letter representing the correct answer to the quiz question.

Once parameter assignments have been made, the loop begins to execute, clearing the screen and then displaying the quiz question. The player's answer is then captured and stored in a variable named reply. Next, an if statement has been set up to analyze the value of reply to see if it is equal to the value assigned to answer, in which case the player has correctly answered the quiz question. If this is the case, the value of $noRight is incremented by one to keep track of the number of correctly answered quiz questions.

The last set of statements to be executed conditionally examines the player's input to ensure that it is valid (i.e. that the player entered either a, b, c, or d and nothing else). In the event this is not the case, the break command is executed, terminating the execution of the loop.

Step 8: Defining the determine_grade Method

The script statements for the Quiz class's fourth method are shown next and should be added to the end of the class. This method determines whether the player has passed the quiz.

```
#Define a method to be used to grade and display quiz results
def determine_grade

  Console_Screen.cls        #Clear the display area

  #To pass the test, the player must correctly answer 3 questions
  if $noRight >= 3 then

    #Inform the player of the good news and assign a ranking
    print "You correctly answered " + $noRight.to_s + " question(s). "
    puts "You have passed the Superman Movie Trivia Quiz!\n\n"
    puts "You have earned a rank of: Good Citizen" if $noRight == 3
    puts "You have earned a rank of: Side Kick" if $noRight == 4
    puts "You have earned a rank of: Superhero" if $noRight == 5
    print "\n\nPress Enter to continue."

  else   #The player has failed the quiz

    #Inform the player of the bad news
    print "You missed " + (5 - $noRight).to_s + " questions. "
    puts "You have failed the Superman Movie Trivia Quiz."
    puts "Perhaps you should watch the movies again before returning to"
```

```
    puts "retake the quiz"
    print "\n\nPress Enter to continue."

  end

  Console_Screen.pause        #Pause the game

end
```

To pass the quiz, the player must correctly answer at least three questions. To determine the player's grade, an `if` expression has been set up to evaluate the value assigned to `$noRight`. If it is greater than or equal to three, the player has passed and a series of `puts` statements are executed that notify the player that he has passed. The `puts` statements also assign the player a ranking based on that grade. A ranking of `Good Citizen` is assigned when three questions have been correctly answered. A ranking of `Side Kick` is assigned when four questions are correctly answered, and a ranking of `Superhero` is assigned if the player answers every question correctly.

If, however, the value of `$noRight` is less than three, the player is informed of the failing score and told how many questions were missed.

Step 9: Defining the display_credits Method

The final method to be added to the `Quiz` class is the `display_credits` method. This method is responsible for displaying information about the quiz and its developer, including the developer's ULR. The statements that make up this method are provided next and should be added to the end of the `Quiz` class.

```
#This method displays the information about the Superman Movie Trivia Quiz
def display_credits

  Console_Screen.cls  #Clear the display area

  #Thank the player and display game information
  puts "\t\tThank you for taking the SUPERMAN MOVIE TRIVIA QUIZ.\n\n\n\n"
  puts "\n\t\t\t Developed by Jerry Lee Ford, Jr.\n\n"
  puts "\t\t\t\t  Copyright 2008\n\n"
  puts "\t\t\tURL: http://www.tech-publishing.com\n\n\n\n\n\n\n\n\n\n"

end
```

Step 10: Initializing Script Objects

Now it is time to initialize an instance of the Screen and Quiz classes. This is accomplished by adding the following statements to the end of the script file.

```
# Main Script Logic -------------------------------------------------

#Initialize global variable that will be used to keep track of the number
#of correctly answered quiz questions
$noRight = 0

Console_Screen = Screen.new  #Instantiate a new Screen object
SQ = Quiz.new       #Instantiate a new Quiz object

#Execute the Quiz class's display_greeting method
SQ.display_greeting
```

In addition to instantiating the Console_Screen and SQ objects, these statements define a global variable named $noRight, which will be used to keep track of the number of correctly answered quiz questions and execute the Quiz class's display_greeting method.

Step 11: Getting Permission to Start the Quiz

The next step in the development of the Superman Movie Trivia Quiz is to add the programming logic responsible for prompting the player for permission to begin the quiz. This is accomplished by adding the following statements to the end of the script file.

```
answer = ""

#Loop until the player enters y or n and do not accept any other input.
loop do

  Console_Screen.cls  #Clear the display area

  #Prompt the player for permission to start the quiz
  print "Are you ready to take the quiz? (y/n): "

  answer = STDIN.gets  #Collect the player's response
  answer.chop!  #Remove any extra characters appended to the string
```

```
    break if answer == "y" || answer == "n"

end
```

As you can see, a loop has been set up that executes until the player provides a valid response
(y or n), at which time the break command is executed to terminate the loop.

Step 12: Administering the Quiz

At this point, all that remains is to add the programming logic that is responsible for either
starting the quiz or for terminating it in the event the player decides not to take it. This is
accomplished by adding the following statements to the end of the script file.

```
#Analyze the player's input
if answer == "n"  #See if the player elected not to take the quiz

  Console_Screen.cls  #Clear the display area

  #Invite the player to return and take the quiz some other time
  puts "Okay, perhaps another time.\n\n"

else  #The player wants to take the quiz

  #Execute the Quiz class's display_instructions method
  SQ.display_instructions

  #Execute the Quiz class's disp_q method and pass it
  #arguments representing a question, possible answers and the letter
  #of the correct answer
  SQ.disp_q("What is the name of the Daily Planet's ace photographer?",
  "a. Jimmy Olsen", "b. Clark Kent", "c. Lex Luthor", "d. Louis Lane",
  "a")

  #Call upon the disp_q method and pass it the second question
  SQ.disp_q("What is the name of Clark Kent's home town?",
  "a. Metropolis", "b. Gotham City", "c. Smallville", "d. New York",
  "c")

  #Call upon the disp_q method and pass it the third question
  SQ.disp_q("In which movie did Superman battle General Zod?",
```

```
"a. Superman", "b. Superman II", "c. Superman III", "d. Superman IV",
"b")

#Call upon the disp_q method and pass it the fourth question
SQ.disp_q("What is the name of Superman's father?",
"a. Nimo", "b. Jarrell", "c. Lex Luthor", "d. Krypton",
"b")

#Call upon the disp_q method and pass it the fifth question
SQ.disp_q("Where had Superman been at the start of 'Superman Returns'?",
"a. Moon", "b. Fortress of Solitude", "c. Earth's Core", "d. Krypton",
"d")

#Call upon the Quiz class's determine grade method to display
#the player's grade and assigned rank
SQ.determine_grade

#Call upon the Quiz class's determine grade method to thank
#the player for taking the quiz and to display game information
SQ.display_credits

end
```

As you can see, these statements are controlled by a large if statement. The first part of the if statement checks to see if the player responds with a value of n when prompted for permission to begin the quiz. These statements clear the screen and then display a message intended to encourage the player to return and take the quiz at another time.

In the event the player decides to take the quiz, the statements in the else portion of the if statement block are executed. As you can see, these statements consist of a series of calls to methods belonging to the SQ and Console_Screen objects. The first method that is called is the display_instructions method, which is then followed by five separate calls to the disp_q method. Each of these five calls passes a different set of arguments, representing a quiz question, four multiple choice answers, and the correct answer. Once all five quiz questions have been processed by the disp_q method, the Quiz class's determine_grade method is called. This method is responsible for determining whether the player passed the quiz. Finally, the display_credits method is called, which clears the screen and displays a message thanking the player for taking time to take the quiz.

Running Your New Ruby Script Game

That's everything! At this point you should be ready to take your new Ruby script for a test drive. If you have not done so yet, save your script file and then execute it. As long as you followed along carefully and did not make any typing mistakes along the way, everything should work as expected. If you run into any errors, make sure that you carefully read the resulting error messages to figure out where things went wrong. If necessary, you may have to review the entire script looking for mistyped or missing scripts statements. Once you've found and fixed any errors, put the script through its paces and then share a copy of it with your friends and see what they think of it.

Summary

In this chapter you learned how to incorporate looping logic into your Ruby scripts to set up the repeated execution of statements and code blocks. You learned how to work with many different types of loops, including loops that are provided as Ruby language constructs, loop modifiers, and loops provided as methods belonging to various Ruby classes. Using what you have learned in this chapter, you will be able to develop Ruby scripts that are capable of processing large amounts of data. You will also be able to develop scripts that can perform specific actions over and over again with a minimal amount of code and effort.

Now, before you move on to Chapter 6, "Working with Collections of Data," I suggest you set aside a little extra time to make a few improvements to the Superman Movie Trivia Quiz by implementing the following list of challenges.

Challenges

1. Currently, the Superman Movie Trivia Quiz consists of just five questions. Consider expanding the number of questions to 10, 25, or 30 to produce a more challenging quiz.
2. The instructions displayed at the beginning of the game are a little sparse. Consider beefing them up to make them more useful.
3. Modify the `Quiz` class's `display_credits` method so that it contains your own name and website information. Also, consider adding information to it to provide the player with information about you and the game.

WORKING WITH
COLLECTIONS OF DATA

So far, every time you have worked with data in this book, it has been using variables to store and manage individual pieces of information. While this is certainly an excellent way to manage small amounts of information, things become very difficult when you start creating scripts that need to work with dozens, hundreds, or even thousands of pieces of data at one time. This chapter will show you how to manage groups of related data, like you might find in a personal address book or a small database, using arrays and hashes. Using the information presented in this chapter, you will learn how to develop Ruby scripts capable of storing, retrieving, and manipulating huge amounts of data with a minimum of programming statements. In addition, you will learn how to create a new Ruby script, the Ruby Number Guessing game.

Specifically, you will learn how to:

- Organize related data using lists
- Use lists as a means of assigning data to arrays
- Create arrays and use them to store, retrieve, and process array items
- Create hashes and use them to store, retrieve, and process key-value pairs
- Create loops that process the items stored in arrays and hashes

PROJECT PREVIEW: THE RUBY NUMBER GUESSING GAME

In this chapter, you will learn how to create a new computer script called the Ruby Number Guessing game. This game challenges the player to guess a randomly generated number from 1 to 100 in as few guesses as possible. The game begins by displaying the welcome message shown in Figure 6.1.

Before starting a new round of play, the game requires that the player provide it with permission to begin, as demonstrated in Figure 6.2.

To begin playing, the player must respond by typing a y and pressing the Enter key. Alternatively, the player can enter a value of n to instruct the game to terminate, as shown in Figure 6.3. Any player input other than y or n is ignored.

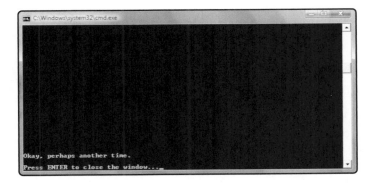

FIGURE 6.3

The player is encouraged to return and play another time.

Assuming the player has elected to play the game, the instructions shown in Figure 6.4 display.

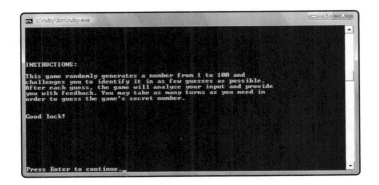

FIGURE 6.4

The game provides the player with instructions on how to play.

Once the player has read and dismissed the instructions by pressing the Enter key, game play begins and the player is prompted to make an initial guess, as shown in Figure 6.5.

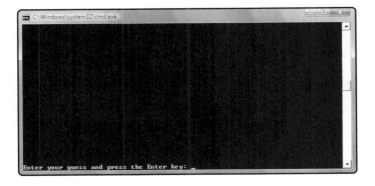

FIGURE 6.5

Valid guesses are between 1 and 100.

After each guess, the game provides the player with a hint that will help him hone in on the game's secret number. Figure 6.6 shows the message that displays when the player's guess is too high.

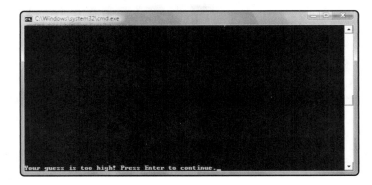

FIGURE 6.6

The game notifies the player that his next guess needs to be lower.

Figure 6.7 shows the message that displays when the player's guess is too low.

FIGURE 6.7

The game notifies the player that his next guess needs to be higher.

The player may make as many guesses as are necessary to finally guess the game's secret number. Once the player guesses the secret number, the message shown in Figure 6.8 displays.

Once the player presses the Enter key, the game prompts the player for permission to play a new game, allowing the player to play as many games as she wants.

FIGURE 6.8

The player has won the game by guessing the secret number.

Processing Related Data as a Unit

All of the examples that you have seen up to this point in the book have involved the storage, manipulation, and retrieval of small amounts of data. As such, variables have been used as the primary means of managing this data. However, as your scripts grow larger and more complex, there will be situations where the number of different pieces of data being managed becomes too large to be effectively managed using variables. Since most of the data managed by a given script is usually related, you can often manage this data in the form of a list.

For example, rather than manipulating the names of 100 individual people using variables, you could add the names to a list and then process the list as a unit. This is a lot easier to manage than trying to process 100 different variables. In Ruby lists can be managed and stored using one of the following structures.

- Arrays
- Hashes

Storing Lists Using Arrays

A *list* is a collection of data. Lists are created as comma-separated items. In Ruby, lists can be used as the basis for populating arrays. An *array* is an indexed list of items. In Ruby, array indexes begin at 0 and are incremented by 1 each time a new item is added. Index numbers can only be whole numbers (integers). In Ruby, arrays are simply viewed as another type of object.

Ruby arrays have an initial element, a final element, and any number of elements in between. Once added to an array, an array element can be referred to by specifying its index position within the array. The following syntax can be used when creating a new array.

VariableName = [Elements]

Here, *VariableName* is the name of a variable to which the array is assigned and *Elements* represents the contents of the array, which are stored as a comma-separated list enclosed within matching square brackets. For example, the following statement creates an array named x and stores five numbers in it.

```
x = [2, 4, 6, 8, 10]
```

If you want to experiment with arrays a bit, you can do so using the irb. For example, start up a new irb session and execute the preceding statement. At this point, the x array has been created and is ready and waiting for you to do something with it. You can then use the inspect method to view the array's contents, as demonstrated here:

```
irb(main):002:0> puts x.inspect
[2, 4, 6, 8, 10]
```

 TRICK inspect is a method associated with most of Ruby's object classes. Its purpose is to provide a text view of an object. In the case of an array, the inspect method will display a list of the elements stored in the array.

Arrays can be used to store any type of object supported by Ruby. For example, the following statement creates a new array called children and stores three text strings in it.

```
children = ["Alexander", "William", "Molly"]
```

Declaring Arrays

Unlike many programming languages, Ruby does not require that you formally declare an array prior to using it. All that you have to do to begin working with a new array is to reference it. In response, Ruby will create a new array. Unlike many programming languages, Ruby does not require that you tell it in advance how big an array will be. Instead, Ruby lets you create and grow an array on the fly, accepting as many or as few items as you want to add to them.

Creating an Array of Strings

As you have already seen, one way to create an array is to assign a list to it, as shown here:

```
children = ["Alexander", "William", "Molly"]
```

A quick way to create an array made up of strings is to use the %w(and) characters, as shown here:

```
children = %w(Alexander William Molly)
```

Here, an array named children has been declared and assigned three string items. The array is created by extracting space-separated string elements. The advantage of using this option when creating string arrays is that you do not have to worry about remembering to provide quotes and commas that are otherwise required when creating an array.

TRICK

You can also use the %W(and) characters to create an array by extracting space-separated string elements while also performing string substitutions for individual words, as shown here:

```
me = "Jerry"

Names = %W(Molly William Alexander #{me} Mary)
puts Names.inspect
```

When executed, this example generates a new array called Names that contains the following items.

```
["Molly", "William", "Alexander", "Jerry", "Mary"]
```

Using the New Method to Create an Array

Yet another way to create an array is to use an object-oriented approach using the Array object's New method.

```
x = Array.new
```

Here, an empty array named x has been created. Using operators and methods shown later in this chapter, you can populate this array.

TRICK

Here is another way of creating an empty array.

```
x = []
```

In this example, an array named x has been created, but has not been assigned a list.

Assigning the Content of One Array to Another

New arrays can also be created by assigning the contents of one array to another array, as demonstrated here:

```
x = [1, 2, 3]
y = x
```

Here an array named x, which contains three numbers, is assigned to a variable named y. As a result of this assignment, y is set up as an array containing a list of three numbers. To prove that the y array was created as described, you can use the inspect method as shown here:

```
puts y.inspect
```

Once executed, this statement will display the following result.

```
[1, 2, 3]
```

Creating a New Array from Two Existing Arrays

Ruby also lets you create a new array by adding two existing arrays together, as demonstrated here:

```
x = [1, 2, 3]
y = [4, 5, 6]
z = x + y
puts z.inspect
```

When executed, this example displays the following output.

```
[1, 2, 3, 4, 5, 6]
```

 TRICK

In an interesting twist on the idea of subtraction, you can use array subtraction to create a new array. Array subtraction takes two arrays, removes any duplicate items, and creates a new array, as demonstrated here:

```
family = %w(Alexander William Molly Daddy Mommy)
parents = %w(Daddy Mommy)
children = family - parents
puts children.inspect
```

Here, two arrays have been defined, one named family with five items and another named parents with two items. A new array named children is then created by subtracting parents from family. When executed, this example displays the following output.

```
["Alexander", "William", "Molly"]
```

As you can see, the duplicate items found in the family and parents array were not added to the new children array.

Adding and Modifying Array Items

In addition to populating an array with items when you initially declare it, Ruby lets you add new items to any array. Ruby also lets you modify existing array items any time you want. One way of doing so is to specify the index number of the item to be replaced or added using the syntax outlined here.

arrayname[indexNo]

Here, *arrayname* is the name of the array and *indexNo* is the index position within the array where the new assignment is to be made.

Modifying an Existing Array Item

To get a feel for how to modify an existing array item, look at the following example, which replaces one of the elements stored in an array.

```
children = ["Alexander", "William", "Molly"]
children[2] = "Mighty One"
puts children.inspect
```

In this example an array named `children` is declared and assigned three initial items. Next, the item stored at index position 2 (`"Molly"`) is replaced with a value of `"Mighty One"`. When executed, this example displays the following output.

```
["Alexander", "William", "Mighty One"]
```

 HINT   Remember, in Ruby arrays start with an index position of 0, so the first item stored in an array has an index position of 0, and the second item stored in the array has an index position of 1.

Adding a New Item to an Array

To add a new item to an existing array, all you have to do is add it using an index number that is one greater than the index number of the last item stored in the array, as demonstrated here.

```
children = ["Alexander", "William", "Molly"]
children[3] = "Dolly"
puts children.inspect
```

When executed, the following output is displayed, showing that the array has been increased by one item.

```
["Alexander", "William", "Molly", "Dolly"]
```

 TRAP   Be careful when adding elements to the end of an array. If you accidentally specify an index number that goes too far beyond the last used index number, you will end up with a range of undefined items, as demonstrated here:

```
children = %w(Alexander William)
children[4] = "Molly"
puts children.inspect
```

When executed, the following output is displayed, showing that the array now contains two `nil` items.

```
["Alexander", "William", nil, nil, "Molly"]
```

Working with the << Method

As has already been stated, in Ruby an array is an object. As such, whenever you work with an array, you can call upon any of the methods associated with Ruby's `Array` class. Once such method is `<<`. Using this method you can add elements to an array by pushing them onto the end of the array, as demonstrated here:

```
Names = []
Names << "Alexander"
Names << "William"
Names << "Molly"
puts Names.inspect
```

Once these statements have been executed, the `Names` array will contain the following list of items.

```
["Alexander", "William", "Molly"]
```

Working with the push Method

If you prefer, you can use the `push` method in place of the `<<` method to add elements to an array by pushing them onto the end of the array, as demonstrated here:

```
Names = []
Names.push("Alexander")
Names.push("William")
Names.push("Molly")
puts Names.inspect
```

Once these statements have been executed, the `Names` array will contain the following list of items.

```
["Alexander", "William", "Molly"]
```

Determining if an Array Is Empty

Before you begin working with an array, you might first want to check to see if anything is in it. One way of accomplishing this is to use the `Array` class's `length` or `size` methods to see if the value that they return is equal to zero. An easier way to accomplish the same thing would be to use the empty? method. This method returns a value of true if the specified array is empty and false if it contains at least one element.

Take a look at the following statements to see an example of how to work with the empty? method:

```
if children.empty? == false then
  children.each {|child| puts child}
else
  puts "The children array is empty"
end
```

Here an array has been created that contains three strings. An if statement is then set up that uses the empty? method to determine if the children array has any items in it. If it does, the each method is used to display the names of every item in the list. If, on the other hand, the array is empty, a text message is displayed instead.

Retrieving Items from an Array

Ruby provides you with a host of different ways to access data stored in an array. This includes the ability to specify particular items as well as ranges of items. Items can also be retrieved based on their locations within arrays.

Retrieving Individual Array Elements

You can retrieve any item located in an array by specifying the name of the array followed by the index number where the item is stored, as demonstrated here:

```
children = ["Alexander", "William", "Molly"]
middleChild = children[1]
```

Here, the first statement declares an array named children and assigns three items to it. The second statement assigns the value of the second item located in the array ("William") to a variable named middleChild.

TRICK Ruby also lets you access the contents of an array by specifying a negative index number. An index number of −1 would refer to the last item in the array while an index number of −2 would refer to the second-to-last item and so on.

Retrieving Individual Array Elements Using the at Method

There is often more than one way to do things in Ruby. For example, when it comes to retrieving items from an array, you can also use the Array class's at method to retrieve an array item based on its index position. This method retrieves an array element using an integer value passed to it as an argument, as demonstrated here:

```
children = %w(Alexander William Molly)
puts children.at(1)
```

Here, the `at` method retrieves a value of "William" from the `children` array, which is then displayed.

Retrieving a Slice

You can use the `Array` class's `slice` method to retrieve a series of elements, referred to as a `slice`, from an array by enclosing a list or range of index numbers within a pair of parentheses, as demonstrated here:

```
children = %w(Alexander William Molly)
boys = children.slice(0..1)
```

When executed, the `slice` method retrieves the first and second items stored in the `children` array and assigns them as items in the `boys` array.

Retrieving the First and Last Elements Stored in an Array

Other ways of retrieving items from an array are provided by the `Array` class's `first` and `last` methods. The `first` method retrieves the first element from the specified array, as demonstrated here:

```
children = %w(Alexander William Molly)
puts children.first
```

When executed, these statements display the following output.

```
Alexander
```

As you may have already guessed, the `Array` class's `last` method can be used to retrieve the last element from the specified array, as shown here:

```
children = %w(Alexander William Molly)
puts children.last
```

When executed, these statements display the following output.

```
Molly
```

Using a Loop to Process the Contents of an Array

As was demonstrated in Chapter 5, you can use a loop to efficiently process the contents of an array using a minimum number of script statements. While you can certainly use the `while` and `until` loop for processing the contents of a loop, the `Array` class's `each` method is tailor-made for processing loops.

For example, the following statements demonstrate how to set up a loop that displays each element in an array named `children`.

```
children = %w(Alexander William Molly)
children.each do |child|
  puts child
end
```

This `each` method automatically repeats once for each item stored in the specified array. In this example, each time the loop iterates, the value of the current array item is assigned to the `child` variable, which is then displayed, resulting in the following output.

```
Alexander
William
Molly
```

Deleting Elements from an Array

Ruby provides you with a number of different methods that you can use to delete items stored in arrays. This includes the ability to delete all of the items stored in an array and to delete items based on their position within the array. You can also delete items based on their value as well as specify items to be deleted using their index position.

Deleting All the Items Stored in an Array

If at some point in a Ruby script you decide that you need to remove all the items stored in an array to begin adding items to the array from scratch, you can use the `Array` class's `clear` method as demonstrated here:

```
children = %w(Alexander William Molly)
children.clear
```

Here, the `clear` method is used to remove all items currently stored in an array named `children`, resulting in an empty array.

Deleting the First Item Stored in an Array

Another way to delete items from an array is with the Array class's shift method. This method deletes the first element stored in an array, shifting the index number of all remaining items elements down by one index position as demonstrated here:

```
children = %w(Alexander William Molly)
x = children.shift
puts children.inspect
```

Here, the shift method is used to retrieve the value of the first element stored in the array, which is assigned to the x variable. At the same time, the shift method also removes the first element from the array, which, in the case of the previous example, results in an array named children that contains the following list of items.

```
["William", "Molly"]
```

Deleting the Last Item Stored in an Array

If you need to, you can delete an item from the end of an array using the Array class's pop method, as demonstrated here:

```
family = %w(Alexander William Molly Daddy Mommy)
family.pop
family.pop
puts family.inspect
```

Here, an array named family has been assigned five items. Next the pop method is used twice, removing the last two items from the array. As a result, the family array is left with the following list of items.

```
["Alexander", "William", "Molly"]
```

Using the Array Class's delete Method

Rather than deleting array items based on their location within an array, you may instead want to delete them based on their value, which you can do using the Array class's delete method. To use this method, you must pass the delete method an argument that identifies which items should be deleted, as demonstrated here:

```
fruit = %w(Apples Oranges Bananas Oranges Grapes)
fruit.delete("Oranges")
```

Here, an array named fruit has been created and assigned five items. Next, the Array class's delete method is executed and passed a value of "Oranges". Based on this input, the delete method removes two items from the fruit array, leaving the array with the following list of items.

```
["Apples", "Bananas", "Grapes"]
```

Deleting Individual Items Using the at Method

Another option for deleting items from an array is to use the `Array` class's `delete_at` method. This method lets you delete any item from an array based on its index position, as demonstrated here:

```
fruit = %w(Apples Oranges Bananas Oranges Grapes)
fruit.delete_at(3)
```

Here an array named `fruit` has been created and assigned five items. Next, the `Array` class's `delete_at` method is executed and passed an argument of 3. In response, the method removes the item from the array stored in index position 3 (e.g., its fourth item). As a result, the `fruit` array ends up containing the following list of items.

```
["Apples", "Oranges", "Bananas", "Grapes"]
```

When an item is deleted using the `delete_at` method, all items that follow it in the array are automatically shifted to the left one position.

 The `Array` class's `insert_at` method is the opposite of the `delete_at` method. The `insert_at` method adds a new item to an array at the specified index number. To make room for the new item, all items already in the array at the specified index location and beyond are automatically shifted one position to the right to make room.

Sorting the Contents of an Array

In Ruby, elements are stored by default in an array based on the order in which they are added to the array. As a result, you may end up with a list of items that are not in the order you want them to be. As such, you may want to use the `Array` class's `sort` method to sort the contents of the array, as demonstrated here:

```
fruit = %w(Apples Oranges Bananas Grapes)
puts fruit.sort.inspect
```

 In the last statement, the output of the `sort` method was used as input for the `inspect` method. When used in this manner, the methods are said to be *chained* together.

In this example, an array named `fruit` is created and assigned five items. The contents of the array are then displayed using the `puts` method. Note that in this example the items are first sorted and then the resulting list is displayed using the `inspect` method resulting in the following output.

```
["Apples", "Bananas", "Grapes", "Oranges"]
```

TRICK
Ruby's `Array` class also provides you with access to a method named `reverse`. This method reverses the order of items stored in a list. So, using this method, you could reverse the order of array items after they have been sorted, as demonstrated here:

```
fruit = %w(Apples Oranges Bananas Grapes)
puts fruit.sort.reverse.inspect
```

Here, the items stored in the `fruit` array are first sorted. Next, the order of the now-sorted items is reversed. Finally, the `inspect` method is used to display the resulting list.

```
["Oranges", "Grapes", "Bananas", "Apples"]
```

Searching an Array

One way of finding something stored in an array is to set up a loop to iterate through the array to look for a specific item. In the case where you have a large array that might contain thousands of items, processing the contents of the array takes time. Before you perform such a resource-intensive operation, it is a good idea to first use the `Array` class's `include?` method to check and see if the array contains any instances of the item you are looking for, as demonstrated here:

```
children = %w(Alexander William Molly)
puts "I found him!" if children.include?("William")
```

Here, the `include?` method is used to search the `children` array to see if it contains a value of `"William"`. Once you determine whether an array contains any instances of the item you are looking for, you can then decide whether you need to loop through the array and process the items in some way.

STORING DATA USING HASHES

As arrays grow in size, it becomes difficult trying to keep up with the index positions where individual items are stored. Because of this, you will usually need to set up a loop to process all of the contents of an array just to find the specific items you need to work with. As an alternative to arrays, Ruby also supports the storage and retrieval of data using hashes.

A *hash*, sometimes referred to as an *associative array* or *dictionary* in other programming languages, is a list of data stored in key-value pairs. Each piece of data stored in a hash is stored as a value and assigned a key, which uniquely identifies the data. Instead of referencing data stored using an index position as with arrays, hashes allow you to reference a value by specifying its key.

Like arrays, hashes are objects and therefore provide you with access to large numbers of methods that you can use to create and interact with hashes. Like arrays, hashes can store any type of object that Ruby supports, including numbers and strings. To access a particular value, you need its associated key. Hashes can be used to store virtually any amount of data, limited only by the computer's available memory. Access to data stored in a hash is relatively fast and does not significantly diminish as additional key-value pairs are added. Hash keys and values can be of any length. Unlike arrays, which store items in the order they are added, hashes do not store their contents in any particular order.

Creating a New Hash File

As with arrays, Ruby provides you with a number of different ways of creating hash files. You can create and populate hash files at the same time. You can spread hash file definitions out over multiple lines and you can even use the Hash class's new method to create new empty hash files.

Defining a New Hash File

The syntax that you need to follow when creating a hash and populating it with an initial set of key-value pairs is outlined here:

```
variableName = {key => value, key => value, ... key => value}
```

Here, *variableName* represents the name of a variable to which the hash is assigned. *key* represents a unique key name associated with a particular value and *value* is a piece of data stored in the hash.

As the following example demonstrates, creating a new hash is pretty straightforward.

```
kids = {"first" => "Alexander", "second" => "William", "third" => "Molly"}
```

In this example a new hash named kids has been created and populated with three key-value pairs. The first key assigned to the hash is named "first" and its associated value is "Alexander". As you can see, keys and their associated values are separated by the => characters and commas are used to separate key-value pairs.

If you prefer, you can replace the => characters with the , character when defining a hash, as shown here:

```
kids = {"first", "Alexander", "second", "William", "third", "Molly"}
```

Once created, you can view the hash using the following statement.

```
puts kids.inspect
```

When executed, this statement displays the following output, showing the structure of the hash that has been created.

```
{"third"=>"Molly", "second"=>"William", "first"=>"Alexander"}
```

Spreading Out a Hash Definition over Multiple Lines

If you prefer, you can rewrite the previous example and spread it across multiple lines to make is easier to understand and expand, as demonstrated here:

```
kids = {"first" => "Alexander",
  "second" => "William",
  "third" => "Molly"
}
```

Using the Hash Class's New Method

If you prefer, you can also create a new empty hash using the Hash class's new method, as demonstrated here:

```
kids = Hash.new
```

Once executed, this statement creates an empty hash to which you can begin adding as many key-value pairs as you see fit.

Adding and Deleting Key-Value Pairs

You can add as many key-value pairs as you want to a hash using the following syntax.

```
hashVariable[key] = value
```

hashVariable is the name of the variable to which the hash has been assigned. *key* is the name of the key to be assigned to the new key-value pair, and *hash* represents the data that is stored. For example, the following statement creates a new hash file and assigns three initial key-value pairs to it.

```
kids = {"first" => "Alexander", "second" => "William", "third" => "Molly"}
```

You can add additional key-value pairs to the hash as shown here:

```
kids["fourth"] = "Dolly"
kids["fifth"] = "Regis"
```

Here, two new key-value pairs have been added to the kids hash. At this point the hash now contains five key-value pairs as shown here:

```
{"third"=>"Molly", "fifth"=>"Regis", "second"=>"William", "first"=>"Alexander",
"fourth"=>"Dolly"}
```

Using One Hash to Populate Another Hash

Another way to create a hash is to copy the contents of one hash into a new hash, as demonstrated here:

```
kids = {"first" => "Alexander", "second" => "William", "third" => "Molly"}
family = kids
```

Now the hash named family contains an exact copy of the key-value pairs stored in the kids hash.

Using the Hash Class's merge Method

Another way to create a new hash is to take the contents of two existing hashes and use them as the basis for creating a new hash. To accomplish this you will need to work with the Hash class's merge method, as demonstrated here:

```
kids = {"first" => "Alexander", "second" => "William", "third" => "Molly"}
parents = {"daddy" => "Jerry", "mommy" => "Mary"}
family = kids.merge(parents)
```

Here, a new hash named family has been created by using the merge method on the kids hash and passing the method the name of the parents hash as an argument. The result is a new hash that contains all of the key-value pairs from both hashes.

 Every key within a hash must be unique. If you accidentally assign a new value to a hash using a key that is already in the hash, Ruby will perform a replacement operation. So take extra care to ensure you create unique key names.

Deleting a Hash's Key-Value Pairs

As with arrays, you can use the Hash class's clear method to remove all key-value pairs from a hash, as demonstrated here:

```
kids = {"first" => "Alexander", "second" => "William", "third" => "Molly"}
kids.clear
```

When executed, the first statement creates a new hash and populates it with three key-value pairs. However, the second statement then executes the Hash class's clear method, deleting all of the key-value pairs from the hash, leaving it empty.

 HINT You can also delete the contents of a hash by assigning an empty list to a hash, as demonstrated here:

```
kids = {"first" => "Alexander", "second" => "William", "third" => "Molly"}
kids = {}
```

Deleting Specific Key-Value Pairs

You can also use the Hash class's delete method to remove a key-value pair from a hash by passing the method the name of a key, as demonstrated here:

```
kids = {"first" => "Alexander", "second" => "William", "third" => "Molly"}
kids.delete("second")
```

When executed, the first statement creates a new hash and populates it with three key-value pairs. The second statement then deletes the key-value pair whose key is "second".

Conditionally Deleting Key-Value Pairs

You can also delete key-value pairs from a hash using the Hash class's delete_if method, as demonstrated here:

```
kids = {"first" => "Alexander", "second" => "William", "third" => "Molly"}
kids.delete_if {|key, value| key >= "third"}
```

The delete_if method takes as an argument an expression. If the expression evaluates as being true for any key-value pair, the key-value pair is deleted from the hash.

Determining the Number of Key-Value Pairs in a Hash

There is no point in trying to retrieve data from a hash or trying to use a loop to process a hash if there are no key-value pairs stored in it. As with arrays, you can use the empty? method to determine if a hash contains any key-value pairs. The empty? method returns a value of true if the specified hash contains no key-value pairs.

To get a better understanding of how the empty? method works, take a look at the following example.

```
kids = {"first" => "Alexander", "second" => "William", "third" => "Molly"}

if kids.empty? == false then
```

```
  puts kids.inspect
else
  puts "The kids hash is empty"
end
```

Here, a hash named `kids` has been created and assigned three key-value pairs. Next the `Hash` class's `empty?` method is used to determine if the hash is empty. Since the hash is not empty, the `inspect` method is executed, showing the hash's contents. However, had the hash in fact been empty, the statement that followed the `else` keyword would have been executed.

 TRICK You can determine the number of key-value pairs stored in a hash using the `Hash` class's `length` or `size` methods, as demonstrated here:

```
kids = {"first" => "Alexander", "second" => "William", "third" =>
"Molly"}
puts kids.size
```

When executed, this example displays the following output.

```
3
```

Accessing Data Stored in Hashes

Data is extracted from a hash in very much the same way that it is extracted from an array, only you specify a key instead of an index number. For example, take a look at the following statement.

```
kids = {"first" => "Alexander", "second" => "William", "third" => "Molly"}
```

Here, a hash named `kids` has been created and assigned three key-value pairs. The following statement demonstrates how to access the value associated with the "third" key.

```
x = kids["third"]
```

Here, a variable named `x` is assigned a value of "Molly".

Looping Through a Hash's Keys

Unlike arrays, hashes are not indexed. Therefore, you cannot set up a loop to process their contents from beginning to end. Hashes have no starting or ending positions. However, Ruby gives you a way around this hash limitation by providing you with access to the `keys` method.

The `keys` method creates a list of all the keys stored within a specified hash. Using this list, you can set up a loop to iterate through and process the hash's keys, as demonstrated here:

```
kids = {"first" => "Alexander", "second" => "William", "third" => "Molly"}

puts "\n\nKeys belonging to the kids hash:\n\n"
kids.keys.each do |child|
    puts child
end
```

Here, a hash named `kids` has been created and assigned three key-value pairs. Next the `puts` method is used to display a string, and then, using chaining, the output of the `keys` method is passed to the `each` method, which displays each key name as it iterates through the list. The output displayed when these statements are executed is shown here:

```
Keys belonging to the kids hash:

third
second
first
```

Looping Through a Hash's Values

Now that you know how to iterate through a list of all the keys stored within a hash, you are just a step away from being able to reach out and grab and then process each key's associated value. As the following example demonstrates, all you have to do to get your hands on the values stored in the hash is precede the reference to the keys with the name of the hash (e.g., *hash*[*key*], or kids[child] in the following example).

```
kids = {"first" => "Alexander", "second" => "William", "third" => "Molly"}
puts "\n\nValues belonging to the kids hash:\n\n"
kids.keys.each do |child|
    puts kids[child]
end
```

The output displayed when these statements are executed is shown here:

```
Values belonging to the kids hash:

Molly
William
Alexander
```

TRICK You can also use the Hash values method to generate a list of all the values stored in a hash.

```
kids = {"first" => "Alexander", "second" => "William", "third" =>
"Molly"}
x = kids.values
puts x.inspect
```

When executed, this example assigns the following list to the x array.

```
["Molly", "William", "Alexander"]
```

Sorting Hash Keys

Because hashes do not store their key-value pairs in any particular order, the order in which keys are retrieved when working with the keys method may not always be optimal. If you want, you can pass the keys method's output to the sort method prior to looking through a hash's keys, as demonstrated here:

```
kids = {"first" => "Alexander", "second" => "William", "third" => "Molly"}
kids.keys.sort.each do |child|
  puts child
end
```

When executed, this example generates the following output, sorted by key name.

```
first
second
third
```

TRICK Ruby's Hash class also supports the reverse method, allowing you to reverse the order of a sort, as demonstrated here:

```
kids = {"first" => "Alexander", "second" => "William", "third" =>
"Molly"}
kids.keys.sort.reverse.each do |child|
  puts child
end
```

BACK TO THE RUBY NUMBER GUESSING GAME

Okay, now it is time to turn your attention back to the development of this chapter's game project, the Ruby Number Guessing game. As with the previous chapter game projects, it is important that you follow along carefully with each step that is outlined in the following sections to avoid making any time-consuming mistakes.

Designing the Game

The development of the Ruby Number Guessing game will be completed in 12 steps, as outlined here:

1. Open your text or script editor and create a new file.
2. Add comment statements to the beginning of the script file to document the script and its purpose.
3. Define a class representing the terminal window.
4. Define a class representing the Ruby Number Guessing game.
5. Add a `display_greeting` method to the `Game` class.
6. Add a `display_instructions` method to the `Game` class.
7. Add a `generate_number` method to the `Game` class.
8. Add a `play_game` method to the `Game` class.
9. Add a `display_credits` method to the `Game` class.
10. Instantiate script objects.
11. Prompt the player for permission to begin the game.
12. Set up the game's controlling logic.

Step 1: Creating a New Ruby File

The first step in developing the Ruby Number Guessing game is to open up your favorite text or code editor and create a new Ruby script file. Save the script file with a name of NumberGuess.rb.

Step 2: Documenting the Script and Its Purpose

Next, add the following comment statements to the script file. These statements provide a high-level overview of the game and its purpose and provide you with a place to record updates to the script should you decide to return and modify it at some point in the future.

```
#--------------------------------------------------------------------
#
# Script Name: NumberGuess.rb
# Version:     1.0
# Author:      Jerry Lee Ford, Jr.
# Date:        October 2007
#
# Description: This Ruby script is a number guessing game that challenges
```

```
#              the player to guess a randomly generated number in as few
#              guesses as possible.
#
#-------------------------------------------------------------------
```

Step 3: Creating the Screen Class

The Ruby Number Guessing game will rely on two custom classes to provide it with a collection of methods that will be used to control interaction with the user and the execution of the game. The code statements belonging to the Screen class are shown next and should be added to the end of the script file.

```
# Define custom classes --------------------------------------------

#Define a class representing the console window
class Screen

  def cls  #Define a method that clears the display area
    puts ("\n" * 25)  #Scroll the screen 25 times
    puts "\a"  #Make a little noise to get the player's attention
  end

  def pause   #Define a method that pauses the display area
    STDIN.gets  #Execute the STDIN class's gets method to pause script
               #execution until the player presses the Enter key
  end

end
```

The Screen class contains two methods. The first method is the cls method. It is made up of two statements. The first statement writes 25 blank lines to the console window to clear the screen and the second statement contains a string that is made up of the \a escape character that when executed results in the play of an audible beep.

The Screen class's second method is named pause and is used to execute the STDIN class's gets method to pause script execution until the player presses the Enter key.

Step 4: Creating the Game Class

The script's second custom class is named Game. It provides access to five methods that are needed to control the overall execution of the game. To begin the creation of this class, add the statements shown next to the end of the script file.

```
#Define a class representing the Ruby Number Guessing Game
class Game


end
```

Step 5: Defining the display_greeting Method

The Game class consists of five methods. The first of these methods is named display_greeting. This method is made up of the script statements shown next, which should be inserted between the Game class's opening and closing statements.

```
#This method displays the game's opening screen
def display_greeting

  Console_Screen.cls  #Clear the display area

  #Display welcome message
  print "\t\t  Welcome to the Ruby Number Guessing Game!" +
  "\n\n\n\n\n\n\n\n\n\n\n\n\nPress Enter to " +
           "continue."

  Console_Screen.pause      #Pause the game

end
```

When called, this method calls upon the Screen class's cls method to clear the screen, displays the game's welcome message, and then pauses the execution of the script using the Screen class's pause method.

Step 6: Defining the display_instructions Method

The next method to be added to the Game class is the display_instructions method. The script statements for this method are shown next and should be added to the end of the class definition, immediately after the previously defined method.

```
#Define a method to be used to present game instructions
def display_instructions

  Console_Screen.cls       #Clear the display area
  puts "INSTRUCTIONS:\n\n"  #Display a heading

  #Display the game's instructions
```

```
puts "This game randomly generates a number from 1 to 100 and"
puts "challenges you to identify it in as few guesses as possible."
puts "After each guess, the game will analyze your input and provide"
puts "you with feedback. You may take as many turns as you need in"
puts "order to guess the game's secret number.\n\n\n"
puts "Good luck!\n\n\n\n\n\n\n\n"
print "Press Enter to continue."

Console_Screen.pause       #Pause the game

end
```

This method uses the Kernel class's puts method to display a series of text strings representing the game's instructions.

Step 7: Defining the generate_number Method

The next method to be added to the Game class is the generate_number method. The script statements for this method are shown next and should be added to the end of the class definition, immediately after the previously defined method.

```
#Define a method that generates the game's secret number
def generate_number

  #Generate and return a random number from 1 to 100
  return randomNo = 1 + rand(100)

end
```

This method is responsible for generating a random number from 1 to 100. To accomplish this, the rand method is executed and passed a value of 100. This results in an integer value between 0 and 99. As such, a value of one is added to the value returned by the rand method to end up with a number in the target range. This integer value is then returned back to the statement that calls upon the generate_number method using the return command.

Step 8: Defining the play_game Method

The next method to be added to the Game class is the play_game method. The script statements for this method are shown next and should be added to the end of the class definition, immediately after the previously defined method.

```ruby
#Define a method to be used to control game play
def play_game

  #Call on the generate_number method to get a random number
  number = generate_number

  #Loop until the player inputs a valid answer
  loop do

    Console_Screen.cls       #Clear the display area

    #Prompt the player to make a guess
    print "\nEnter your guess and press the Enter key: "

    reply = STDIN.gets  #Collect the player's answer
    reply.chop!          #Remove the end of line marker
    reply = reply.to_i  #Convert the player's guess to an integer

    #Validate the player's input only allowing guesses from 1 to 100
    if reply < 1 or reply > 100 then
      redo  #Redo the current iteration of the loop
    end

    #Analyze the player's guess to determine if it is correct
    if reply == number then    #The player's guess was correct
      Console_Screen.cls        #Clear the display area
      print "You have guessed the number! Press Enter to continue."
      Console_Screen.pause      #Pause the game
      break
    elsif reply < number then  #The player's guess was too low
      Console_Screen.cls        #Clear the display area
      print "Your guess is too low! Press Enter to continue."
      Console_Screen.pause      #Pause the game
    elsif reply > number then  #The player's guess was too high
      Console_Screen.cls        #Clear the display area
      print "Your guess is too high! Press Enter to continue."
      Console_Screen.pause      #Pause the game
    end
```

```
    end

end
```

This method begins by calling upon the `Game` class's `generate_number` method, which generates a random number from 1 to 100. This value is then assigned to a variable named `number`. The rest of the statements that make up the method are enclosed inside a loop that has been set up to execute forever.

Within the loop, the screen is cleared and then the player is prompted to try and guess the game's secret number. The player's guess is captured and stored in a variable named `reply`. The value stored in `reply` is then converted to an integer using the `to_i` method. This way, if the player entered something other than an integer, an error will not occur when the script begins to analyze the player's input using the statements that follow.

Next, the value assigned to `reply` is analyzed to see if it is less than 1 or greater than 100. If this is the case, the `redo` command is executed, restarting the current iteration of the loop to prompt the player to guess again.

If a valid guess was provided by the player, the value of `reply` is then analyzed to see if it is equal to the game's secret number, lower than the secret number, or higher than the secret number. If the player has guessed the game's secret number, a message is displayed notifying the player that the number has been guessed and then the `break` command is executed, terminating the execution of the `play_game` method's loop. If, however, the player's guess is too low or too high, the player is given a hint to help guide her next guess and the `play_game` method's loop is repeated, giving the player the chance to make another guess.

Step 9: Defining the display_credits Method

The last method to be added to the `Game` class is the `display_credits` method. This method will display information about the game and its author, including the author's URL. The statements that make up this method are shown next and should be appended to the end of the `Game` class.

```
#This method displays the information about the Ruby Number Guessing game
def display_credits

  Console_Screen.cls  #Clear the display area

  #Thank the player and display game information
  puts "\t\tThank you for playing the Ruby Number Guessing Game.\n\n\n\n"
  puts "\n\t\t\t Developed by Jerry Lee Ford, Jr.\n\n"
```

```
    puts "\t\t\t\t  Copyright 2008\n\n"
    puts "\t\t\tURL: http://www.tech-publishing.com\n\n\n\n\n\n\n\n\n\n"

end
```

Step 10: Initializing Script Objects

The next step in the development of the Ruby Number Guessing game is to initialize instances of the Screen and the Game classes. This is done by appending the following statements to the end of the script file.

```
# Main Script Logic ---------------------------------------------------

#Initialize a global variable that will be used to keep track of the
#number of correctly answered quiz questions
$noRight = 0

Console_Screen = Screen.new  #Instantiate a new Screen object
SQ = Game.new                #Instantiate a new Quiz object

#Execute the Quiz class's display_greeting method
SQ.display_greeting

answer = ""
```

In addition to instantiating the Console_Screen and SQ objects, these statements define a variable named answer, which will be used in the next section to control the execution of the loop that will be used to prompt the player for permission to begin a new round of play.

Step 11: Getting Permission to Start the Game

The programming logic that is responsible for prompting the player for permission to begin a new round of play is outlined here:

```
#Loop until the player enters y or n and do not accept any other input
loop do

  Console_Screen.cls  #Clear the display area

  #Prompt the player for permission to start the quiz
  print "Are you ready to play the Ruby Number Guessing Game? (y/n): "
```

```
answer = STDIN.gets  #Collect the player's response
answer.chop!  #Remove any extra characters appended to the string

#Terminate the loop if valid input was provided
break if answer == "y" || answer == "n"
```

```
end
```

These statements, which should be added to the end of the script file, are controlled by a loop that has been set up to run forever. Upon each iteration of the loop, the player is prompted to enter a value of y or n, to indicate whether a new round of play should be initiated or the game should be terminated. Any input other than a y or n is ignored. Once a valid response has been collected from the user, the break command is executed, terminating the loop and allowing the rest of the script to continue running.

Step 12: Controlling Game Play

The remainder of the script file is controlled by a larger if code block. The script statements that it executes depend on whether the player decided to terminate the game or play another round.

```
#Analyze the player's input
if answer == "n"  #See if the player elected not to take the quiz

  Console_Screen.cls  #Clear the display area

  #Invite the player to return and take the quiz some other time
  puts "Okay, perhaps another time.\n\n"

else  #The player wants to take the quiz

    #Execute the Quiz class's display_instructions method
    SQ.display_instructions

  loop do

    #Execute the Quiz class's disp_q method and pass it
    #arguments representing a question, four possible answers, and the
    #letter representing the correct answer
    SQ.play_game
```

```
    Console_Screen.cls  #Clear the display area

    #Prompt the player for permission to start the quiz
    print "Would you like to play again? (y/n): "

    playAgain = STDIN.gets  #Collect the player's response
    playAgain.chop!  #Remove any extra characters appended to the string

    break if playAgain == "n"

  end

  #Call upon the Quiz class's determine_credits method to thank
  #the player for taking the quiz and to display game information
  SQ.display_credits

end
```

If the player decides to stop playing the game, the script statement located at the top of the `if` code block is executed, clearing the screen and inviting the player to return and play another time. If, however, the player decides to play a new round, the statements that follow the `else` keyword are processed, in which case the Game class's `display_instructions` method is called. Next a loop is set up to facilitate the execution of as many rounds of play as the player wants. Each time the loop repeats, it calls on the `play_game` method, which is responsible for managing the actual playing of the game. Once the `play_game` method has finished executing, the screen is cleared and the player is asked if she would like to play another game. If the player responds by entering an n and pressing the Enter key, the `break` command is executed, terminating the loop and allowing the `display_credits` method to be called, after which the script terminates. If the player responds by entering a value of y and then pressing the Enter key, the loop iterates and a new round of play is initiated.

Running Your New Ruby Script Game

Okay, that's everything you need to create and execute the Ruby Number Guessing game. As long as you followed along carefully and did not make any typos when keying in the script statements, everything should work as advertised. In the event that you do run into errors, make sure that you carefully read the resulting error messages to ascertain where you made your mistakes. If necessary, go back and review the script and look for typos and missing scripts statements.

Summary

In this chapter, you learned how to store related items in arrays and hashes. You learned how to use methods belonging to arrays and hashes to manipulate and process their contents. In doing so, you learned how to add, delete, and sort array and hash data. You also learned how to tell when arrays and hashes are empty and to use loops to iterate through them and display their contents. Now, before you move on to Chapter 7, "Working with Regular Expressions," I suggest you set aside a little extra time to make a few improvement to the Ruby Number Guessing game by implementing the following list of challenges.

CHALLENGES

1. Consider adding logic to the game to keep track of the total number of games played as well as the total number of guesses made. Use this information to display game statistics at the end of each round of play that show the player how many games have been played and the average number of guesses that have been made per game.

2. Consider modifying the game to allow the player to specify the range of numbers that the game should use when generating the game's secret number (e.g., 1–10, 1–100, 1–1,000, or even 1–1,000,000).

3. As currently written, the Ruby Number Guessing game provides the player with a hint whenever her guess is too low or too high. The game also rejects any input that is not numeric and not within the range of 1 to 100 but does so without explaining to the player why invalid guesses are being rejected. Consider modifying the game to include helpful messages that let the player know what is going on when guesses fall outside of the 1 to 100 range.

Part

III

Advanced Topics

WORKING WITH REGULAR EXPRESSIONS

I n previous chapters, you learned how to create an assortment of different computer games. In most of these games, you more or less accepted whatever input the player provided, with little or no validation. In this chapter, this changes because you will learn how to use regular expressions. Using regular expressions, you can perform a detailed analysis of user input to determine if it meets criteria you specify. Using regular expressions, you will also be able to pick apart and process the contents of data regardless of its source, including text files and databases. You will also learn how to perform text-substitution operations and to deal with differences in case. On top of all this, this chapter will show how to create a new Ruby script, the Word Guessing game.

Specifically, you will learn how to:

- Set up basic regular expression patterns
- Set up regular expression patterns to match groups of characters
- Set up regular expression patterns to match individual or multiple instances of characters
- Use metacharacters when setting up regular expression patterns
- Perform text substitution and to ignore differences in case

PROJECT PREVIEW: THE WORD GUESSING GAME

In this chapter, you will learn how to create a new computer script called the Word Guessing game. This game challenges the player to try to guess a secret word in three or fewer guesses. Before making any guesses, the player is allowed to specify five consonants and one vowel, which, if present in the word, are revealed, providing the player with a clue as to what the word might be.

The Word Guessing game begins by displaying the message shown in Figure 7.1, welcoming the player to the game.

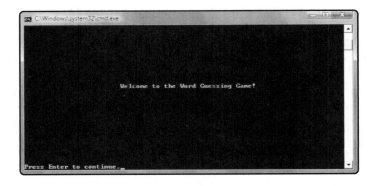

FIGURE 7.1

The Word Guessing game's welcome message.

The player is then prompted for permission to start a round of play, as demonstrated in Figure 7.2.

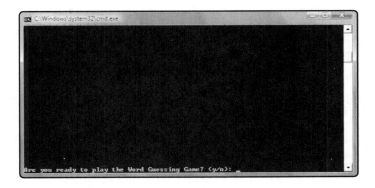

FIGURE 7.2

The player is prompted for permission to start a new game.

Before the first round of play begins, instructions for playing the game are presented as shown in Figure 7.3.

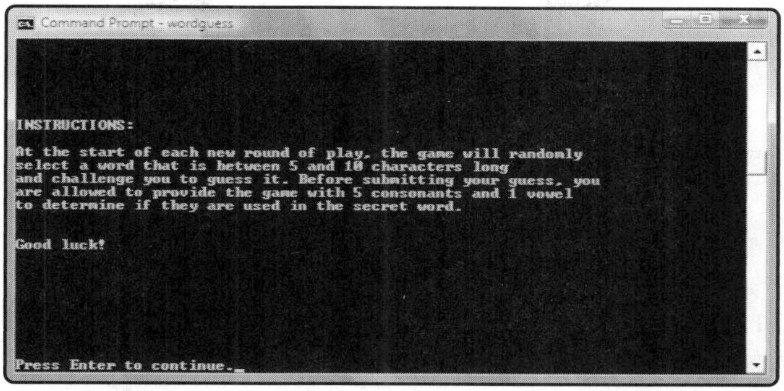

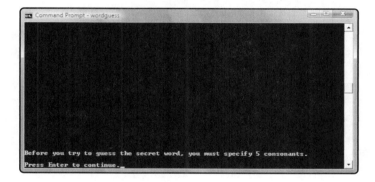

FIGURE 7.3

The player is told how to play the game.

Next, the player is asked to specify five consonants, as demonstrated in Figure 7.4.

FIGURE 7.4

To make things easier, the player gets to provide a list of consonants that will be revealed if they are part of the secret word.

Consonants are collected one at a time, as shown in Figure 7.5. If the player attempts to enter a vowel, number, special character, or more than one character at a time, her input is rejected, and she will be prompted to try again.

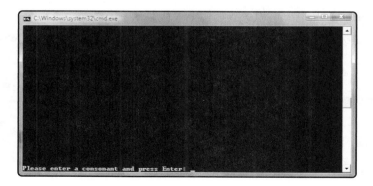

FIGURE 7.5

Using regular expressions, the player's input is carefully evaluated before being accepted.

Once all five consonants have been collected, the player is prompted to specify a vowel. The game then displays a clue to its secret word and challenges the player to try to guess it, as demonstrated in Figure 7.6.

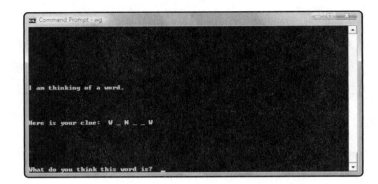

Figure 7.7 shows the message that is displayed if the player guesses the secret word.

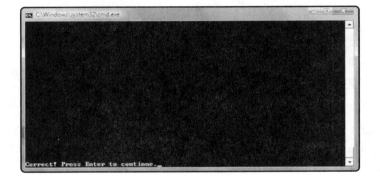

If the player's first guess is incorrect, two more chances are given to guess the secret word. Figure 7.8 shows the message that is presented before the player is permitted to make a final guess.

If the player is unable to guess the game's secret word, the screen shown in Figure 7.9 is displayed letting the user know that the current round of play is over and revealing the secret word to the player.

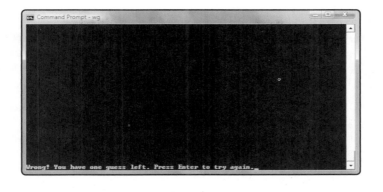

FIGURE 7.8

The game is ready to let the player make one last guess.

FIGURE 7.9

The player has failed to guess the game's secret word.

At the end of each round of play, the game prompts the player for permission to start another round. Depending on the player's response, the game is either terminated or a new secret word is selected, and play begins again.

THE BASICS OF WORKING WITH REGULAR EXPRESSIONS

Data processed in computer scripts can come from many different sources, including databases, files, as input passed from other scripts and programs, and from the users, as is the case with computer games. While you can certainly trust in the source of the data to provide your scripts with valid data, you often do so at your own peril. In most cases, you will want to build data-validation logic into your own scripts, rejecting any data that is not in the proper format.

You can perform a certain amount of data validation using conditional logic and methods belonging to Ruby classes. However, to create really granular data-validation routines, you will need to take things a step further and use regular expressions. A *regular expression* is a pattern used to identify matching character data.

In previous chapter projects, you performed limited amounts of data validation. In these scripts, you were able to simplify data validation by restricting valid data to very limited and specific sets of characters, rejecting any data provided by the player that did not match the script's precise requirements. For example, in the Superman Movie Trivia Quiz, you rejected as invalid any player input that was not an a, b, c, or d when processing quiz questions, as shown here:

```
#Analyze the player to determine if it was valid
if reply == "a" or reply == "b" or reply == "c" or reply == "d" then
   break  #Terminate the execution of the loop
end
```

When processing this type of restricted input, you can use basic conditional logic to process the player input. The following statements, taken from the Ruby Number Guessing game, provide another example of how input data validation was implemented.

```
#Validate the player's input only allowing guesses from 1 to 100
if reply < 1 or reply > 100 then
   redo  #Redo the current iteration of the loop
end
```

Here, numeric data is validated using conditional logic, and any value that is below 1 or greater than 100 is rejected. This type of data validation worked well in this example because the input allowed by the script was restricted to a very specific range (1 to 100). Things become a lot trickier when you begin writing scripts that can accept and process many different types of input. For example, this chapter's game project is the Word Guessing game. This game will accept any alphabetic characters as input. Given the number of letters in the alphabet, it is not practical to use either of the two previous data-validation examples as models for solving this problem. Instead, as you will see, this script will validate incoming data using several different validation techniques, including regular expressions.

Regular expressions are not just limited to data validation. Regular expressions can also be used to search for data within strings and to perform string substitutions. For example, using regular expressions, you can define patterns that:

- Perform search and replace operations on strings
- Keep counts of instances of patterns
- Extract a substring from a larger string

LEARNING HOW TO MATCH BASIC PATTERNS

In most cases, regular expression patterns are processed from left to right. Matches occur when patterns are found anywhere within a source string. By default, matches are case sensitive, although you can override this behavior. Also, every character inside a pattern is taken literally, with the exception of metacharacters, to which regular expressions assign a special meaning.

Matching Basic Patterns

The most basic type of regular expression is one that matches up against a specific pattern or a set of characters. This type of pattern can be set up using the // match operator, which has the following syntax.

```
/pattern/
```

For example, take a look at the following pattern.

```
/USA/
```

This pattern will match the occurrence of the characters USA if found anywhere in a string. If found, a value of true is returned. Otherwise, a value of false is returned. To see how this pattern might be used, take a look at the following set of statements.

```
if "Welcome to New York Harbor, USA." =~ /USA/ then
  puts "Welcome to America!"
end
```

Here, the source string "Welcome to New York Harbor, USA." is searched using a pattern of /USA/. Since the string contains the words USA, a match occurs and the following output is displayed when the statements are executed.

```
"Welcome to America!"
```

Take note of the use of the =~ operator, which is the equivalent of the equals operation in a regular expression.

 In addition to the =~ operator, you should also be familiar with the !~ operator, which is the regular expression equivalent of the not equals operator.

Matching Alternate Patterns

In addition to matching basic patterns as discussed in the previous section, you can set up regular expression patterns that can look for any of a possible set of matches. To set up this type of pattern, you need to use the | character to separate each possible match, as demonstrated here:

```
if "Welcome the USA!." =~ /USA|America/ then
  puts "We have a match!"
end
```

Here, a search pattern has been set up that looks for either the string USA or the string America. If either string is found in the source string, the match is successful.

Using this alternate pattern-matching approach, you can set up a pattern that searches for as many different alternate patterns as you want, as demonstrated here:

```
if "Remember to call your mother." =~ /tall|call|wall|ball|fall|mall/ then
  puts "We have a match!"
end
```

As you can see, alternate pattern matches can be very convenient. However, they can quickly grow a little long-winded. To make things easier, you can shorten things up using parentheses to separate unique parts of the search pattern from common parts, as demonstrated here:

```
if "Remember to call your mother." =~ /(t|c|w|b|f|m)all/ then
  puts "We have a match!"
end
```

Here, /(t|c|w|b|f|m)all/ is just a shorthand way of writing /tall|call|wall|ball|fall|mall/.

UNDERSTANDING HOW TO WORK WITH METACHARACTERS

Normally, any character that you include in a regular expression pattern will match the same character if found in the source string. However, metacharacters are an exception to this rule. A *metacharacter* is a character that alters the way a pattern match occurs, as demonstrated in the following example.

```
if "My name is Jerry. My father's name is Mr. Ford." =~ /Mr./ then
  print "We have a match!"
end
```

Here, the source string is searched using the pattern /Mr./. The result is a match. However, the match has occurred for a reason that may not be immediately obvious. On the surface, it appears that the pattern matched because the string Mr. is equal to the string Mr. in the source string. However, something different is actually happening here. Specifically, when used in a regular expression, the . character is viewed as a metacharacter. Metacharacters have a special meaning. In particular, the . metacharacter is used to match up against any individual character. As a result, a pattern of /Mr./ results in a match with Mr., Mrs, and Mrx, etc., which is clearly not what was intended in the previous example.

While metacharacters can be extremely useful, sometimes they can get in the way. In these situations, you can escape the metacharacter by preceding it with a \ character. When escaped, the metacharacter is taken literally. Therefore, using the \ escape character, you can force a regular expression to treat the . character like a period and not like a metacharacter, as demonstrated here:

```
if "My name is Jerry. My father's name is Mr. Ford." =~ /Mr\./ then
  print "We have a match!"
end
```

Table 7.1 lists a number of metacharacters that you will want to become familiar with.

	TABLE 7.1 REGULAR EXPRESSION METACHARACTERS	
Character	**Description**
.	Matches any character
^	Looks for a match at the beginning of a line
$	Looks for a match at the end of a line
\A	Looks for a match at the beginning of a string
\Z	Looks for a match at the end of a string
\d	Matches any numeric character
\w	Matches any alphabetic, numeric, or underscore character
\D	Matches any non-numeric character
\W	Matches any non-alphabetic, non-numeric, or non-underscore character
\s	Matches white space
\S	Matches non-white space

You will learn more about how to work with metacharacters as you read through the rest of this chapter.

Matching Individual Characters

As you just learned, you can use the . metacharacter as part of a pattern to match any individual character (except for the new line character). By using multiple instances of the . metacharacter, you can create patterns that match more than one character, as demonstrated here:

```
if "My name is Jerry. My father's name is Mr. Ford." =~ /f...er/ then
  print "We have a match!"
end
```

Here, a pattern has been set up to match the lowercase letter f followed by any two characters and the letters er.

Matching a Pattern at the Beginning of a String

By default, a regular expression looks anywhere within a string for a match. However, using the ^ metacharacter, you can create regular expression patterns that only look at the beginning of a line for a match. For example, a pattern of /^My name/ will result in a match only if it is found at the beginning of the source, as demonstrated here:

```
if "My name is Jerry. My father's name is Mr. Ford." =~ /^My name/ then
  print "We have a match!"
end
```

Matching a Pattern at the End of a String

The $ metacharacter is the opposite of the ^ metacharacter, performing a match only if the pattern is found at the end of the line, as demonstrated here:

```
if "My name is Jerry. My father's name is Mr. Ford." =~ /Ford\.$/ then
  print "We have a match!"
end
```

 If necessary, you can combine the ^ and & metacharacters when creating regular expression patterns. For example, you could combine the ^, $, and . metacharacters to create a pattern that matches only if the source string is made up of a single character, as shown here:

```
/^.$/
```

Matching One or Not at All

There may be some situations in which you need to look for a character or a group of characters that occur either once or not at all, with either possibility resulting in a match. You can set this up using the ? metacharacter modifier, which matches zero or none of the preceding characters, as demonstrated here:

```
if "My name is Jerry. My father's name is Mr. Ford." =~ /Mrs?/ then
  print "We have a match!"
end
```

Here, a pattern of /Mrs?/ has been specified. This pattern will match a string of Mrs, and if the s is not present, it will also match Mr. You can use the ? metacharacter modifier on groups of characters just as easily, as shown here:

```
if "My father's name is Mr. Ford." =~ /father('s name)?/ then
  print "We have a match!"
end
```

As you can see, the trick here is to use parentheses to enclose the group of characters. In this example, a match will occur if either father or father's name is found in the source string.

Matching Zero or More Times

Another metacharacter modifier that you need to know about is the * character. This character is similar to the . metacharacter except that the * metacharacter matches zero or more instances of the preceding character. For example, a pattern of /f*r/ would match any of the following set of characters:

- father
- friendlier
- for
- r

 Another useful metacharacter modifier is the + character, which matches one or more instances of the preceding character.

Matching Any of a Collection of Characters

Another type of pattern that you may need to work with is one that searches for a range of characters. This can be set up using *character classes*, which are enclosed inside a matching pair of square brackets ([]). Any characters placed inside the [] characters are regarded as a single character. Ruby's support for regular expressions includes support for the character class patterns shown in Figure 7.2.

TABLE 7.2 CHARACTER CLASS PATTERNS

Pattern	Description
/[abc]/	Matches any specified lowercase letter (a, b, c)
/[abcdefghijklmnopqrstuvwxyz]/	Matches any lowercase letter
/[0123456789]/	Matches any number between 0 and 9
/[0 - 9]/	Shorthand option for matching any number between 0 and 9
/[a - z]/	Shorthand option for matching any of the lowercase letters
/[A - Z]/	Shorthand option for matching any of the uppercase letters

To see an example of how to work with character class patterns, look at the following example.

```
print "Please enter a vowel and press Enter: "
input = STDIN.gets
input.chop!

if input =~ /[aeiou]/ then
  puts "A vowel has been submitted."
end
```

Here, the user is prompted to enter a vowel (i.e., a, e , i, o, or u). A conditional check is then performed using a regular expression of /[aeiou]/. As a result, a match occurs if the user enters a response that includes at least one vowel.

OTHER COMMON USES OF REGULAR EXPRESSIONS

Ruby's support for regular expressions is quite extensive. As a result, there is a lot more that you can do with regular expressions than what has been discussed so far in this chapter. For example, using regular expressions, you can perform case-insensitive pattern searches. In addition, you can also perform complex string substitutions, where one or more instances of a search pattern are used to replace characters in a source string.

Regular expressions represent an enormous topic. So much so that entire books have been dedicated to this one topic. If you are interested in learning more about regular expressions, check out *Mastering Regular Expressions, Second Edition* (ISBN: 0596002890). You might also want to visit http://en.wikipedia.org/wiki/Regular_expression.

Overcoming Differences in Case

So far, all of the regular expression patterns that you have used have worked because the case used inside the pattern matched the case used in the source string. It won't always work out this well. To eliminate case as an issue, you can disable case-sensitivity using the optional i modifier, as demonstrated here:

```
if "Welcome to New York Harbor, USA." =~ /usa/i then
  puts "Welcome to America!"
end
```

When used, the i modifier allows the pattern to match characters in the source string, regardless of the case that is in use. So this example results in a match, even though lowercase characters have been specified in the pattern and uppercase characters are used in the source string. If you were to remove the i modifier from the above example, a case-sensitive match would be attempted and the result would be no match.

String Substitution

In addition to finding and validating string contents, you can modify strings using character substitution with the String class's sub method. This method accepts as an argument a search pattern, which can be any regular expression pattern or string, and a replacement pattern. The sub method has the following syntax.

```
string.sub(search, replace)
```

This method searches *string* and substitutes the first instance of *search* that it finds with *replace*. To get a feel for how this method works, take a look at the following example.

```
x = "Once upon a time there was a small boy who climbed a small tree."
puts x.sub("small", "big")
```

Here, a string is assigned to a variable named x. Next, the sub method is called and passed "small" as the search pattern and "big" as the replacement pattern. As a result, the following output is displayed when these statements are executed.

```
Once upon a time there was a big boy who climbed a small tree.
```

Here, the first instance of the word small has been replaced with the word big. However, the source string contained two instances of the word small and the second instance was not replaced. If you want to replace all instances of the search pattern, you need to work with the String class's gsub method instead. Like the sub method, the gsub method accepts as an argument a search pattern, which can be any regular expression pattern or string, and a replacement pattern. Using gsub, you could rewrite the previous example as shown here:

```
x = "Once upon a time there was a small boy who climbed a small tree."
puts x.gsub("small", "big")
```

When executed, this example displays the following output.

```
Once upon a time there was a big boy who climbed a big tree.
```

BACK TO THE WORD GUESSING GAME

All right, that's enough about regular expressions for now. It is time to turn your attention back to the creation of this chapter's game project, the Word Guessing game. Remember to follow along carefully, watch for typos, and not omit any steps.

Designing the Game

The development of the Word Guessing game will be completed in 15 steps as outlined here:

1. Open your text or script editor and create a new file.
2. Add comment statements to the beginning of the script file to document the script and its purpose.
3. Define a class representing the terminal window.
4. Define a class representing the Number Guessing game.
5. Add a `display_greeting` method to the `Game` class.
6. Add a `display_instructions` method to the `Game` class.
7. Add a `select_word` method to the `Game` class.
8. Add a `get_consonants` method to the `Game` class.
9. Add a `get_vowel` method to the `Game` class.
10. Add a `prompt_for_guess` method to the `Game` class.
11. Add a `play_game` method to the `Game` class.
12. Add a `display_credits` method to the `Game` class.
13. Instantiate script objects.
14. Prompt the player for permission to begin the game.
15. Set up the game's controlling logic.

Step 1: Creating a New Ruby File

The first step in developing the Word Guessing game is to start your preferred text or code editor, create a new Ruby script file, and save the script file with a name of WordGuess.rb.

Step 2: Documenting the Script and Its Purpose

Now let's add a few comment statements to the beginning of the script file to provide a high-level overview of the game and to explain what it does. To do this, add the following statements to the end of the script file.

```
#----------------------------------------------------------------
#
# Script Name: WordGuess.rb
# Version:     1.0
# Author:      Jerry Lee Ford, Jr.
# Date:        October 2007
#
# Description: This Ruby script demonstrates how to work with regular
```

```
#           expressions through the development of a computer game
#           that challenges the player to guess a mystery word after
#           being first allowed to guess 5 consonants and 1 vowel.
#
#-------------------------------------------------------------------
```

Step 3: Creating the Screen Class

The Word Guessing game will utilize two custom classes that will provide it with a collection of methods required to control user interaction and the execution of the game. The code statements for the script's first custom class, the Screen class, are shown next and should be added to the end of the script file.

```
# Define custom classes ------------------------------------------------

#Define a class representing the console window
class Screen

  def cls  #Define a method that clears the display area
    puts ("\n" * 25)  #Scroll the screen 25 times
    puts "\a"  #Make a little noise to get the player's attention
  end

  def pause    #Define a method that pauses the display area
    STDIN.gets  #Execute the STDIN class's gets method to pause script
                #execution until the player presses the Enter key
  end

end
```

The Screen class contains two methods. The cls method writes 25 blank lines to the console window to clear the screen and then makes an audible beep sound. The pause method uses the STDIN class's gets method to pause script execution until the player presses the Enter key.

Step 4: Creating the Game Class

The code statements that make up the Game class are shown next and should be added to the end of the script file. This class contains eight methods that are needed to control the game's execution. To begin the creation of the Game class, add the following statements to the end of the script file.

```
#Define a class representing the Word Guessing Game
class Game


end
```

Step 5: Defining the display_greeting Method

The first of the methods defined in the Game class is display_greeting and as the name implies, it is responsible for displaying the game's welcome message. The statements that make up this method are shown next and should be inserted between the game class's opening and closing statements.

```
#This method displays the game's opening message
def display_greeting

  Console_Screen.cls  #Clear the display area

  #Display welcome message
  print "\t\t\tWelcome to the Word Guessing Game!" +
  "\n\n\n\n\n\n\n\n\n\n\n\n\nPress Enter to " +
            "continue."

Console_Screen.pause       #Pause the game
end
```

Step 6: Defining the display_instructions Method

The next method to be added to the Game class is the display_instructions method. The script statements for this method are shown next and should be added to the class definition, immediately after the previously defined method.

```
#Define a method to be used to present game instructions
def display_instructions

  Console_Screen.cls      #Clear the display area
  puts "INSTRUCTIONS:\n\n" #Display a heading

  #Display the game's instructions
  puts "At the start of each new round of play, the game will randomly"
  puts "select a word that is between 5 and 10 characters long"
  puts "and challenge you to guess it. Before submitting your guess, you"
```

```
puts "are allowed to provide the game with 5 consonants and 1 vowel to"
puts "determine if they are used in the secret word.\n\n\n"

puts "Good luck!\n\n\n\n\n\n\n\n\n"
print "Press Enter to continue."

Console_Screen.pause        #Pause the game

end
```

This method displays a series of text strings that provide the player with instructions for playing the game.

Step 7: Defining the select_word Method

The next method to be added to the Game class is the select_word method. This method's script statements are shown next and should be added to the end of the class definition, immediately after the display_instructions method.

```
#Define a method that generates the secret word
def select_word

  #Define an array of 20 words from which the game will randomly select
  words = ["W I N D O W", "S T A T I O N", "H A M B U R G E R",
           "E X P R E S S I O N", "W A L L E T", "C A M E R A",
           "A I R P L A N E", "C A N D L E", "C O M P U T E R",
           "P I C T U R E", "F R A M E", "S H E L F", "B O W L I N G",
           "P O L I T E", "S T A T E M E N T", "N E G A T I V E",
           "M E T H O D", "F I S H I N G", "C O M P E N S A T E",
           "H A P P Y"]

  #Generate and return a random number between 0 and 19
  randomNo = rand(19)

  #Return a randomly selected word to the calling statement
  return words[randomNo]

end
```

This method begins by defining an array named words and populates the array with 20 text strings representing game words. Spaces have been added between each letter in each word to facilitate the eventual splitting up of the characters that make up each word into an array later in the script file.

Next, a random number between 0 and 19 is generated. The final statement in the method returns a word extracted from the words array back to the statement that called upon the method to execute.

Step 8: Defining the get_consonants Method

The code statements for the get_consonants method are shown next and should be added to the end of the class definition, immediately after the select_word method. This method is responsible for prompting the player to provide a list of five consonants, which the game will use to disclose matching letters in its secret word prior to prompting the player to try to guess it.

```
#Define a method that collects the player's consonant guesses
def get_consonants

  list = Array.new  #define an array in which to store the consonants

  #Give the player an idea of what is coming
  puts "Before you try to guess the secret word, you must specify " +
      "5 consonants.\n\n"
  print "Press Enter to continue."

  Console_Screen.pause     #Pause the game

  5.times do  #Iterate 5 times

    Console_Screen.cls      #Clear the display area

    #Prompt the player to enter a consonant
    print "\nPlease enter a consonant and press Enter: "

    input = STDIN.gets  #Collect the player's input
    input.chop!         #Remove the end of line marker

    #Only accept consonant characters
    if input !~ /[bcdfghjklmnpqrstvwxyz]/i then
      Console_Screen.cls        #Clear the display area
```

```
      print "Error: " + input + " is not a consonant. Press Enter to " +
      "continue."
      Console_Screen.pause        #Pause the game
      redo  #Repeat the current execution of the loop
    end

    #Only accept one character of input per guess
    if input.length > 1 then # !~ /./ then
      Console_Screen.cls        #Clear the display area
      print "Error: You may only enter one character at a time. Press " +
      "Enter to continue."
      Console_Screen.pause         #Pause the game
      redo  #Repeat the current execution of the loop
    end

    #Do not allow the player to submit the same guess twice
    if list.include?(input.upcase) == true then
      Console_Screen.cls         #Clear the display area
      print "Error: You have already guessed " + input + ". Press " +
      "Enter to continue."
      Console_Screen.pause         #Pause the game
      redo  #Repeat the current execution of the loop
    else
      list.push(input.upcase)  #Convert the consonant to uppercase and
    end                        #add it to the list of consonants

  end

  return list  #Return the list of consonants to the calling statement

end
```

This method begins by defining a new array named list, which will be used to store a list of consonants supplied by the player. Next, a message is displayed that explains to the player that she is about to be prompted to provide five consonants. A loop is then set up that executes five times (once for each consonant that is collected).

Within the loop, the player is prompted to enter a constant. The user's input is then validated in a series of three conditional checks. The first conditional check sets up a regular expression that performs a case-insensitive comparison of the player's input against a list of all the consonants in the alphabet. The player's input is rejected if it does not match one of the consonants listed in the regular expression.

The second conditional check uses the `String` class's `length` method to determine whether the player entered more than one character and rejects the input if she did. The third conditional check uses the `String` class's `include?` method to determine if the player's input (converted to uppercase) has already been submitted (e.g., has been added to the `list` array) and rejects it if this is the case. However, if the player's input is valid at the end of the third conditional check, it is added to the end of the `list` array using the `push` method (after being converted to all uppercase).

> There are two important points to note in the previous set of conditional checks. First, any time one of the conditional checks rejects the player's input, the `redo` command is executed. As a result, the current execution of the loop runs again, preventing the loop from iterating. Second, only valid input that has been converted to uppercase is added to the `list` array. The contents of this array will be used later in the script to disclose any matching letters in the game's secret word, thus helping the player to figure it out.

The last statement in the `get_consonants` method returns a copy of the contents of the `list` array to the statement that invoked the method.

Step 9: Defining the get_vowel Method

The code statements for the `get_vowel` method are shown next and should be added to the end of the class definition, immediately after the `get_consonants` method. This method is responsible for prompting the player to provide a vowel, which the game will use to disclose matching letters in its secret word prior to prompting the player to try to guess it.

```
#Define a method that collects the player's vowel guess
def get_vowel

  #Give the player an idea of what is coming
  puts "Before you try to guess the secret word, you must specify " +
  "1 vowel.\n\n"

  1.times do  #Iterate 1 time

    Console_Screen.cls      #Clear the display area
```

```
#Prompt the player to enter a vowel
print "\nPlease enter a vowel and press Enter: "
input = STDIN.gets  #Collect the player's input
input.chop!          #Remove the end of line marker

#Only accept vowel characters
if input !~ /[aeiou]/i then
  Console_Screen.cls        #Clear the display area
  print "Error: " + input + " is not a vowel. Press Enter to " +
  "continue."
  Console_Screen.pause      #Pause the game
  redo  #Repeat the current execution of the loop
end

#Only accept one character of input per guess
if input.length > 1 then # !~ /./ then
  Console_Screen.cls        #Clear the display area
  print "Error: You may only enter one character at a time. Press " +
  "Enter to continue."
  Console_Screen.pause      #Pause the game
  redo
end

input = input.upcase  #Convert the vowel to uppercase
return input  #Return the vowel to the calling statement

  end

end
```

As you can see, the program statements that make up this method are very similar to those in the previous method, except only two conditional validation checks are performed on the user's input and the user's input is returned to the calling statement as a individual value and not as a list.

Step 10: Defining the prompt_for_guess Method

The code statements for the prompt_for_guess method are shown next and should be added to the end of the class definition, immediately after the get_vowel method. This method is responsible for formatting the display of the secret word and then managing the game's interaction with the player as the player attempts to guess the word.

```ruby
#Define a method that collects player guesses
def prompt_for_guess(shortWord, word, consonants, vowel)

  Console_Screen.cls        #Clear the display area

  consonants.push(vowel)  #To make things easy, add the vowel to the
                          #list of consonants

  wordArray = word.split(" ") #Split the secret word into an array

  i = 0  #Initial the variable with a starting value of zero

  #Loop once for each letter in the word (stored in an array)
  wordArray.each do |letter|

    match = false  #Initial the variable with a starting value of false

    #Loop once for each consonant stored in the consonants array
    consonants.each do |character|

      #Compare the current character from the consonants array to the
      #current letters in the wordArray array
      if character == letter then
        match = true  #Set variable value to indicate a match
        break  #Terminate loop execution when a match occurs
      end

    end

    #If there is no matching character in the consonants array for the
    #current letter in the wordArray array, replace that letter in the
    #wordArray with an underscore character
    if match == false then
      wordArray[i] = "_"  #Replace the current character with an
    end                   #underscore
```

```
  match = false  #Reset the value of the match variable

  i = i + 1  #Increment the variable's value by 1

end

#Once the contents of the array have been formatted with underscores,
#convert the contents of the array back into a word
word = wordArray.join(" ")

#Allow the player up to three guesses
3.times do |i|  #i equals 0 on the first iteration of the loop

  Console_Screen.cls      #Clear the display area

  #Prompt the player to try to guess the secret word
  puts "I am thinking of a word.\n\n\n\n\n\n"
  print "Here is your clue:  " + word + "\n\n\n\n\n\n\n\n"
  print "What do you think this word is?  "
  reply = STDIN.gets  #Collect the player's reply
  reply.chop!          #Remove the end of line marker
  reply = reply.upcase  #Convert the reply to all uppercase

  #Analyze the player's guess
  if reply == shortWord then  #The player guessed the secret word

    Console_Screen.cls      #Clear the display area
    print "Correct! Press Enter to continue."
    Console_Screen.pause      #Pause the game
    break  #Terminate the execution of the loop

  else  #The player did not guess the secret word

    Console_Screen.cls      #Clear the display area

    #Display a message based on how many turns remain
    if i == 1 then
      print "Wrong! You have one guess left. Press Enter to " +
```

```
        "try again."
      elsif i == 2
        print "Sorry, you lose.\n\n"
        print "The word was " + shortWord + ". Press Enter to continue."
      else
        print "Wrong! Press Enter to try again."
      end

      Console_Screen.pause       #Pause the game

    end

  end

end
```

The `prompt_for_guess` method processes four arguments. `shortWord` is a copy of the game's secret word with no spaces in it. `word` is a copy of the game's secret word with spaces inserted between each letter. `consonants` is a list of five consonants previously supplied by the player, and `vowel` is a string representing the vowel specified by the player when the `get_vowel` method was executed.

The `prompt_for_guess` method begins by adding `vowel` to the `consonants` array. This is done to simplify things by grouping all of the player's input into a single array, making the data easy to process. Next a new array named `wordArray` is created and assigned a list of letters extracted from `word`.

 HINT   In order to extract each letter from the string stored in `word` and assign it as an item in the `wordArray` array, the `String` class's `split` method was used. This method splits the contents of `string` into an array using a specified delimiter. In the case of the `word` variable, the delimiter was the blank space located between each letter.

Next, a value of zero is assigned to a variable named `i`. This variable will be used later in the method to keep track of which item (letter) is being examined in the `wordArray` array when it is being processed by a loop and compared to each of the six letters provided by the player (five consonants and a vowel).

A loop is then set up that loops though each item stored in the `wordArray` array. Within this loop a second loop has been set up that loops through each item stored in the `consonants` array. The inner loop compares the currently selected item (letter) from the wordArray array against each of the items (letters) in the consonants array. If a match is found, the inner loop is terminated using the break command and a value of true is assigned to a variable named match.

Next, a conditional statement is executed that replaces the current character in the wordArray array with an underscore if no match was found in the consonants array. The value of match is then set back to false and the value of i is incremented by one. Once every item in wordArray has been compared to every item in consonants, the contents of wordArray are converted back into a string again using the Array class's join method.

The join method takes as an argument a delimiter that is then used to pad array items to create a string. In the previous statement, the join method is passed a single blank space.

Next, a loop is set up that provides the player with three chances to guess the game's secret word. Each time the loop iterates, it displays a copy of the secret word. Any letters in the word that match up against the consonants and vowel that the player specified are revealed and all other letters are hidden (represented by underscore characters). The player is then prompted to guess the secret word.

The player's guess is converted to all uppercase characters and compared against the value of shortWord to see if there is a match, in which case the player has successfully guessed the word. If this happens, the break command is executed, terminating the execution of the loop. Otherwise, the player is informed of her error and given another chance to make a guess. After using up all three chances without correctly guessing the secret word, the loop terminates.

Because Ruby is a case-sensitive programming language, it views upper-and lowercase letters as being different from one another. To keep things simple, the game converts all letters to uppercase, eliminating any concerns about comparing one string against another.

Step 11: Defining the play_game Method

The next method to be added to the Game class is the play_game method. The statements belonging to this method are shown next and should be added to the end of the class definition, immediately after the prompt_for_guess method.

```
#Define a method to control game play
def play_game
```

```
word = select_word   #Call on the method that retrieves a random word

Console_Screen.cls       #Clear the display area

consonants = get_consonants #Call on the method that prompts the player
                            #to enter a list of consonants

Console_Screen.cls       #Clear the display area

#Call on the method that prompts the player to enter a vowel
vowel = get_vowel

#Remove blank spaces from the word to create a short version of the word
shortWord = word.gsub(" ", "")

#Call the method that processes player guesses
prompt_for_guess(shortWord, word, consonants, vowel)

Console_Screen.cls       #Clear the display area

end
```

This method begins by calling on the select_word method to retrieve a word for the player to guess. Next, the get_consonants method is called to retrieve a list of five consonants, and the get_vowel method is called to prompt the player to identify a vowel. Next, the String class's gsub method is used to generate a short version of the secret word (without spaces) and the prompt_for_guess method is executed. This method is passed shortWord, word, consonants, and vowel as arguments and uses these objects to prompt the player to try to guess the secret word.

Step 12: Defining the display_credits Method

The last method to be added to the Game class is the display_credits method. This method displays the game's credits, including the author's URL. The statements that make up this method are shown next and should be appended to the end of the Game class.

```
#This method displays the information about the Word Guessing game
def display_credits

  Console_Screen.cls  #Clear the display area
```

```
#Thank the player and display game information
puts "\t\t    Thank you for playing the Word Guessing Game.\n\n\n\n"
puts "\n\t\t\t Developed by Jerry Lee Ford, Jr.\n\n"
puts "\t\t\t\t Copyright 2008\n\n"
puts "\t\t\tURL: http://www.tech-publishing.com\n\n\n\n\n\n\n\n\n\n"
```

```
end
```

Step 13: Initializing Script Objects

Now it is time to initialize instances of the Screen and the Game classes. This is done by appending the following statements to the end of the script file.

```
# Main Script Logic --------------------------------------------------

Console_Screen = Screen.new  #Instantiate a new Screen object
WordGuess = Game.new         #Instantiate a new Game object

#Execute the Game class's display_greeting method
WordGuess.display_greeting

answer = ""  #Initialize variable and assign it an empty string
```

In addition to instantiating the Console_Screen and SQ objects, these statements define a variable named answer, which will be used to control the execution of the loop that prompts the player for permission to begin a new round of play.

Step 14: Getting Permission to Start the Game

The script statements responsible for prompting the player for permission to start a new round of play are outlined here:

```
#Loop until the player enters y or n and do not accept any other input
loop do

  Console_Screen.cls  #Clear the display area

  #Prompt the player for permission to start the quiz
  print "Are you ready to play the Word Guessing Game? (y/n): "

  answer = STDIN.gets  #Collect the player's answer
  answer.chop!  #Remove any extra characters appended to the string
```

```
#Terminate the loop if valid input was provided
break if answer =~ /y|n/i
```

```
end
```

These statements, which should be added to the end of the script file, are controlled by a loop that has been set up to run forever. Each time the loop iterates, the player is prompted to enter a value of y or n, to tell the game whether a new round of play should be initiated or the game should be terminated. Any input other than a y or n is ignored. As soon as valid input has been provided, the `break` command is executed and the loop terminates, allowing the rest of the script to execute.

Step 15: Controlling Game Play

The rest of the statements that make up the Word Guessing game are shown next and should be added to the end of the script file. These statements are responsible for controlling the overall execution of the game.

```
#Analyze the player's input
if answer == "n"  #See if the player elected not to take the quiz

  Console_Screen.cls  #Clear the display area

  #Invite the player to return and take the quiz some other time
  puts "Okay, perhaps another time.\n\n"

else  #The player wants to play the game

    #Execute the game class's display_instructions method
    WordGuess.display_instructions

  loop do  #Loop forever

    #Execute the Game class's play_game method
    WordGuess.play_game

    #Find out if the player wants to play another round
    print "Would you like to play again? (y/n): "
```

```
    playAgain = STDIN.gets  #Collect the player's response
    playAgain.chop!  #Remove any extra characters appended to the string

    #Terminate the loop if valid input was provided
    break if playAgain =~ /n/i

  end

  #Call upon the Game class's determine_credits method
  WordGuess.display_credits

end
```

As you can see, these statements are controlled by a large if code block. The script statements that it executes depend on whether the player decides to terminate the game or play another round. If the player elects not to play, a message is displayed that encourages her to return and play another time. If the player elects to play, the Game class's display_instructions method is executed. Next, a loop executes the Game class's play_game method, initiating a new round of play. Once the current round of play has finished, control returns to the loop, which prompts the player to play again. If the player decides to play again, the loop iterates. Otherwise the break command is executed, terminating the loop and allowing the display_credits method to execute.

Running Your New Ruby Script Game

Okay, you now have everything needed to create and execute the Word Guessing game. Assuming that you did not make any typos along the way and that you did not accidentally skip any steps, the script should run as described at the beginning of this chapter. If, however, you should run into an error or two, be sure to carefully read the text of the error messages to get an idea of what and where the problems reside. If all else fails, go back and review the script and look for typos and missing script statements.

SUMMARY

In this chapter, you learned how to use regular expressions as a tool for analyzing data. You learned how to create regular expressions that can match simple character patterns and groups of characters. You learned how to incorporate metacharacters to create more stream-lined and powerful regular expressions. You also learned how to use regular expressions to extract data from a string and to perform string substitution. Finally, you learned how to use regular expressions to negate differences in case.

Now, before you move on to Chapter 8, "Object-Oriented Programming," I suggest you set aside a little extra time to make a few improvements to the Word Guessing game by implementing the following list of challenges.

CHALLENGES

1. The Word Guessing game currently draws upon 20 words when selecting the game's secret word. As a result of having a small pool of words from which to choose, the same word may be used more than once during any given session of play. Consider doubling or even tripling the number of words available to the game.

2. As it is currently written, the text that is used to provide instructions and guide player moves is a little dry and cryptic. Consider rewording this text to make things more user-friendly.

OBJECT-ORIENTED PROGRAMMING

I n Chapter 3, you learned a number of elementary object-oriented programming concepts, including how to define new classes and instantiate objects based on those classes. You learned how to define properties and methods within those classes and to interact with these properties and methods once you instantiated objects based on these classes. In subsequent chapters you learned how to work with an assortment of predefined Ruby classes, include the string, numeric, array, and hash classes. In this chapter, you will learn more object-oriented programming concepts, including how to initialize objects upon instantiation, restrict access to object variables using different variable scopes, overwrite class methods, and restrict access to class methods. On top of all this, you will learn how to create a new Ruby script, the Ruby Rock, Paper, Scissors game.

Specifically, you will learn:

- How to pass data to new objects as they are instantiated
- How to work with instance and class variables
- About abstraction, encapsulation, inheritance, and polymorphism
- How to override Ruby's built-in classes

PROJECT PREVIEW: THE RUBY ROCK, PAPER, SCISSORS GAME

This chapter's script project is the Ruby Rock, Paper, Scissors game. This Ruby game is a computerized version of the classic Rock, Paper, Scissors game but pits the player against the computer. There are three possible moves that the player and the computer can make: rock, paper, or scissors. After both the computer and the player have selected their moves, the results are analyzed based on the following rules.

- Rock crushes scissors to win
- Paper covers rock to win
- Scissors cut paper to win
- Matching moves result in a tie

The Ruby Rock, Paper, Scissors game begins by displaying the message shown in Figure 8.1.

 FIGURE 8.1

The opening message invites the player to play the game.

After dismissing the opening screen, the player is prompted for permission to start a new round of play, as shown in Figure 8.2.

FIGURE 8.2

The player is prompted for permission to start the game.

If the player decides to play, the instructions shown in Figure 8.3 display. The instructions provide a brief overview of the rules of the game.

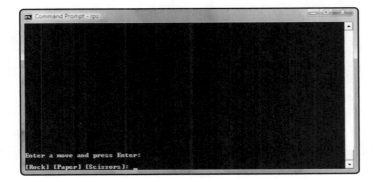

FIGURE 8.3

The instructions for the Ruby Rock, Paper, Scissors game.

Once the player presses the Enter key to dismiss the game's instructions, the screen shown in Figure 8.4 displays, prompting the player to specify a move.

FIGURE 8.4

To make a move the player must type Rock, Paper, or Scissors and press the Enter key.

As soon as the player selects a move, the game randomly selects a move on behalf of the computer. The player's move is then compared to the computer's move to determine the result, as demonstrated in Figure 8.5.

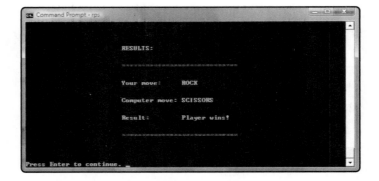

FIGURE 8.5

The player's selection of Rock beats the computer's selection of Scissors.

At the end of each round of play, the game prompts the player for permission to play again, as shown in Figure 8.6.

FIGURE 8.6

The player may play as many rounds as she wants.

Once the player has had her fill and decides to stop playing, the screen shown in Figure 8.7 displays and the game ends.

FIGURE 8.7

The closing message encourages the player to visit the developer's website.

UNDERSTANDING KEY OBJECT-ORIENTED TERMS

Object-oriented programming is a key feature of Ruby. As has been stated, in object-oriented programming, data and code are stored together as objects. In Ruby, objects are created from classes. A *class* provides a template that specifies properties, methods, and data that are available for interacting with and controlling an object.

You have worked extensively with classes throughout this book. Ruby provides you with access to a huge collection of predefined classes. For example, you have already learned how to work with various methods belonging to the String class and various types of numeric classes to manipulate text and perform mathematic calculations. Every time you have used the puts or print method to display text, you have worked with methods belonging to the Kernel class. Arrays and hashes have their own classes as well, both of which are packed full of helpful methods.

Object-oriented programming helps to simplify the coding process by promoting code reuse, allowing you to define classes from which you can then generate any number of objects. Object-oriented programming also provides a number of other key features, including abstraction, encapsulation, inheritance, and polymorphism.

Abstraction

Abstraction is a term that refers to the process of organizing program code into classes. This includes the specification of both properties and methods. Using the class as a template, you can create instances of objects, as demonstrated here.

```
class Automobile

  attr_accessor :color

  def drive
    puts "Vroom!!!"
  end

end
```

Here, a class named Automobile has been defined and assigned one property and one method. Once defined, a new object can be created from this class, as shown here.

```
myCar = Automobile.new
```

Once created, you can assign a value to the object's color property, as shown here.

```
myCar.color = "Blue"
```

Once set, you can access the object's `color` property whenever you need to. You can also execute the object's `drive` method, as shown here.

```
puts "I love to drive my little " + myCar.color + " car."
myCar.drive
```

When executed, these two statements display the following results.

```
I love to drive my little Blue car.
Vroom!!!
```

Encapsulation

Another key feature of object-oriented programming is encapsulation. *Encapsulation* is a programming technique that restricts access to one or more of the properties and methods defined within a class. Encapsulation helps to make script code more reliable by restricting which parts of a script can access class properties and methods. Encapsulation also supports data protection by allowing you to include additional program code that validates data passed to methods (to ensure that it meets expected criteria).

By default, any properties and methods that you add to a class are public, meaning that they can be accessed from outside of the class. To control access to the properties and methods within a class, you can insert any of the following keywords within the class.

- `public`. Makes any properties or methods that follow publicly available throughout the script.
- `private`. Restricts access to any properties or methods that follow to just within the object itself.
- `protected`. Restricts access to any properties or methods that follow to just objects of the same class or objects of subclasses of the class.

Access to any properties or methods that are defined after the occurrence of one of these words is governed by that keyword, which remains in effect until either the end of the class is reached or a different level of encapsulation is specified. For an example of how to restrict access to a method located in a custom class, look at the following Ruby script, which prompts the user to enter the name of a superhero. In response, the script displays that hero's secret identity (if it is known).

```
class Hero

  def initialize(name)
```

```ruby
      secret_identity(name)
  end

  def display_identity
    puts "\n\nThis hero's secret identity is " + @identity + "\n\n"
    print "Press Enter to continue."
  end

  private

  def secret_identity(name)

    if name =~ /Superman/i then
      @identity = "Clark Kent"
    elsif name =~ /Batman/i then
      @identity = "Bruce Wayne"
    elsif name =~ /Spiderman/i then
      @identity = "Peter Parker"
    else
      @identity = "Unknown"
    end

  end

end

loop do

  puts ("\n" * 25)
  puts "\n\nWelcome to the superhero identity tracker!\n\n"
  print "Enter a superhero's name or type Q to quit: "

  input = STDIN.gets
  input.chop!

  break if input =~ /q/i

  puts ("\n" * 25)
```

```
myHero = Hero.new(input)
myHero.display_identity

STDIN.gets

end
```

Here, a class named Hero has been defined. Within the class three methods have been set up. The first method is named `initialize`. It executes as soon as an object is instantiated using this class. This method accepts as an argument a string representing a superhero's name. When the method executes, it calls upon the class's third method, passing it the superhero's name. The second method in the class is the `display_identity` method, which prompts the user to type in the name of a hero. When it is called upon to execute, it displays a text string that contains a variable named `@identity`, which is populated with data supplied by the third method.

The third method is the `secret_identity` method. It is preceded by the `private` keyword, preventing it from being directly accessed from outside of the class. Within the method, an `if` code block is executed that analyzes the value of the superhero's name to see if it matches one of several known superhero names. If a match occurs, the value of `@identity` is assigned a text string containing the superhero's secret identity. If no match is found, a value of `"Unknown"` is assigned instead.

The rest of the script is made up of a loop that has been set up to run forever. Each time the loop repeats, it prompts the player to either enter a superhero's name or a q, thereby terminating the execution of the script. Figure 8.8 shows the initial screen that is displayed when this example is run. As you can see, the user is prompted to enter the name of a superhero to see if the script has the hero's secret identity on record.

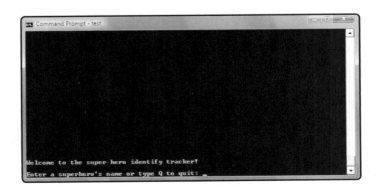

FIGURE 8.8

The user is prompted to enter a hero's name or to type q to quit.

After entering a name, the output shown in Figure 8.9 displays. Depending on whether the script is able to determine the hero's secret identity, either the hero's real name is displayed or the user is told that the hero's identity is currently unknown.

This hero's secret identify is Peter Parker
Press enter to continue._

FIGURE 8.9

The superhero's secret identity is revealed.

Inheritance

As you learned in Chapter 3, inheritance is also a key feature of object-oriented programming. *Inheritance* occurs when one class is derived from another class. The derived class, sometimes referred to as the child class, inherits all of the properties and methods of the parent class. In addition, you can modify any inherited properties and methods or even add new ones to customize the child class.

With inheritance, it is possible to build an entire family of classes consisting of parents, children, siblings, grandchildren, and so on. When defining classes using inheritance, programmers place properties and methods common to all classes in the top-most class, thus allowing all classes derived from this class to inherit them and place properties and methods specific to individual classes within those classes. The advantage of this approach is that it not only allows you to customize classes as you see fit but it also helps to simplify the development and maintenance of Ruby scripts. As a result, if you need to make a change to a method that is a common method, all you have to do is change it in the parent class and all classes derived from that class will automatically inherit that change.

As a demonstration of how inheritance works, take a look at the following script.

```
class Hero

  attr_accessor :power, :weakness

  def catch_phrase
```

```
    print "Halt in the name of the law! "
  end

end

class UnderDog < Hero

  def bark
    puts "Woof!"
  end

end

class Superman < Hero
  attr_accessor :cape
end

class Batman < Hero
  attr_accessor :mask
end

UD = UnderDog.new
SM = Superman.new
BM = Batman.new

SM.power = "Flight"
SM.weakness = "Kryptonite"
SM.cape = "red"

SM.catch_phrase
puts "Or I will fly over there in my " + SM.cape + " cape and capture you!"
```

Here, a class named Hero has been created that defines two properties and a method. Next, a new class named UnderDog has been defined as a child class of the Hero class. The UnderDog class is then assigned an additional method. Two additional classes are then created that, like the UnderDog class, inherit all of the properties and methods from the Hero class. Unique properties have been included in the definitions for both of these classes.

Finally, three objects are instantiated, one from each class, and the object based on the Superman class is then assigned various property assignments, after which its `catch_phrase` method is executed, resulting in the following output.

```
Halt in the name of the law! Or I will fly over there in my red cape and
capture you!
```

Polymorphism

Yet another object-oriented programming feature is polymorphism. *Polymorphism* is the ability to define something in different forms. One way that this is implemented within Ruby is in Ruby's ability to execute the same method on many different types of objects and to get results that are appropriate for each type of object. An excellent example of this type of behavior is provided by Ruby's + method. When used to work with two strings, the + method concatenates the two strings together, as demonstrated here.

```
puts "Once upon " + "a time in a far away land..."
```

When executed, this statement displays the following output.

```
Once upon a time in a far away land...
```

When used with two numbers, the + method adds them together, as demonstrated here:

```
puts 5 + 4
```

When executed, this statement displays a value of 9.

When used with two arrays, the + method merges them together to create a new array, as demonstrated here:

```
x = [1, 2, 3] + [4, 5, 6]
puts x.inspect
```

When executed, this statement displays the following output.

```
[1, 2, 3, 4, 5, 6]
```

Should you have a need to use it, this type of polymorphic programming can be easily replicated in your own custom methods, as demonstrated here:

```
class Hero
  attr_accessor :power, :weakness
  def catch_phrase
    puts "Here I come to save the day!"
```

```
    end
end

class UnderDog < Hero
end

class Superman < Hero
  def catch_phrase
    puts "Up, up and away!"
  end
end

class Batman < Hero
  def catch_phrase
    puts "Quick, to the batcave!"
  end
end
```

Here, a class named Hero has been defined and assigned two properties and one method named catch_phrase. Next, three child classes are created based on the Hero class. The first child class is name UnderDog and it simply inherits the properties and methods of its parent class. The next two classes inherit these same features but then overwrite the catch_phrase method with their own custom version of the method. As a result, if you instantiate objects based on each of the three child objects, and then execute their catch_phrase methods, you will see different results.

```
UD = UnderDog.new
SM = Superman.new
BM = Batman.new

UD.catch_phrase
SM.catch_phrase
BM.catch_phrase
```

When executed this example displays the following output.

```
Here I come to save the day!
Up, up and away!
Quick, to the batcave!
```

INITIALIZING OBJECTS UPON INSTANTIATION

If you want, you can instantiate an object and initialize one or more object properties in one single step. To do so, Ruby provides you with access to a special method named initialize. When included inside a class definition, the initialize method is automatically executed any time an object is instantiated. By including an initialize method in a class definition, you can pass arguments to the class when you instantiate it, and these arguments will automatically be passed to the initialize method, where they are then mapped to variables, as demonstrated in the following example.

```
class Noise

  def initialize(occurrences)
    @occurrences = occurrences
  end

  def make_sound
    @occurrences.times {print "\a"}
  end

end
```

Here, a class named Noise has been set up that contains two methods. The first method is named initialize. It has been set up to process a single argument, which it then assigns to a variable named @occurrences. The second method is named make_sound. When called, it plays a beep sound a specified number of times, as determined by the value assigned to @occurrences.

 @occurrences is an example of an instance variable. It restricts variable access to the object in which it resides. You'll learn more about instance variables a little later in this chapter.

Like any class, you may instantiate as many object instances of it as you want. The following statements instantiate two objects based on the Noise class.

```
shortSound = Noise.new(1)
longSound = Noise.new(10)
```

The first statement creates an object named shortSound, using the new method to create a new instance of the Noise object. Note that a value of 1 has been passed as an argument. As a result, when the new object is created, @occurrences is assigned a value of 1, and the times method, located in the make_sound method, will play the beep sound one time.

The second statement creates a variable named `longSound`. The only difference between this object and the `shortSound` object is that the `longSound` object will play the beep sound 10 times when the `make_sound` method is called. Once both objects have been instantiated, you can call upon them to execute, as shown here.

```
shortSound.make_sound
STDIN.gets
longSound.make_sound
```

Here, the `shortSound` object's `make_sound` method is executed, playing a single beep sound after which the script pauses until the Enter key is pressed. At this time the `longSound` object's `make_sound` method is executed, playing 10 consecutive beep sounds.

UNDERSTANDING VARIABLE SCOPE

As you learned back in Chapter 3, Ruby supports four different types of variables: local, global, instance, and class. Each of these variables is capable of storing a single instance of any type of object supported by Ruby. The difference between them is the scope within which they can be accessed.

Working with Local Variables

You have worked with local variables in numerous instances. A local variable is one that can be accessed only within the scope in which it is created. For example, the following example defines a class named `Greeting`, which contains a method named `display_msg`.

```
class Greeting

  def display_msg
    puts "Hello " + myName
  end

end
```

As a local variable, `myName` can only be accessed in the method in which it has been defined. Therefore, if you specify the use of a variable named `myName`, as demonstrated next, outside of the method, Ruby will regard that variable reference as being a totally different variable with its own scope.

```
Msg = Greeting.new
myName = "Jerry Ford"
Msg.display_msg
```

When executed, this example results in an `Undefined local variable or method error` because even though the value of `myName` was set in the previous statement, it remains unassigned in the `Greeting` class.

Working with Global Variables

One way around the problem shown in the previous example is to use a global variable. Global variables are accessible throughout a Ruby script and have an unlimited scope. To create a global variable, all you have to do is precede its name with the $ character, as demonstrated in the following example.

```
class Greeting

  def display_msg
    puts "Hello " + $myName
  end

end


Msg = Greeting.new
$myName = "Jerry Ford"


Msg.display_msg
```

Since the `myName` variable has been changed from a local to a global variable, no errors will occur if the `display_msg` method is called when the following statements are executed.

```
Msg = Greeting.new
myName = "Jerry Ford"
Msg.display_msg
```

Instead, the following output is displayed.

```
Hello Jerry Ford
```

HINT   The problem with using global variables is that they go against object-oriented programming principles. Specifically, they expose data located in different parts of a script file, opening up the possibility that it might be accidentally changed from a different part of the script file. Instead, it is much better to isolate different parts of a script file from one another, limiting access to variables to just the parts of the script that need to access them. Following this practice results in more modular code that is less prone to error and easier to maintain. Instead of using global variables to make the previous example work, it is a better idea to use local variables and to pass any values needed in different parts of a script as arguments, as demonstrated here:

```
class Greeting

  def display_msg(userName)
    puts "Hello " + userName
  end

end

Msg = Greeting.new
name = "Jerry Ford"

Msg.display_msg(name)
```

Here, a value is assigned to a variable called name, which is then passed an argument to the display_msg method. This method then uses userName, which is local to the method, to display the following output.

```
Hello Jerry Ford
```

Working with Instance Variables

When working with variables that are defined within different methods belonging to the same class definition, it can sometimes be helpful to increase variable scope of variables to allow them to be referenced by all methods residing inside the class definition. This approach still keeps pretty tight control over variable scope while making it easier to work with variables within objects instantiated from those classes. For example, earlier in this chapter you looked at a class named Noise, which contains two methods, initialize and make-sound. These two methods needed to share access to an argument passed during object instantiation. To accommodate this requirement, an instance variable was used, as shown here:

```
class Noise

  def initialize(occurrences)
    @occurrences = occurrences
  end

  def make_sound
    @occurrences.times {print "\a"}
```

```
     end

end
```

Instance variables begin with the @ character, global variables begin with the $ character, and local variables begin with a letter or underscore character.

Working with Class Variables

The last type of variable supported by Ruby is the class variable. Class variables are similar to instance variables except that whereas the scope of instance variables is limited to the object they are defined in, class variables are accessible to all instances of the same class.

Class variable names are easily identified because they begin with the @@ characters, as demonstrated in the following example.

```
class Superman

  def initialize

    if defined?(@@myHero) then
        puts "Error: Only one instance of Superman is permitted at a time."
    else
        @@myHero = "Is alive"
        puts "Up, up and away!"
    end

  end

end
```

Here, a class named Superman has been defined. The class contains a single method named initialize, which automatically executes when an object is created using this class. The following statement creates an object based on the Superman class.

```
clarkKent = Superman.new
```

When executed, the clarkKent object creates a class variable named @@myHero and assigns it a value. If an attempt is made to create a second object based on the Superman class, as demonstrated next, an error message will be displayed.

```
louisLane = Superman.new
```

The error message is displayed because of the @@myHero variable, which is accessible to any objects created from the Superman class and is found using the defined? operator.

HINT   In the previous example, the defined? operator looks for the existence of a variable and returns a value of true if it is found and false if it is not found.

TAKING ADVANTAGE OF RUBY'S BUILT-IN CLASSES

Ruby is a true object-oriented programming language. Everything is viewed as an object, even strings and numbers. For example, using the class method, you can display the object type for any object, as demonstrated here:

```
irb(main):001:0> puts "Hello".class
String
```

Likewise, you can use the class method to display the object type for different types of numeric objects, as demonstrated here:

```
irb(main):002:0> puts 1.class
Fixnum
```

```
irb(main):003:0> puts 1.1.class
Float
```

When you create objects that match up against a predefined Ruby class, such as a string, number, array, or hash, you instantly get access to all of the predefined methods that Ruby defines for those objects because your objects automatically inherit the properties and methods belonging to these classes. As a result, your programming experience is significantly simplified because you do not have to reinvent the wheel with every new Ruby script you write. For example, since every array automatically has access to all the methods defined by the Array class, you can sort the contents of an array by calling on the Array class's sort method. As such, you have instant access to reliable source code that works without errors. Best of all, you didn't have to take the time required to write your own custom sort method. You can even chain together different object's methods to pass one method's output to another method as input, as demonstrated here:

```
myArray = [2, 8, 3, 5, 1]
puts myArray.sort.reverse.inspect
```

Here, the first statement creates an array object named myArray and assigns it a collection of numbers in no particular order. The second statement chains together a series of array methods that sorts the contents of the array, reverses their order, and then displays them as a string.

```
[8, 5, 3, 2, 1]
```

The advantage of chaining together methods in this manner is that you can perform power actions with a minimal amount of programming code. The less code you have to write, the lower the chances you'll make an error, and the easier your Ruby scripts are to maintain. You can also include your own custom functions as part of a chain.

MODIFYING RUBY CLASSES

Ruby is an exceptionally flexible programming language, so much so that you can even modify its parts by removing, redefining, or adding to them. Ruby unleashes you from a strict set of limits, allowing you to customize the language to suit your own preferences and needs. For example, you can add more operator methods to Ruby's `Numeric` class. In Ruby, mathematical calculations are typically performed by defining an expression like the one shown here:

```
x = 1 + 3
```

Here, a variable named x is assigned the value returned by the expression of 1+ 3. The following statement demonstrates another way of formulating the previous example.

```
x = 1.+ 3
```

Here, a value of 4 is assigned to x using an expression that uses dot notation to execute the `Numeric` class's + method, adding 1 and 3 together. If you want to, you can add new methods to the `Numeric` class that you can use in place of Ruby's +, -, *, \, and other related methods, as demonstrated here:

```
class Numeric
  def add(x)
    self.+(x)
  end
end
```

 Take note of the use of the word `self` in the previous example. Self is used here as a shorthand way of referring to the current object.

Here, a custom class named `Numeric` has been defined, which contains a single method named add. By adding this class to a Ruby script, you can use the newly defined add method in place of the + method to perform addition, as demonstrated here:

```
x = 1.add 3
```

When executed, this statement will set x equal to 4.

If you want, you can expand the custom Numeric class to include a range of additional common mathematical operators that use English names, as shown here:

```ruby
class Numeric

  def add(x)
    self.+(x)
  end

  def subtract(x)
    self.-(x)
  end

  def multiply(x)
    self.*(x)
  end

  def divide(x)
    self./(x)
  end


end
```

BACK TO THE RUBY ROCK, PAPER, SCISSORS GAME

Okay, now it is time to turn your attention back to the development of this chapter's game project, the Ruby Rock, Paper, Scissors game. This game is a computerized version of the classic Rock, Paper, Scissors game in which the player is challenged to go head-to-head against the computer.

Designing the Game

As with all of the game projects covered so far in this book, the development of the Ruby Rock, Paper, Scissors game will follow a specific series of steps, as outlined here.

1. Open your text or script editor and create a new file.
2. Add comment statements to the beginning of the script file to document the script and its purpose.

3. Define a class representing the terminal window.
4. Define a class representing the Rock, Paper, Scissors game.
5. Define the `display_greeting` method.
6. Define the `display_instructions` method.
7. Define the `play_game` method.
8. Define the `get_player_move` method.
9. Define the `get_computer_move` method.
10. Define the `analyze_results` method.
11. Define the `display_results` method.
12. Define the `display_credits` method.
13. Initialize script objects.
14. Get permission to start the game.
15. Control overall game play.

As you follow along, make sure that you do not skip a step and that you look out for typos.

Step 1: Creating a New Ruby File

The first step in the development of the Ruby Rock, Paper, Scissors game is to open your favorite text or script editor and create and save a new Ruby script file. Name this file RPS.rb and store it in the same folder as the rest of your Ruby script files.

Step 2: Documenting the Script and Its Purpose

The next step in the development of the Ruby Rock, Paper, Scissors game is to add the following comment statements to the beginning of the file. These statements provide high-level documentation about the script and its author.

```
#- - - - - - - - - - - - - - - - - - - - - - - - - - - - - - - - - - - - - - - - - - - -
#
# Script Name: RPS.rb
# Version:     1.0
# Author:      Jerry Lee Ford, Jr.
# Date:        October 2007
#
# Description: This Ruby game is a computerized version of the classic
#              Rock, Paper, Scissors game in which the player
#              goes head-to-head against the computer.
#
#- - - - - - - - - - - - - - - - - - - - - - - - - - - - - - - - - - - - - - - - - - - -
```

Step 3: Defining a Screen Class

The Ruby Rock, Paper, Scissors game will make use of two custom classes. These classes will provide access to a collection of methods that are required to control the game and interact with the player. Next are the script statements for the first of these two classes.

```
# Define custom classes -------------------------------------------------

#Define a class representing the console window
class Screen

  def cls  #Define a method that clears the display area
    puts ("\n" * 25)  #Scroll the screen 25 times
    puts "\a"   #Make a little noise to get the player's attention
  end

  def pause   #Define a method that pauses the display area
    STDIN.gets  #Execute the STDIN class's gets method to pause script
                #execution until the player presses the Enter key
  end

end
```

These statements make up the Screen class, which is responsible for providing methods that control the clearing of the console screen and the pausing of the game.

Step 4: Creating the Game Class

The script's second custom class is the Game class. It contains eight methods that provide access to an assortment of functionality. To begin the development of the Game class, you will need to append the following statements to the end of the script file.

```
#Define a class representing the Ruby Rock, Paper, Scissors game
class Game

end
```

Step 5: Defining the display_greeting Method

The first of the Game class's methods is the display_greeting method. This method is responsible for displaying the game's opening welcome message. The statements that make up this method are listed next and should be inserted between the class's opening and closing statements.

```
#This method displays the game's opening message
def display_greeting

  Console_Screen.cls  #Clear the display area

  #Display welcome message
  print "\t\t\tLet's Play Ruby Rock, Paper, Scissors!" +
  "\n\n\n\n\n\n\n\n\n\n\n\n\n\nPress Enter to " +
          "continue. "

  Console_Screen.pause      #Pause the game

end
```

Step 6: Defining the display_instructions Method

The next method that is defined within the Game class is the display_instructions method. Its statements are shown next and should be inserted into the Game class, immediately after the display_greeting method.

```
#Define a method to be used to present game instructions
def display_instructions

  Console_Screen.cls      #Clear the display area
  puts "INSTRUCTIONS:\n\n" #Display a heading

  #Display the game's instructions
  puts "This game pits the player against the computer. To play, you must"
  puts "enter one of the following moves when prompted: Rock, Paper, or"
  puts "Scissors.\n\n"
  puts "The game will then randomly select a move for the computer and "
  puts "the result of the game will be analyzed according to the following"
  puts "rules. \n\n"
  puts "* Rock crushes Scissors, Rock equals Rock, and Rock is covered by"
  puts "  Paper\n\n"
  puts "* Paper covers Rock, Paper equals Paper, and Paper is cut by"
  puts "  Scissors\n\n"
  puts "* Scissors cut Paper, Scissors equals Scissors, and Scissors are"
  puts "  crushed by Rock. \n\n\n"
  puts "Good luck!\n\n\n"
```

```
  print "Press Enter to continue. "
  Console_Screen.pause        #Pause the game

end
```

As you can see, this method displays the game's instructions using a series of puts statements.

Step 7: Defining the play_game Method

The third of the Game class's methods is the play_game method. The statements that make up this method are shown next and should be inserted into the Game class, immediately after the display_instructions method.

```
#Define a method to control game play
def play_game

  Console_Screen.cls        #Clear the display area

  #Call on the method responsible for collecting the player's move
  playerMove = get_player_move

  #Call on the method responsible for generating the computer's move
  computerMove = get_computer_move

  #Call on the method responsible for determining the results of the game
  result = analyze_results(playerMove, computerMove)

  #Call on the method responsible for displaying the results of the game
  display_results(playerMove, computerMove, result)

end
```

The statements that make up this method are responsible for managing the overall execution of an individual round of play. As you can see, this is accomplished through a series of calls to other methods. The calls to the playerMove and computerMove methods retrieve the player's and the computer's moves, which are then passed to the analyze_results method. This method determines the winner of the current round of play and passes back its result. This result is then passed to the display_results method, which informs the player of the result.

Step 8: Defining the get_player_move Method

The next method defined within the Game class is the get_player_move method. The statements that make up this method are shown next and should be inserted into the Game class, immediately after the play_game method.

```
#Define the method responsible for collecting the player's move
def get_player_move

  '
  Console_Screen.cls        #Clear the display area

  loop do  #Loop forever

    Console_Screen.cls  #Clear the display area

    #Prompt the player to select a move
    puts "Enter a move and press Enter:\n\n"
    print "[Rock] [Paper] [Scissors]: "

    @choice = STDIN.gets  #Collect the player's answer
    @choice.chop!  #Remove any extra characters appended to
                        #the string

    #Terminate the loop if valid input was provided
    break if @choice  =~ /Rock|Paper|Scissors/i

  end

  #Convert the player move to uppercase and return it to the calling
  #statement
  return @choice.upcase

end
```

This method is responsible for collecting the player's move. It does so using a loop that runs forever. Each time the loop repeats, it displays a prompt that instructs the player to respond by entering a move (Rock, Paper, or Scissors). The player's input is analyzed using a regular expression. If the player's input matches one of the three words listed in the regular expression, the break command is executed, terminating the loop and allowing the game to continue. If, on the other hand, the player fails to provide valid input, the break command is not executed and the loop repeats, prompting the player to try again.

Step 9: Defining the get_computer_move Method

The next method defined within the Game class is the get_computer_move method. The statements that make up this method are shown next and should be inserted into the Game class, immediately after the get_player_move method.

```ruby
#Define the method responsible for making the computer's move
def get_computer_move

  #Define an array containing a list of three possible moves
  moves = ["ROCK", "PAPER", "SCISSORS"]

  #Generate and return a random number between 0 and 2
  randomNo = rand(3)

  #Return a randomly selected move to the calling statement
  return moves[randomNo]

end
```

This method is responsible for generating a move on behalf of the computer. This is accomplished using the rand method to generate a random number between 0 and 2. This number is then used to retrieve one of three moves stored in an array named moves. Once a move has been selected, it is returned to the statement that called upon the get_computer_move method.

Step 10: Defining the analyze_results Method

The next method defined within the Game class is the analyze_results method. This method is responsible for comparing the player's move and the computer's move, passed to the method as arguments, to determine the results of the current round of play. The statements that make up this method are shown next and should be inserted into the Game class, immediately after the get_computer_move method.

```ruby
#Define the method responsible for analyzing and returning the result of
#the game
def analyze_results(player, computer)

  #Analyze the results of the game when the player selects ROCK
  if player == "ROCK" then
    return "Player wins!" if computer == "SCISSORS"
    return "Tie!" if computer == "ROCK"
    return "Computer wins!" if computer == "PAPER"
```

```
  end

  #Analyze the results of the game when the player selects PAPER
  if player == "PAPER" then
    return "Player wins!" if computer == "ROCK"
    return "Tie!" if computer == "PAPER"
    return "Computer wins!" if computer == "SCISSORS"
  end

  #Analyze the results of the game when the player selects SCISSORS
  if player == "SCISSORS" then
    return "Player wins!" if computer == "PAPER"
    return "Tie!" if computer == "SCISSORS"
    return "Computer wins!" if computer == "ROCK"
  end

end
```

As you can see, this method consists of three conditional tests that evaluate the player's and computer's moves to determine whether the game was won, lost, or tied. Based on the result of this analysis, a text string is returned back to the statement that called upon the method to execute.

Step 11: Defining the display_results Method

The next method defined within the Game class is the display_results method. This method is responsible for displaying the results of the game, as passed to it as an argument, along with the player's and the computer's moves. The statements that make up this method are shown next and should be inserted into the Game class, immediately after the analyze_results method.

```
#Define the method responsible for displaying the result of the game
def display_results(player, computer, result)

  #Display arguments passed to the method using the following template
  Console_Screen.cls        #Clear the display area
  puts "\n\n\t\t\tRESULTS:"
  puts "\n\n\t\t\t============================="
  puts "\n\n\t\t\tYour move:      " + player
  puts "\n\n\t\t\tComputer move: " + computer
  puts "\n\n\t\t\tResult:         " + result
```

```
puts "\n\n\t\t\t=============================="
puts "\n\n\n\n"
print "Press Enter to continue. "
Console_Screen.pause        #Pause the game

end
```

Step 12: Defining the display_credits Method

The last method defined within the Game class is the `display_credits` method. This method displays additional information about the game, including the developer's URL. The statements that make up this method are shown next and should be appended to the end of the Game class, just before its closing `end` statement.

```
#This method displays information about the Ruby Rock, Paper, Scissors game
def display_credits

  Console_Screen.cls  #Clear the display area

  #Thank the player and display game information
  puts "\t    Thank you for playing the Ruby Rock, Paper, Scissors game."
  puts "\n\n\n\n"
  puts "\n\t\t\t Developed by Jerry Lee Ford, Jr.\n\n"
  puts "\t\t\t\t  Copyright 2007\n\n"
  puts "\t\t\tURL: http://www.tech-publishing.com\n\n\n\n\n\n\n\n\n\n"

end
```

Step 13: Initializing Script Objects

Now that both of the script's custom classes have been defined and populated with their respective methods, it is time to instantiate instances of both classes. This is accomplished by appending the following statements to the end of the script file.

```
# Main Script Logic ------------------------------------------------------

Console_Screen = Screen.new  #Instantiate a new Screen object
RPS = Game.new                #Instantiate a new Game object

#Execute the Game class's display_greeting method
RPS.display_greeting
```

```
answer = ""   #Initialize variable and assign it an empty string
```

In addition to instantiating the `Console_Screen` and `RPS` objects, these statements define a variable named `answer` and assign it an empty string as an initial value. This variable will be used to control the execution of the loop defined in the next section.

Step 14: Getting Permission to Start the Game

The script statements responsible for prompting the player for permission to start a new round of play are outlined here:

```
#Loop until the player enters y or n and do not accept any other input
loop do

  Console_Screen.cls  #Clear the display area

  #Prompt the player for permission to start the game
  print "Are you ready to play Ruby Rock, Paper, Scissors? (y/n): "

  answer = STDIN.gets  #Collect the player's answer
  answer.chop!  #Remove any extra characters appended to the string

  #Terminate the loop if valid input was provided
  break if answer =~ /y|n/i

end
```

As you can see, a loop has been set up to control the execution of statements that prompt the player for permission to start a round of play. At the end of each iteration of the loop, a regular expression is used to evaluate the player's input, executing the `break` command if that input is valid.

Step 15: Controlling Game Play

The rest of the Ruby Rock, Paper, Scissors script is made up of the statements shown here. These statements are responsible for managing the overall execution of the game.

```
#Analyze the player's answer
if answer == "n"  #See if the player wants to quit

  Console_Screen.cls  #Clear the display area
```

```ruby
    #Invite the player to return and play the game some other time
    puts "Okay, perhaps another time.\n\n"

else  #The player wants to play the game

    #Execute the Game class's display_instructions method
    RPS.display_instructions

  playAgain = ""

  loop do  #Loop forever

    #Execute the Game class's play_game method
    RPS.play_game

    loop do  #Loop forever

      Console_Screen.cls  #Clear the display area
      #Find out if the player wants to play another round
      print "Would you like to play again? (y/n): "

      playAgain = STDIN.gets  #Collect the player's response
      playAgain.chop!  #Remove any extra characters appended to the string

      #Terminate the loop if valid input was provided
      break if playAgain =~ /n|y/i

    end

    #Terminate the loop if valid input was provided
    break if playAgain =~ /n/i

  end

  #Call upon the Game class's determine_credits method
  RPS.display_credits

end
```

As you can see, these statements are controlled by an `if` code block. If the player elects not to play the game, a message is displayed that invites the player to return and play another time. If instead the player decides to play, the `Game` class's `display_instructions` method is called on to execute. Next a loop is set up to control the overall execution of the game. Within the loop the `Game` class's `play_game` method is called, starting a new round of play. Once the `play_game` method has finished, the loop resumes execution and prompts the player to play again. Once the player decides to stop playing, the `break` command is executed, terminating the loop. This allows the `display_credits` method to execute after which the game ends.

Running Your New Ruby Script Game

All right, you now have everything you need to complete the development of the Ruby Rock, Paper, Scissors game. If you have not done so yet, save your new Ruby script. As long as you have followed along carefully with each of the previously discussed steps, and you didn't make any inadvertent typing errors along the way, your new scripts should be ready for testing. As you test the Ruby Rock, Paper, Scissors game, begin by playing it exactly as the game should be played. Once you are confident that everything is working correctly, try playing the game the wrong way, feeding in inappropriate input to ensure that the game handles it appropriately.

SUMMARY

In this chapter, you learned a lot more about Ruby's support for object-oriented programming. This included learning about programming concepts such as abstraction, inheritance, encapsulation, and polymorphism. You learned how to initialize objects upon instantiation and how to work with instance and class variables. You also learned how to modify Ruby by developing your own version of various Ruby class methods.

Now, before you move on to Chapter 9, "File and Folder Administration," I suggest you set aside a little extra time to make a few improvements to the Ruby Rock, Paper, Scissors game by implementing the following list of challenges.

CHALLENGES

1. Currently, the Ruby Rock, Paper, Scissors game requires that the player type out the words Rock, Paper, and Scissors in full when making moves. Consider making things easier on the player by also accepting r, p, and s as valid moves.

2. Consider modifying the Ruby Rock, Paper, Scissors game so that it collects statistics about game play, including such things as the number of games played and the number of games won, lost, and tied.

CHAPTER 9

FILE AND FOLDER ADMINISTRATION

I n this chapter, you will learn the ins and outs of how to use Ruby to develop scripts that interact with the computer's file system. In doing so, you will learn how to develop scripts that can create, rename, and delete files and folders. You will learn how to determine a file's size and to iterate through a folder's contents. You will also learn how to write data to text files. This will include learning how to write data to new files as well as how to overwrite or append data to existing text files. Finally, you will learn how to read and process data stored in files. On top of all this, you will learn how to create a new Ruby script, the Ruby Blackjack game.

Specifically, you will learn how to:

- Create and delete text files
- Read from and write to text files
- Create and delete folders
- Examine and process folder contents

PROJECT PREVIEW: THE RUBY BLACKJACK GAME

In this chapter, you will learn how to create a new Ruby script called the Ruby Blackjack game. This game will create a virtualized casino blackjack dealer against whom the player will compete in an effort to build a hand that comes as close as possible to 21 without going over. As shown in Figure 9.1, the game begins by displaying a welcome message.

FIGURE 9.1

The Ruby Blackjack game's opening welcome message.

The player is then prompted for permission to begin play, as shown in Figure 9.2.

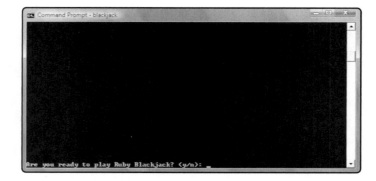

FIGURE 9.2

The player must respond with a y to begin the game.

Once permission has been given, instructions for playing the game are displayed, as shown in Figure 9.3.

Both the player and the dealer are dealt an initial card, after which the player is prompted to play out the rest of her hand, as demonstrated in Figure 9.4.

The player may ask for as many additional cards as she wants, as long as the total value of her hand does not exceed 21. If this happens, the player busts and loses the hand, as demonstrated in Figure 9.5.

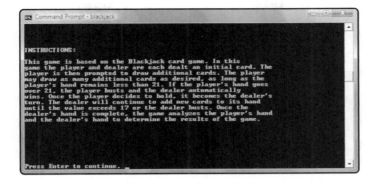

FIGURE 9.3

The object of the game is to get a hand that is as close as possible to 21 without going over.

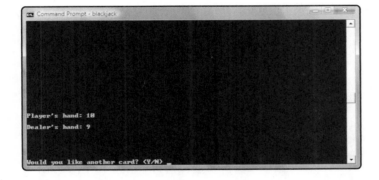

FIGURE 9.4

Once initial cards are dealt, the player always goes first.

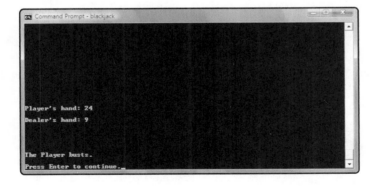

FIGURE 9.5

The player's hand has exceeded a total of 21, resulting in a loss.

After each round of play, the player is prompted for permission to start a new hand, as shown in Figure 9.6.

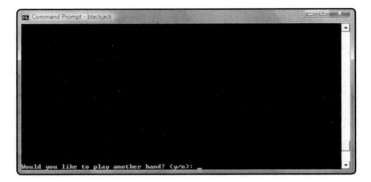

FIGURE 9.6

The player may play as many hands as she wants.

Figure 9.7 shows an example of a game in which the player has won. Here the player's hand is a perfect 21.

FIGURE 9.7

The player has won this hand.

Once the player has decided to stop playing, the game ends after displaying the screen shown in Figure 9.8.

FIGURE 9.8

The game's final screen displays information about the game and its author.

Understanding File Input and Output

The movement of data from one source to another on a computer is commonly referred to as data input and output. The actual movement of the data occurs as a stream between the sending and the receiving resources. By default, the computer looks to the keyboard for standard input or STDIN and sends standard output or STDOUT to the computer's monitor.

You can redirect STDIN and STDOUT as necessary to pull data from a different input source and to reroute data to a different output destination. Redirection is accomplished using pipe operators. The > pipe operator allows you to pass the output from one source, such as a Ruby script, to another source, like a text file. For example, suppose you created a Ruby script named Hello.rb that contained the following statement.

```
puts "Hello World!"
```

When executed from the command line, the words Hello Word! are displayed on the computer screen. However, using the > pipe operator, you could instead redirect the script's output to a text file, as demonstrated here:

```
ruby Hello.rb > Hello.txt
```

When the Hello.rb script is executed this time, its output is redirected to a file named Hello.txt located in the current working directory (i.e., the same directory where the script resides). If the Hello.txt file does not exist, it is created and then written to. If a file of the same name already exists, its contents are overwritten.

In a similar fashion, you can use the < pipe operator to redirect standard input from one resource to another. For example, suppose you had a Ruby script named DispMsg.rb that consisted of the following statement.

```
message = STDIN.gets
```

If you execute this script from the command prompt, the script would immediately pause and wait for input to be provided by the user. Once something is typed and the Enter key is pressed, the script assigns the input to the message variable and then terminates. However, using the < pipe operator, you can instead redirect STDIN from a file source, as demonstrated here:

```
ruby Dispmsg.rb < Hello.txt
```

Here, the Dispmsg.rb script reads the first line of text stored in a file named Hello.txt and then assigns it to the message variable.

HINT If an empty file were used as input in the previous example, a value of *nil* (Ruby's way of representing a value of nothing) would be assigned to the message variable.

Both the > and the < pipe operators are provided by the operating system and can be used as an elementary way of writing to and reading from text files. However, Ruby provides a number of more elegant and sophisticated ways of working with and administering files.

ADMINISTERING TEXT FILES AND FOLDERS

Ruby offers a number of different ways to perform file and folder administration. Ruby provides you with everything you need to create, rename, and delete files and folders. This functionality is provided through the Ruby File and Dir classes, which supply you with access to various file and folder administration methods.

Verifying Whether a File or Folder Exists

Before you begin any file or folder administration task, it is a good idea to first check and see if the file or folder with which you intend to work already exists. Files and folders can disappear from a computer for a host of different reasons. They may, for example, be accidentally deleted or moved to a different location. If after checking for the existence of a folder and finding out that it does not exist, you may want to terminate the script's execution or you may instead want to create a new folder. The same logic can be applied to files.

To determine if a file or folder exists, you need to use the File class's exist? method, which supports the following syntax.

```
File.exist?(Name)
```

Name represents the name and path of the file or directory being looked for. To get a better feel for how to use the exist? method, look at the following example.

```
puts "Found it!" if File.exist?("Hello.txt")
```

Here, a statement has been set up to look for a file named Hello.txt located in the current working directory. If the file is found, a message is displayed. A more realistic example might involve modifying this statement to display a message in the event the file is not found. For example, the following statements provide an example that does something similar to this, only this time the focus of attention is on a folder named TestDir instead of a file.

```
if File.exist?("TestDir") then

  puts "All is well."
```

```
else

  print "The TestDir folder is missing. Enter y to recreate it: "
  answer = STDIN.gets
  answer.chop!

  if answer =~ /y/i then
   Dir.mkdir("TestDir")
  end

end
```

Here, if the folder is not found, a message is displayed prompting the user for permission to create a new copy of the folder. If the user agrees, the `Dir` class's `mkdir` method is used to create the folder.

Retrieving Information about a File or Folder

The `File` and `Dir` classes provide you with access to a number of methods that you can use to get information about files and folders. Using these methods, you can determine whether a specified resource is a file, folder, or something else. You can also determine whether a file is empty or how large it is, and you can retrieve a list of all the files and folders stored in a folder.

Determining if a Resource Is a File or a Folder

Using the `File` class's `directory?` method, you can determine if a resource is a file or something else (file, socket, pipe, etc.). This method supports the following syntax.

`File.directory?(Name)`

Name represents the name and path of the resource to be checked. To get a better feel for how to work with the `directory?` method, look at the following example.

```
if File.directory?("TestDir") then
  puts "It's a folder."
else
  puts "It is something else."
end
```

Here, the current working `directory?` method is used to determine whether TestDir is a file or a folder. The `directory?` method returns a value of `true` if the specified resource is a folder and value of `false` if it is not. Based on the results of the analysis, one of two text messages is displayed.

The `File` class also contains a method named `file?`, which can be used to determine whether a resource is a file or something else. As you can see from the following syntax, the `file?` method is very similar to the `directory?` method.

```
File.file?(Name)
```

Name represents the name and path of the resource to be checked. To get a better feel for how to work with the `file?` method, look at the following example.

```
if File.file?("Hello.txt") then
  puts "It's a file."
else
  puts "It is something else."
end
```

Here, the example looks for a file named Hello.txt located in the current working directory.

Checking a File's Size

Before reading from a file or overwriting an existing file with a new file, you may want to first check to see if the file has anything in it. Based on this analysis, you could avoid trying to read from an empty file or decide to write new data to the end of a file in append mode instead of overwriting any existing data.

To determine if a file has any data in it, you can use the `File` class's `size` method, which has the following syntax. This method returns a count of the specified file's size in bytes.

```
File.size(Name)
```

Name represents the name and path of the resource to be checked. To get a better feel for how to work with the `size` method, look at the following example.

```
puts "File Hello.txt is " + File.size("Hello.txt").to_s + " bytes in size."
```

Here, a text string is displayed that shows the size of a file named Hello.txt located in the current working directory.

In addition to the `size` method, you can also use the `size?` method to determine the size of a file. The syntax for this method is shown next. This method returns the size of the file, in bytes. However, if the file is empty, a value of `nil` is returned instead.

```
File.size?(Name)
```

Name represents the name and path of the resource to be checked. To get a better feel for how to work with the size method, look at the following example.

```
if File.size?("Hello.txt") > 0 then
  puts "Processing file"
else
  puts "File processing skipped"
end
```

Here, the size? method is used to determine whether a file should be processed. If the size of the file is greater than zero bytes, it is processed. Otherwise it is not processed.

Examining Folder Contents

Ruby gives you the ability to list the contents in a folder using the Dir class's entries method, which returns the contents of the list as an array. You can then iterate through the array and work with each individual file or folder as necessary. The entries method has the following syntax.

```
Dir.entries(Name)
```

Name represents the name and path of the directory to be processed. To get a better feel for how to work with the entries method, look at the following example.

```
puts Dir.entries(".")
```

Here, the puts method is used to display the contents of the current working directory, as provided by the entries method. When executed, this statement will display output similar to that shown here.

```
c:\Ruby_scripts>test

.

..
BlackJack.rb
Crazy8Ball.rb
NumberGuess.rb
RPS.rb
RubyJoke.rb
SupermanQuiz.rb
TallTale.rb
Test.rb
TypingChallenge.rb
WordGuess.rb
```

In Ruby, the . character can be used as a shortcut for representing the current working directory.

You can also produce a list of all the files stored in a folder using the `Dir` class's `foreach` method, as demonstrated here:

```
Dir.foreach(".") do |resource|
  puts resource
end
```

Here, a loop has been set up that iterates through every file and folder stored in the current working directory. The advantage of using the `foreach` method in this manner is that it provides you with the ability to take multiple actions against folder contents by allowing you to place as many statements as you want inside the loop.

Creating New Folders

As you will see in a few minutes, Ruby allows you to create new files and write any amount of data to them. Ruby also provides you with the ability to create new folders using the `Dir` class's `mkdir` method, which has the following syntax.

```
Dir.mkdir(Name)
```

Name is used to specify the name and path of the folder that you want to create. To get a better feel for how to work with the `mkdir` method, look at the following example.

```
Dir.mkdir("TestDir")
```

When executed, this statement creates a new folder named TestDir. However, if a folder of the same name already exists, an error will occur, so you may want to check to see if a folder of the same name already exists, as shown here:

```
if File.exist?("TestDir") then
  Dir.mkdir("TestDir")
end
```

Deleting Files and Folders

Ruby also offers you the ability to delete both files and folders. To do so, you will need to work with the `File` and `Dir` class's `delete` method. The `File` class's `delete` method has the following syntax.

```
File.delete(Name,... Name)
```

The `Dir` class's `delete` method's syntax is identical, as shown here:

```
Dir.delete(Name,... Name)
```

Name represents any number of files or folders that you want to delete. To get a better feel for how to work with the `delete` method, look at the following example.

```
Dir.delete("TestDir")
```

Here, a folder named `TestDir` is deleted if it exists.

 If you attempt to delete a file or folder that does not exist, or if you try to delete a folder that is not empty, an error will occur.

Renaming Files

Ruby also provides you with the ability to rename a file or folder using the `File` class's `rename` method, which has the following syntax.

```
File.rename(OldName, NewName)
```

OldName represents the current name of the file to be renamed and *NewName* represents the new file name that is to be assigned to the file. To get a better feel of how to work with the `rename` method, look at the following example.

```
File.rename("Hello.txt", "Greeting.txt")
```

This example renames a file named Hello.txt to Greeting.txt. If the specified file or folder does not exist, an error will occur.

WORKING WITH FILES AND FOLDERS ON DIFFERENT OPERATING SYSTEMS

All of the examples that you have looked at in this chapter have operated based on the assumption that the example scripts were being executed from the same folder where target files and folders resided (e.g., the current working directory). Of course, this will not always be the case. As a result, you need to be able to specify the path to the files and directories you want to work with.

On Microsoft Windows, you can include paths in your script statements, as demonstrated here:

```
puts File.exists?('C:\Test_Files\Hello.txt')
```

The reason that single quotes were used in this example is because they prevent any character interpolation from occurring. As a result, the \ characters are taken literally and everything works just fine. If you wanted to work with double quotes instead, you would have to escape each instance of the \ character to get expected results, as demonstrated here:

```
puts File.exists?("c:\\Ruby_Scripts\\xxx.txt")
```

Here, the File class's exists? method has been instructed to look in the C:\Test_Files folder for a file named Hello.txt.

If instead of Microsoft Windows, you were working on a computer running UNIX or Linux, you could rewrite the previous example as shown here:

```
puts File.exists?('/Test_Files/Hello.txt')
```

Here, the File class's exists? method has been instructed to look in a folder named Test_Files, which is located at the root of the computer file systems, for a file named Hello.txt.

Note that while Microsoft Windows uses backslashes when specifying path information, UNIX and Linux use forward slashes.

If you need to develop scripts that will run on different operating systems, then you will need a way of determining which type of operating system your script is executing on. One way of addressing this challenge is to take advantage of Ruby's RUBY_PLATFORM special variable, as demonstrated here:

```
if RUBY_PLATFORM =~ /win32/ then
  puts File.exists?('C:\Test_Files\Hello.txt')
else
  puts File.exists?('/Test_Files/Hello.txt')
end
```

Here, the value assigned to RUBY_PLATFORM is checked to see if it contains the characters win32. If it does, the script is executing on a Windows computer. Otherwise, it is assumed that the script is executing on a computer running some flavor of UNIX or Linux.

RUBY_PLATFORM is a special Ruby variable. A *special variable* is a variable that is automatically created and maintained by Ruby and which can be referenced by any Ruby scripts. RUBY_PLATFORM contains a string that identifies the name of the operating system on which a script is executing. Using the regular expression shown in the previous example, you can easily distinguish between a Windows and a non-Windows computer.

Reading from and Writing to Text Files

In addition to taking advantage of the operating system's ability to pipe data to and from text files using the ‹ and › pipe operators, Ruby offers a number of different options for writing data to and reading it from files using methods belonging to the File class.

One way of interacting with files is to use the File class's new method to set up a reference to it. Once this reference has been established, you can refer to the file as necessary to perform read and write operations. One way to set up a file reference is to use the syntax outlined here:

```
Reference = File.new(Name, Mode)
```

Reference is a placeholder for a variable that will be used to refer back to the target file. *Name* represents the file that you want to interact with and *Mode* represents one of the options listed in Table 9.1 that specify the mode in which you want the file opened.

TABLE 9.1   FILE CLASS MODE SPECIFICATIONS

Mode	Description
r	Opens the file in read-only mode, placing the location pointer at the beginning of the file.
r+	Opens the file for both reading and writing, placing the location pointer at the beginning of the file.
w	Opens the file in write-only mode, overwriting any existing text by placing the pointer at the beginning of the file. If the specified file does not exist, it is created.
w+	Opens the file for both reading and writing, overwriting any existing text by placing the pointer at the beginning of the file. If the specified file does not exist, it is created.
a	Opens the file in append mode, placing the pointer at the end of the file to preserve any pre-existing text.
a+	Opens the file in append mode, allowing for both reading and writing, placing the pointer at the end of the file to preserve any pre-existing text.

Writing Data to Text Files

One way of writing data to a text file is to use the File class's new method and to specify a write mode operation, as demonstrated here:

```
outFile = File.new("Demo.txt", "w")
  outFile.puts "Ho Ho Ho"
  outFile.puts "Merry Christmas!"
outFile.close
```

In this example, a file reference has been set up to open a file named Demo.txt using write mode. Once established, the file reference (outFile) can be used to write data to the file using the puts method. In this example, two lines of text were written to the file. If the target file does not exist, it is created and then written to. If, however, it does exist, it is opened and then overwritten. Take special note of the last statement in the example. This is a requirement for any file that is opened by creating a file reference. Failure to explicitly close any open file reference may result in the corruption of the file.

> Up to this point in the book, you have used the puts method exclusively for the purpose of displaying text on the computer screen (e.g., default STDOUT). However, in this example, by pre-appending the file reference to the puts method using dot notation, you have redirected the puts method's output to the specified file.

Figure 9.9 shows the contents of the text file that is created when the example is executed.

FIGURE 9.9

A text file programmatically created and written to by a Ruby script.

Appending Data to the Ends of Text Files

Appending data to the end of a file is very similar to writing it except that in append mode, any data already written to the file is preserved. This makes append mode the appropriate option to use when adding to the end of text files, as demonstrated here:

```
outFile = File.new("Demo.txt", "a")
  outFile.puts "And a happy new year!"
outFile.close
```

In this example, the Demo.txt file is reopened and an additional line of text is written to it before it is again closed. Figure 9.10 shows how the contents of the text file have been modified once the example has executed.

FIGURE 9.10

Examining the
contents of the
text file once
additional data has
been appended
to it.

Reading Data from Text Files

Reading data stored in text files is no more difficult than writing to text files. For starters, the file must be opened in read mode. You can then read data from the text file, as demonstrated here:

```
File.new("Demo.txt", "r").each do |line|
  puts line
end
```

In this example, the Demo.txt file has been opened for reading using the File class's new method. Next, the each method is used to iterate through and display each line of text that is in the file. When executed, the following output is displayed.

```
Ho Ho Ho
Merry Christmas!
And a happy new year!
```

In addition to processing the contents of a text file using a loop, you can also use the gets method to retrieve data from the file a line at a time, as demonstrated here:

```
inputFile = File.new("Demo.txt", "r")
puts inputFile.gets
inputFile.close
```

Here, the Demo.txt file has been opened in read mode. Next, the gets method is used to read the first line of the file, which is then displayed by the puts method. The last statement closes the open file. When executed, these statements generate the following output.

```
Ho Ho Ho
```

As you can see, working with a file reference when reading a file is pretty straightforward. However, every time you open a file to read it, you must remember to close the file to prevent the file from becoming corrupt. To help make things even easier on you, Ruby provides a couple of quick and easy shortcut methods that you can use to read file contents without having to worry about closing the files when you are done. These methods include the `read` and `readlines` methods.

To use the `read` method, all you have to do is pass the method the name of the file that you want read, as demonstrated here:

```
inputFile = File.read("Demo.txt")
```

In this example, the Demo.txt file is opened and read and all of its contents are stored in a variable named `inputFile`. You can then process the data stored in `inputFile` as you see fit. For example, you might manipulate it using regular expression or simply display it as demonstrated here:

```
puts inputFile
```

When executed, this statement displays the data stored in the `inputFile` variable, as shown here:

```
Ho Ho Ho
Merry Christmas!
And a happy new year!
```

The `readlines` method is similar to the `read` method, only instead of reading the contents of a file into a single variable, the file's contents are read line by line into an array, allowing you to reference and manipulate them using any of the `Array` class's methods. For example, the following statement uses the `readlines` method to read the Demo.txt file and store its contents in an array named `inputArray`.

```
inputArray = File.readlines("Demo.txt")
```

Once loaded into the array, you can process the array's contents as you see fit. For example, the following statements could be used to loop through the array and print out its content, one item at a time.

```
inputArray.each do |line|
  puts line
end
```

TRICK   In addition to opening a file for reading using the `File` class's `new` method, you can also use the `File` class's `open` method. The advantage of using the `open` method over the `new` method is that the `open` method does not require you to close the file once it has been read. You can use the `open` method in conjunction with other methods, including the `each`, `read`, and `readlines` methods. For example, the following statement uses the `open` method in conjunction with the `readlines` method to read all of the lines stored in Demo.txt and store them in an array named `inputArray`.

```
inputArray = File.open("Demo.txt").readlines
```

The `File` class's `open` method can also be used for write operations, as demonstrated here:

```
File.open("Demo.txt", "a") do |output|
  output.puts "\nThe End"
end
```

Here, the `open` method is used to open the Demo.txt file in append mode and then to write a single line of text to the end of the file. Once the write operation is completed, the file is automatically closed. The contents of the text file are modified, as shown here:

```
Ho Ho Ho
Merry Christmas!
And a happy new year!

The End
```

BACK TO THE RUBY BLACKJACK GAME

Okay, now it is time to turn your attention back to the development of this chapter's game project, the Ruby Blackjack game. As with all previous games, this script will be developed in a modular fashion. As you work your way through this script, take particular note of the manner in which script variables are kept localized and how programming logic is kept separate and organized into distinct methods.

Designing the Game

The development of the Ruby Blackjack game will be completed in 15 steps, as outlined here:

1. Open your text or script editor and create a new file.
2. Add comment statements to the beginning of the script file to document the script and its purpose.
3. Define a class representing the terminal window.
4. Define a class representing the Blackjack game.
5. Define the `display_greeting` method.
6. Define the `display_instructions` method.
7. Define the `play_game` method.

8. Define the `get_new_card` method.
9. Define the `complete_player_hand` method.
10. Define the `play_dealer_hand` method.
11. Define the `determine_winner` method.
12. Define the `display_credits` method.
13. Instantiate custom script objects.
14. Get confirmation before continuing game play.
15. Control high-level game play.

Remember to follow along carefully and make sure that you do not skip any steps as you work your way through this script.

Step 1: Creating a New Ruby File

Let's begin the creation of the Ruby Blackjack game by starting up your favorite text or script editor and creating a new Ruby script file. Save this file with a file name of Blackjack.rb and store it in the same folder as the rest of your Ruby script files.

Step 2: Documenting the Script and Its Purpose

Okay, now let's add the usual list of comment statements to the beginning of the script file to document the script file and explain what it does. To do this, add the following statements to the end of the script file.

```
#---------------------------------------------------------------
#
# Script Name: BlackJack.rb
# Version:     1.0
# Author:      Jerry Lee Ford, Jr.
# Date:        October 2007
#
# Description: This Ruby game is a virtualized casino card game in which
#              the player competes against the dealer (computer) in an
#              effort to build a hand that comes as close as possible to 21
#              without going over.
#
#---------------------------------------------------------------
```

Step 3: Defining a Screen Class

The Ruby Blackjack game will make use of two custom classes, which will provide you with access to collections of methods required to control user interaction and the overall execution of the game. The code statements for the script's first class, the Screen class, are shown next and should be added to the end of the script file.

```
#Define a class representing the console window
class Screen

  def cls  #Define a method that clears the display area
    puts ("\n" * 25)  #Scroll the screen 25 times
    puts "\a"   #Make a little noise to get the player's attention
  end

  def pause    #Define a method that pauses the display area
    STDIN.gets  #Execute the STDIN class's gets method to pause script
               #execution until the player presses the Enter key
  end

end
```

The Screen class defines two methods. The cls method writes 25 blank lines to the console window and then plays a beep sound. The pause method pauses script execution whenever it is called and waits for the player to press the Enter key.

Step 4: Creating the Game Class

The Game class contains eight methods, which provide you with control over the game's execution. To begin the creation of the Game class, append the following statements to the end of the script file.

```
#Define a class representing the Ruby Blackjack game
class Game

end
```

Step 5: Defining the display_greeting Method

The first method defined in the Game class is display_greeting. It is responsible for displaying the game's welcome message. The statements that make up this method are shown next and should be inserted inside the Game class's opening and closing statements.

```
#This method displays the game's opening message
def display_greeting
```

```
Console_Screen.cls   #Clear the display area

#Display a welcome message
print "\t\t\tWelcome to the Ruby Blackjack Game!" +
"\n\n\n\n\n\n\n\n\n\n\n\n\nPress Enter to " +
        "continue. "


Console_Screen.pause      #Pause the game

end
```

Step 6: Defining the display_instructions Method

The next method defined in the Game class is the display_instructions method. This method displays the game instructions using a series of text strings. The statements that make up this method are shown next and should be added to the Game class definition, immediately after the display_greeting method.

```
#Define a method to be used to display game instructions
def display_instructions

  Console_Screen.cls       #Clear the display area
  puts "INSTRUCTIONS:\n\n"  #Display a heading

  #Display the game's instructions
  puts "This game is based on the Blackjack card game. In this"
  puts "game the player and dealer are each dealt an initial card. The"
  puts "player is then prompted to draw additional cards. The player"
  puts "may draw as many additional cards as desired, as long as the"
  puts "player's hand remains less than 21. If the player's hand goes"
  puts "over 21, the player busts and the dealer automatically"
  puts "wins. Once the player decides to hold, it becomes the dealer's"
  puts "turn. The dealer will continue to add new cards to its hand"
  puts "until the value exceeds 17 or the dealer busts. Once the"
  puts "dealer's hand is complete, the game analyzes the player's hand"
  puts "and the dealer's hand to determine the results of the game."
  puts "\n\n\n\n\n\n\n"
  print "Press Enter to continue. "
```

```
Console_Screen.pause          #Pause the game
```

end

Step 7: Defining the play_game Method

The next method defined in the Game class is the play_game method, which is responsible for managing an individual round of play. The statements that make up this method are shown next and should be added to the end of the class definition, immediately after the display_instructions method.

```
#Define a method to control game play
def play_game

  Console_Screen.cls          #Clear the display area

  #Assist the player and dealer with an initial starting card
  playerHand = get_new_card
  dealerHand = get_new_card

  #Call the method responsible for dealing new cards to the player
  playerHand = complete_player_hand(playerHand, dealerHand)

  #If the player has not busted, call the method responsible for managing
  #dealer's hand
  if playerHand <= 21 then
    dealerHand = play_dealer_hand(dealerHand)
  end

  #call the method responsible for determining the results of the game
  determine_winner(playerHand, dealerHand)

end
```

This method begins by calling on the get_new_card method two times to assign an initial card to both the player's and dealer's opening hand. Since the player always goes before the dealer, the complete_player_hand method is called next and is passed the value of the player's and dealer's hand as an argument. The complete_player_hand method is responsible for adding new cards to the player's hand until the player busts or decides to stick with the cards currently in her hand, after which it returns a value representing the current value of the player's hand. This value is then examined to see if it exceeds 21, in which case the player has gone bust. If the player has not gone bust, the play_dealer_hand method is called and passed the current value of the dealer's hand as an argument. The play_dealer_hand method is responsible for playing out the dealer's hand and then returning the result of that hand. The last statement in the player_game method calls up on the determine_winner method, passing it the current value of the player's and dealer's hands. The determine_winner method analyzes these two arguments to determine the result of the game.

Step 8: Defining the get_new_card Method

The next method to be added to the Game class is the get_new_card method, whose statements are shown here:

```
#Define a method responsible for dealing a new card
def get_new_card

  #Assign a random number from 1 to 13 as the value of the card being
  #created
  card = 1 + rand(13)

  #A value of 1 is an ace, so reassign the card a value of 11
  return 11 if card == 1

  #A value of 10 or more equals a face card so reassign the card a value
  #of 10
  return 10 if card >= 10

  return card   #Return the value assigned to the new card

end
```

When called, this method generates a random number from 1 to 13, which it assigns to a variable named card. If the value of card is set equal to 1, the card is considered to be an ace. As such, the value of card is reassigned a value of 11. On the other hand, if the value of card is greater than or equal to 10, it is assumed that the card is either a 10 or a face card (Jack, Queen, or King) and as such the value of card is set equal to 10. Once the value assigned to card is finally established, it is returned back to the statement that called upon the method to execute.

Step 9: Defining the complete_player_hand Method

The next method defined in the Game class is the complete_player_hand method, which is responsible for assisting the player in completing her hand. The statements that make up this method are shown next and should be added to the end of the class definition, immediately after the get_new_card method.

```
#Define a method responsible for dealing the rest of the player's hand
def complete_player_hand(playerHand, dealerHand)

  loop do  #Loop forever

    Console_Screen.cls  #Clear the display area

    #Show the current state of the player's and dealer's hands
    puts "Player's hand: " + playerHand.to_s + "\n\n"
    puts "Dealer's hand: " + dealerHand.to_s + "\n\n\n\n\n\n"
    print "Would you like another card? (Y/N) "

    reply = STDIN.gets  #Collect the player's answer
    reply.chop!  #Remove any extra characters appended to the string

    #See if the player decided to ask for another card
    if reply =~ /y/i then
      #Call method responsible for getting a new card and add it to the
      #player's hand
      playerHand = playerHand + get_new_card
    end

    #See if the player has decided to stick with the current hand
    if reply =~ /n/i then
      break  #Terminate the execution of the loop
    end

    if playerHand > 21 then
      break  #Terminate the execution of the loop
    end

  end
```

```
#Return the value of the player's hand
return playerHand
```

```
end
```

This method is passed two arguments, playerHand and dealerHand, which represent the current value of the player's and dealer's hands. The value of both hands is displayed and the player is then asked if she would like another card. If the player elects to add another card to her hand, the value assigned to playerHand is incremented, adding the result returned by the get_new_card method to the value of playerHand. The player may add as many cards as desired to her hand, provided that the total value of her hand does not exceed 21. Once the player busts or decides not to draw more cards, the method ends by returning the current value of the player's hand back to the statement that called upon the method to execute.

Step 10: Defining the play_dealer_hand Method

The next method defined in the Game class is the play_dealer_hand method, which is responsible for completing the dealer's hand. The statements that make up this method are shown next and should be added to the end of the class definition, immediately after the complete_player_hand method.

```
#Define a method responsible for managing the dealer's hand
def play_dealer_hand(dealerHand)

  loop do  #Loop forever

    #If the value of the dealer's hand is less than 17 then give the
    #dealer another card
    if dealerHand < 17 then
      #Call method responsible for getting a new card and add it to the
      #dealer's hand
      dealerHand = dealerHand + get_new_card
    else
      break  #Terminate the execution of the loop
    end

  end
```

```
  #Return the value of the dealer's hand
  return dealerHand

end
```

This method takes as an argument the current value of the dealer's hand. The method then repeatedly calls upon the `get_new_card` method, adding new cards to the dealer's hand until the total value of the dealer's hands exceeds 17, at which time the method returns the current value of the dealer's hand to the calling statement and then ends.

Step 11: Defining the determine_winner Method

The next method defined in the `Game` class is the `determine_winner` method, which is responsible for determining the results of the game. The statements that make up this method are shown next and should be added to the end of the class definition, immediately after the `play_dealer_hand` method.

```
#Define a method responsible for analyzing the player's and dealer's
#hands and determining who won
def determine_winner(playerHand, dealerHand)

  Console_Screen.cls  #Clear the display area

  #Show the value of the player's and dealer's hands
  puts "Player's hand: " + playerHand.to_s + "\n\n"
  puts "Dealer's hand: " + dealerHand.to_s + "\n\n\n\n\n\n"

  if playerHand > 21 then  #See if the player has busted
    puts "The Player busts!\n\n"
    print "Press Enter to continue."
  else  #See if the player and dealer have tied
    if playerHand == dealerHand then
      puts "Tie!\n\n"
      print "Press Enter to continue."
    end
    #See if the dealer has busted
    if dealerHand > 21 then
        puts "The Dealer busts!\n\n"
        print "Press Enter to continue."
    else
```

```
      #See if the player's hand beats the dealer's hand
      if playerHand > dealerHand then
        puts "The Player wins!\n\n"
        print "Press Enter to continue."
      end
      #See if the dealer's hand beats the player's hand
      if playerHand < dealerHand then
        puts "The Dealer wins!\n\n"
        print "Press Enter to continue."
      end
    end
  end

  Console_Screen.pause        #Pause the game

end
```

This method is passed two arguments, representing the current value of the player's and dealer's hands. It then displays both of these values and, using a series of nested if statements, determines the overall result of the game. Based on the analysis, the method displays an appropriate message.

Step 12: Defining the display_credits Method

The last method to be added in the Game class is the display_credits method. This method is responsible for displaying the game's credits, including the author's URL. The statements that make up this method are shown next and should be added to the end of the Game class.

```
#This method displays information about the Ruby Blackjack game
def display_credits

  Console_Screen.cls  #Clear the display area

  #Thank the player and display game information
  puts "\t\t    Thank you for playing the Ruby Blackjack game.\n\n\n\n"
  puts "\n\t\t\t Developed by Jerry Lee Ford, Jr.\n\n"
  puts "\t\t\t\t  Copyright 2007\n\n"
  puts "\t\t\tURL: http://www.tech-publishing.com\n\n\n\n\n\n\n\n\n\n"

end
```

Step 13: Initializing Script Objects

Now that both of the script's custom classes have been defined, it is time to initialize instances of both classes. This is done by appending the following statements to the end of the script file.

```
# Main Script Logic ---------------------------------------------------

Console_Screen = Screen.new  #Instantiate a new Screen object
BJ = Game.new  #Instantiate a new Game object

#Execute the Game class's display_greeting method
BJ.display_greeting

answer = ""  #Initialize variable and assign it an empty string
```

In addition to instantiating the `Console_Screen` and `BJ` objects, these statements call upon the `Game` class's `display_greeting` method, which is responsible for prompting the player for permission to start the game, and then define a variable named `answer`, which will be used to manage the execution of a loop.

Step 14: Getting Permission to Start the Game

The following script statements are responsible for prompting the player for permission to begin the game and should be added to the end of the script file.

```
#Loop until the player enters y or n and do not accept any other input
loop do

  Console_Screen.cls  #Clear the display area

  #Prompt the player for permission to start the game
  print "Are you ready to play Ruby Blackjack? (y/n): "

  answer = STDIN.gets  #Collect the player's answer
  answer.chop!  #Remove any extra characters appended to the string

  #Terminate the loop if valid input was provided
  break if answer =~ /y|n/i

end
```

These statements are controlled by a loop that runs forever. Upon each iteration of the loop, the player is prompted for permission to start a new round of play. Any input other than a y or n is ignored. Once valid input is provided, a break command is executed, terminating the loop and allowing the rest of the script to execute.

Step 15: Controlling Game Play

The rest of the statements that make up the Ruby Blackjack game are shown next and should be appended to the end of the script file. These statements are responsible for managing the overall execution of the game.

```ruby
#Analyze the player's answer
if answer == "n"  #See if the player wants to quit

  Console_Screen.cls  #Clear the display area

  #Invite the player to return and play the game some other time
  puts "Okay, perhaps another time.\n\n"

else  #The player wants to play the game

  #Execute the Game class's display_instructions method
  BJ.display_instructions

  playAgain = ""  #Initialize variable and assign it an empty string

  loop do  #Loop forever

    #Execute the Game class's play_game method
    BJ.play_game

    loop do  #Loop forever

      Console_Screen.cls  #Clear the display area
      #Find out if the player wants to play another round
      print "Would you like to play another hand? (y/n): "

      playAgain = STDIN.gets  #Collect the player's response
      playAgain.chop!  #Remove any extra characters appended to the string
```

```
      #Terminate the loop if valid input was provided
      break if playAgain =~ /n|y/i

end

#Terminate the loop if valid input was provided
break if playAgain =~ /n/i

end

#Call upon the Game class's determine_credits method
BJ.display_credits

end
```

These statements are controlled by a large `if` code block. The script statements that are executed depend on the player's input. If the player decides not to play the game, a message is displayed encouraging the player to return and play another time. If, on the other hand, the player decides to play, the `Game` class's `display_instructions` method is executed. Next, a loop executes that repeatedly calls upon the `Game` class's `play_game` method. Each time the `play_game` method finishes executing, control returns to the loop, which prompts the player to play again. The player may play as many times as she wants. Once she decides to stop playing, a `break` command is executed, terminating the loop and allowing the `display_credits` method to execute.

Running Your New Ruby Script Game

Okay! You now have everything you need to create and execute the Ruby Blackjack game. As long as you followed along carefully and kept an eye on your typing, everything should work exactly as expected. If you run into any errors, carefully examine the resulting error message to determine where the problem may reside. If necessary, go back and review the script and look for typos or missing scripts statements.

SUMMARY

In this chapter, you learned how to interact with the computer's file system. This included learning how to read from and write to text files. In doing so, you learned how to overwrite existing files or append data to the end of them when writing text. You also learned how to read data from text files a line at a time or all at once. This chapter showed you how to rename and delete files and folders as well as how to determine the size of a file and how to iterate through all the items in a folder.

Now, before you move on to Chapter 10, "Debugging," I suggest you set aside a little extra time to make a few improvements to the Ruby Blackjack game by implementing the following list of challenges.

CHALLENGES

1. One popular variation of Blackjack involves making the player the winner in the event she is able to build a hand of five cards without busting. Consider modifying the Ruby Blackjack game to incorporate this feature.

2. Rather than allowing the player to play the game forever, consider assigning the player a starting sum of money ($10) and allowing the player to play until she either decides to quit of goes broke (at $1 per hand).

3. As currently set up, both the player and the computer start each game with a single card. However, in most Blackjack games, the player is supposed to start each hand with two cards. Modify the game to correct this deficiency.

4. The Ruby Blackjack game is a little short on descriptive text. Consider making things a little more interesting by adding more text.

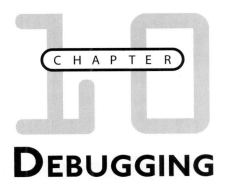

DEBUGGING

U p to now your main tools for dealing with script errors have been the careful review of error messages and the careful review of the statements that make up your script files. Given that this book has provided you with explicit instruction on how to create and execute all of its examples and game scripts, these tools have hopefully been all you needed. However, as you venture out on your own and as your scripts become more complex, your script errors will become more difficult to track down. The purpose of this chapter is to provide you with additional instruction on how to track down and deal with script errors. You will learn how to add error-handling logic to your Ruby scripts. You will also learn how to work with Ruby's built-in debugger to debug and test the execution of your script files. On top of all this, you will learn how to create a new Ruby script, the Ruby Tic-Tac-Toe game.

Specifically, you will learn:

- About syntax, runtime, and logical errors
- How to create error handlers that react to and handle errors
- How to track the logical execution flow of statements within your script files
- How to use Ruby's debugger to run and monitor the execution of Ruby scripts

PROJECT PREVIEW: THE RUBY TIC-TAC-TOE GAME

In this chapter, you will learn how to create a new computer script called the Ruby Tic-Tac-Toe game. This Ruby script is designed to bring together all of the programming concepts presented throughout the book. The game begins by displaying a welcome screen, as shown in Figure 10.1.

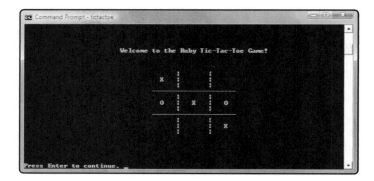

Next, the players are prompted for permission to begin a new round of play, as demonstrated in Figure 10.2.

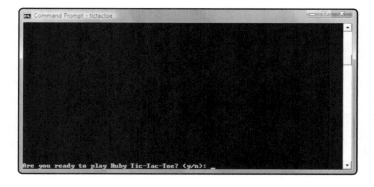

Once the players have decided to play, the instructions shown in Figure 10.3 are displayed, outlining the rules for playing the game.

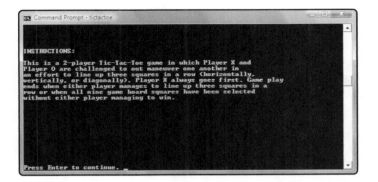

FIGURE 10.3

The Tic-Tac-Toe game's instructions explain the objective of the game.

Moves are made by entering the coordinates of a Tic-Tac-Toe game board square. As Figure 10.4 shows, Player X always goes first.

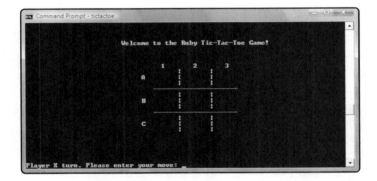

FIGURE 10.4

Player X is prompted to make the game's first move.

As game play progresses, letters identifying each player's moves are displayed on the Tic-Tac-Toe game board, as demonstrated in Figure 10.5.

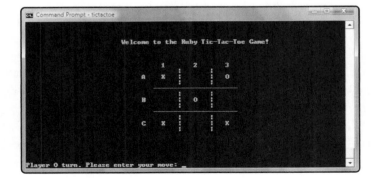

FIGURE 10.5

The game manages the switching of player turns.

After each move, the game examines the game board looking for a winner. To win, a player must line up three squares in a row, vertically, horizontally, or diagonally. Figure 10.6 shows an example of a game that has been won by Player X.

At the end of each game, the players are prompted for permission to start another game. Once the players have had enough and decide to quit playing, the screen shown in Figure 10.7 displays.

ANALYZING DIFFERENT TYPES OF SCRIPT ERRORS

Undoubtedly, you have run into your fair share of errors as you have made your way though this book. You may have made a few typos when testing some of the many examples presented in this book or you may have accidentally skipped a step or two when creating the book's game scripts. That's okay. Even the most experienced programmers run into errors. Dealing with programming errors, sometimes referred to as bugs, is simply a part of every programmer's life. The trick is learning how to identify and fix bugs when they occur, which is the focus of this chapter.

Watching Out for Syntax Errors

Errors can occur for a number of reasons. One category of errors that you should be familiar with is syntax errors. *Syntax errors* are errors that occur if you do not correctly follow Ruby's syntactical rules when writing your script statements. A syntax error will occur if you mistype a Ruby keyword or if you fail to add matching quotation marks or parentheses as required by your statements.

Ruby checks scripts for syntax errors before executing them. As such, any script that contains a syntax error will not compile and execute until the error has been corrected. Generally, all you need to track down and fix most syntax errors is the information provided by Ruby's error messages.

Preventing Runtime Errors

Another category of errors that you need to be aware of is *runtime errors*. These errors occur when a script attempts to perform an illegal action. For example, a runtime error will occur if you attempt to divide a number by zero, as demonstrated here:

```
puts 10 / 0
```

When executed, this statement produces the following error and then terminates the execution of the script.

```
C:/Ruby_scripts/Test.rb:2:in `/': divided by 0 (ZeroDivisionError)
        from C:/Ruby_scripts/Test.rb:2
```

Runtime errors can sometimes be buried deep inside seldom-used methods and may not make their presence known until a particular set of circumstances occurs. As a result, it is extremely important that you thoroughly test your Ruby scripts, ensuring that every part of every method works as expected.

Unfortunately, runtime errors can also occur for a host of reasons that are completely outside of your control. For example, if your script needs to access a network drive and the drive or network crashes, your script will experience a runtime error when it tries to access the drive. In these types of situations, the best you may be able to do is try to gracefully handle the situation, perhaps by displaying a more user-friendly error message, which you can do using the error handling techniques discussed later in this chapter.

Looking Out for Logical Errors

A final type of error that you need to be familiar with is *logical errors*. A logical error is an error that occurs because of a mistake made in the formulation of the logic used to accomplish a particular task. For example, a logical error would occur if you wrote a statement that you intended to use to multiply two numbers together but instead you accidentally divided one number by the other. As a result, your script's output would clearly be different from what you wanted.

The best way to avoid logical errors is to carefully plan out the design of your scripts before you start writing them. However, even the most experienced programmers sometimes make logical errors. Using the debugging techniques discussed in this chapter, you will be able to monitor the execution of your Ruby scripts to track down and correct logical errors.

HANDLING EXCEPTIONS

Any time an error occurs within a Ruby script, an exception is generated. When an exception occurs, the interpreter displays an error message and forces the immediate termination of the script. Sometimes the error messages that are reported are rather cryptic and even down-right confusing. Rather than accept this default behavior, Ruby allows you to handle exceptions when they occur, giving you the ability to deal with the error.

Dealing with errors may mean displaying friendly and more useful error messages. Dealing with errors may also mean finding ways of allowing scripts to continue execution without the user even knowing anything went wrong. For example, you might include additional logic within a script to retry a given operation a number of times. Alternatively, suppose you had a script that needed to access a file on a network drive and that network drive became unavailable while the script was executing. Instead of displaying an error and terminating, you might add an error handler to the script that allows the script to use default data instead.

Creating Exception Handlers

When an exception is generated, it is said to be raised. Whenever an exception is raised, Ruby looks for an exception handler capable of handling the exception. If it finds one, control is transferred to the handler. Otherwise, an error message is displayed and the script terminates. For example, suppose you created a script made up of the following statement.

```
puts x
```

When executed, the following error would be reported.

```
Test.rb:2: undefined local variable or method `x' for main:Object (NameError)
```

As you can see, the error occurred because the script attempted to reference an undefined variable.

To define an error handler, you need to first identify a location within your Ruby script where you think an error may be able to occur and then precede it with the `begin` keyword. Next, place the `rescue` keyword after the location and then add any statements intended to deal with the exception immediately after the `rescue` keyword. Finally, add the `end` keyword. If you want, you could prevent the previous error from terminating the script by developing an exception handler for it as shown here:

```
begin
  puts x
rescue
  #No actions defined
end
```

As you can see, the statement with the error in it has been placed between the `begin` and `rescue` keywords. As a result, when the error occurs, the error handler traps it. Since there are no statements included between the `rescue` and `end` keywords, the error is simply disregarded. As such, if there were any statements remaining in the script, the script would continue running allowing those statements to execute.

Accessing Error Information

Exceptions that occur within Ruby scripts are managed as objects that come from the `Exception` class and its family of subclasses. Using the => operator, you can access information about an exception and use it as demonstrated here:

```
begin
  puts x
rescue => e
  puts "\n\nSorry. An error has occurred. Please report the following"
  puts "error information to the help desk.\n\n"
  puts "ERROR CLASS: " + e.class.to_s
  puts "ERROR MESSAGE: " + e
end
```

In this example, a user-friendly error message is displayed in place of the default error message. The user-friendly message identifies both the class and text of the error and requests that the user inform the help desk of the error, as demonstrated here:

```
Sorry. An error has occurred. Please report the following
error information to the help desk.
```

```
ERROR CLASS: NameError
ERROR MESSAGE: undefined local variable or method `x' for main:Object
```

Handling Different Types of Errors

The previous error handler represents a generic error handler in that it will catch any type of error that occurs. If you want, you can create error handlers designed to handle specific types of errors, as demonstrated here:

```
begin
  puts x
rescue NameError
  puts "A name error has occurred!"
rescue ArgumentError
  puts "Incorrect use of arguments!"
rescue RangeError
  puts "A range error has occurred!"
rescue
  puts "Unexpected error!"
end
```

Here, separate `rescue` statements have been defined, each of which is designed to handle a different type of error. The first three `rescue` statements trap specific types of errors. The last `rescue` statement will trap any error that does not match up against the three previously defined error types.

TRACKING THE LOGICAL FLOW OF YOUR SCRIPTS

Sometimes the contents of Ruby's error messages leave something to be desired, and as a result, errors can be a bit tricky to track down. One way of determining what is happening in a script is to strategically embed `print` and `puts` statements throughout the script that identify when specified methods are executed and display the contents of variables whose values you suspect may not be getting set correctly. To demonstrate how you might apply this advice, take a look at the following method (a modified version of a method borrowed from Chapter 9's Ruby Blackjack game).

```
def play_game

  puts "Method play_game starting execution."

  Console_Screen.cls
```

```
playerHand = get_new_card
dealerHand = get_new_card

puts "Initial value of playerHand = " + playerHand
puts "Initial value of dealerHand = " + dealerHand

playerHand = complete_player_hand(playerHand, dealerHand)

puts "Updated value of playerHand = " + playerHand

if playerHand <= 21 then
  dealerHand = play_dealer_hand(dealerHand)
  puts "Updated value of dealerHand = " + dealerHand
end

determine_winner(playerHand, dealerHand)
puts "Calling determine_winner"

puts "Method play_game has complete execution."

end
```

By embedding puts statements throughout your script as demonstrated in this method, you can monitor the execution of your script file, monitoring when each method executes while also keeping an eye on the values assigned to variables during script execution. Once you are confident that your script is working as expected, you can either remove the extra puts statements or comment them out, but keep them available should you later need to conduct further testing.

FINDING BUGS USING THE RUBY DEBUGGER

The use of print and puts statements as a debugging tool is fine for small scripts. However, as your Ruby scripts grow larger and more complex, this approach becomes too difficult and time consuming to implement. To monitor and debug larger Ruby scripts, you need to learn how to work with Ruby's built-in debugger. The debugger allows you to monitor and control the execution of your scripts on a statement-by-statement basis, pausing whenever necessary to check on the value of variables.

Starting the Debugger

Ruby's debugger is a built-in component. As such, it is always ready and available for use. Ruby's debugger provides you with an alternative environment for executing your scripts. However, before you can use the debugger to run a Ruby script, the script must be syntax error free. Once you have tracked down and fixed all syntax errors, you can use the debugger to run and monitor your Ruby script. To use the debugger, you must start it using the following syntax.

```
ruby -r debug [options] [script] [arguments]
```

As you can see, the debugger is loaded by starting the Ruby interpreter with the -r debug option. If necessary, you may include any other needed Ruby options followed by the name of the script that you want to debug and any arguments that you may need to pass to that script.

The best way to learn how to work with Ruby's debugger is to just start using it. Of course, to use it, you must have a Ruby script that you want to monitor and debug. For the rest of the discussion in this section, the following Ruby script will be used to demonstrate how to work with the debugger.

```
x = 1
loop do
  puts x
  x += 1
  puts "We are half way there!" if x == 3
  break if x == 5
end
```

If you were to run this script normally, without invoking the debugger, it would generate the following output.

```
1
2
We are half way there!
3
4
```

Now let's load the script and execute it using the Ruby debugger. To do so, execute the following command at the operating system command prompt.

```
ruby -r debug test.rb
```

In response, Ruby will load your script in the debugger and generate the following output.

```
Debug.rb
Emacs support available.

test.rb:1:x = 1
(rdb:1)
```

The first several lines indicate that the debugger is active. The third line identifies the line number of the next statement in the script that is about to run. Since the script has only just been loaded into the debugger, this statement in the script has yet to execute. The last line displays the debugger's command prompt.

To give you a good understanding of how to work with the debugger, let's use it to run the Test.rb script. If you have not done so, create and save your own version of the Test.rb script and then start its execution in the debugger, as shown here:

```
ruby -r debug test.rb
```

In response, the debugger loads and prepares to execute the script, as shown here:

```
Debug.rb
Emacs support available.

test.rb:1:x = 1
(rdb:1)
```

Let's allow the first script statement to be executed. This is accomplished by executing the step command, as shown here:

```
(rdb:1) step
test.rb:2:loop do
(rdb:1)
```

As you can see, the debugger now shows that script statement 2 is ready for execution. Before executing it, let's check on the value assigned to the x variable now that the first statement has been run. One way of doing this is to simply type the name of the variable at the debugger prompt, as demonstrated here:

```
(rdb:1) x
1
(rdb:1)
```

As you can see, x has been assigned a value of 1. Another way of examining the value assigned to x is to type `var local` and press Enter, as shown here:

```
(rdb:1) var local
  x => 1
(rdb:1)
```

The `var local` command tells the debugger to list all local variables within the current scope. (Type `var global` to view global variables and `var instance` to view instance variables.)

As you work your way through your script, it is easy to lose track of exactly where you are. To get your bearings, you can enter the `list` command and in response, the debugger will display the next statement to be executed as well as a number of statements that surround it, as demonstrated here:

```
(rdb:1) list
[-3, 6] in test.rb
   1  x = 1
=> 2  loop do
   3    puts x
   4    x += 1
   5    puts "We are half way there!" if x == 3
   6    break if x == 5
(rdb:1)
```

Rather than stepping through a script line by line, you may instead want to set a breakpoint. A *breakpoint* is a marker placed in a script that pauses script execution when it is reached. Once paused, you can execute any debugger commands.

To set up a breakpoint, you use the `break` command, passing the line number where you want to set the break as an argument. Let's set up a break point for the fourth line in the script file, as shown here:

```
(rdb:1) break 4
Set breakpoint 1 at test.rb:4
(rdb:1)
```

Now that the breakpoint has been set, type the `cont` command at the debugger prompt, as shown here:

```
(rdb:1) cont
1
Breakpoint 1, toplevel at test.rb:4
```

```
test.rb:4:   x += 1
(rdb:1)
```

The cont command runs the program without any stepping, stopping execution when a breakpoint is reached or the scripts ends. As you can see, after the cont command was executed, the script executed the second and third statements and then paused before executing the fourth statement (where the breakpoint was set).

Next, let's step through the fourth statement and then check on the value assigned to x, as shown here:

```
(rdb:1) step
test.rb:5:   puts "We are half way there!" if x == 3
(rdb:1) x
2
(rdb:1)
```

The value of x is now set equal to 2. Now, let's remove the breakpoint that you just set by either typing del and the number that was previously assigned to the breakpoint or by telling del to delete all breakpoints, as demonstrated here:

```
(rdb:1) del
Clear all breakpoints? (y/n) y
(rdb:1)
```

 TRICK You can type in the word break all by itself to generate a list of all currently set breakpoints and to see the line number associated with each breakpoint.

Now that the breakpoint has been removed, let's set a conditional breakpoint and then allow the script to run without stepping through it. The watch command is used to set conditional breakpoints, as shown here:

```
(rdb:1) watch x = 3
Set watchpoint 4
(rdb:1) cont
Watchpoint 4, toplevel at test.rb:5
test.rb:5:   puts "We are half way there!" if x == 3
(rdb:1)
```

Here, the conditional breakpoint has been set up to execute once the value assigned to x is set equal to 3. Then the cont command was used to continue script execution, pausing again when the value of x has become 3.

Now, let's display and then remove the conditional breakpoint, as shown here:

```
(rdb:1) break
Breakpoints:

Watchpoints:
  4 x = 3

(rdb:1) del
Clear all breakpoints? (y/n) y
(rdb:1) break
Breakpoints:

Watchpoints:

(rdb:1)
```

Let's wrap up the current debug session by telling the debugger to terminate, as shown here:

```
(rdb:1) quit
Really quit? (y/n) y
```

As you can see, the `quit` command instructs the Ruby debugger to terminate, returning you to the operating system's command prompt. By executing debugger commands, you can exercise detailed control over the execution of a Ruby script. You can control when statements execute and keep track of the order in which things are occurring. In addition, you can inspect the values assigned to variables to ensure that they are being appropriately set. As a result, by carefully stepping through the execution of a Ruby script and monitoring its activity, you can spot places where things are not working as you expect them to. Once you have identified the source of your script errors, you can make changes to your scripts and test them again.

BACK TO THE RUBY TIC-TAC-TOE GAME

Okay, now it is time to turn your attention back to the development of this chapter's game project, the Ruby Tic-Tac-Toe game. As you work on this script take note of the manner in which variables are used. In particular, keep an eye on the global variables that are used to represent each of the game board's nine squares. While the rest of the variables used in the script are all local variables and are passed when necessary as arguments to methods, the variables representing the game board squares have been made global because there are so many of them and because they are used extensively throughout this script.

Designing the Game

The development of the Ruby Tic-Tac-Toe game will be completed in 16 steps, as outlined here:

1. Open your text or script editor and create a new file.
2. Add comment statements to the beginning of the script file to document the script and its purpose.
3. Define a class representing the terminal window.
4. Define a class representing the Tic-Tac-Toe game.
5. Define the `display_greeting` method.
6. Define the `display_instructions` method.
7. Define the `display_game_board` method.
8. Define the `validate_player_move` method.
9. Define the `play_game` method.
10. Define the `clear_game_board` method.
11. Define the `check_results` method.
12. Define the `display_game_results` method.
13. Define the `display_credits` method.
14. Instantiate custom script objects.
15. Get the player's permission to begin game play.
16. Control high-level game play.

Step 1: Creating a New Ruby File

The first step in the development of the Ruby Tic-Tac-Toe game is to open your favorite text or script editor and create a new Ruby script file named TicTacToe.rb, storing it in the same folder as your other Ruby game scripts.

Step 2: Documenting the Script and Its Purpose

Now that you have created your new script file, let's add the following comments to it. These statements provide documentation about the game and its purpose.

```
#-------------------------------------------------------------------
#
# Script Name: TicTacToe.rb
# Version:     1.0
# Author:      Jerry Lee Ford, Jr.
# Date:        October 2007
#
# Description: This Ruby script is a 2-player version of the popular
#              Tic-Tac-Toe game in which players try to out
```

```
#              maneuver one another in an effort to line up three game
#              board squares in a row (horizontally, vertically, or
#              diagonally).
#
#-------------------------------------------------------------------
```

Step 3: Defining a Screen Class

The Ruby Tic-Tac-Toe game utilizes two custom classes. These classes provide the script with a set of methods that control interaction with the user and the game. The code statements for the script's first class, the Screen class, are shown next and should be added to the end of the script file.

```
# Define custom classes -------------------------------------------

#Define a class representing the console window
class Screen

  def cls  #Define a method that clears the display area
    puts ("\n" * 25)  #Scroll the screen 25 times
    puts "\a"   #Make a little noise to get the player's attention
  end

  def pause    #Define a method that pauses the display area
    STDIN.gets  #Execute the STDIN class's gets method to pause script
              #execution until the player presses the Enter key
  end

end
```

The Screen class is made up of two methods. The first method is named cls and when executed, will write 25 blank lines to the console window to clear the screen. In addition, a beep sound is played each time the screen is cleared. The pause method uses the STDIN class's gets method to pause the execution of the script until the player presses the Enter key.

Step 4: Creating the Game Class

The statements that define the Game class are shown next and should be added to the end of the script file. This method contains nine methods. To begin the creation of the Game class, add the following statements to the end of the script file.

```
#Define a class representing the Ruby Tic-Tac-Toe game
class Game

end
```

Step 5: Defining the display_greeting Method

The first method to be defined in the Game class is the display_greeting method. This method is responsible for displaying the game's welcome screen. The statements that make up this method are shown next and should be inserted into the Game class.

```
#This method displays the game's opening message
def display_greeting

  Console_Screen.cls  #Clear the display area

  #Display the game's welcome screen
  puts "\t\t\tWelcome to the Ruby Tic-Tac-Toe Game!\n\n\n\n"
  puts "\t\t\t         |       |"
  puts "\t\t\t      X  |       |"
  puts "\t\t\t         |       |"
  puts "\t\t\t      ---------------------"
  puts "\t\t\t         |       |"
  puts "\t\t\t      0  |   X   |   0"
  puts "\t\t\t         |       |"
  puts "\t\t\t      ---------------------"
  puts "\t\t\t         |       |"
  puts "\t\t\t         |       |   X"
  puts "\t\t\t         |       |"
  print "\n\n\n\n\nPress Enter to continue. "

  Console_Screen.pause      #Pause the game

end
```

Step 6: Defining the display_instructions Method

The next method to be added to the Game class is the display_instructions method. The script statements that make up this method are shown next and should be added to the game class definition, immediately after the display_greeting method.

```
#Define a method to be used to display game instructions
def display_instructions

  Console_Screen.cls        #Clear the display area

  puts "INSTRUCTIONS:\n\n"  #Display a heading

  #Display the game's instructions
  puts "This is a 2-player Tic-Tac-Toe game in which Player X and"
  puts "Player O are challenged to out maneuver one another in"
  puts "an effort to line up three squares in a row (horizontally,"
  puts "vertically, or diagonally). Player X always goes first. Game play"
  puts "ends when either player manages to line up three squares in a"
  puts "row or when all nine game board squares have been selected"
  puts "without either player managing to win."
  puts "\n\n\n\n\n\n\n\n\n\n\n"
  print "Press Enter to continue. "

  Console_Screen.pause       #Pause the game

end
```

Step 7: Defining the display_game_board Method

The next method to be added to the Game class is the display_game_board method. The script statements that make up this method are provided next and should be added to the game class definition, immediately after the display_instructions method.

```
#Define a method to display the game board and collect player moves
def display_game_board(player)

  move = ""  #Assign a default value

  loop do  #Loop forever

    Console_Screen.cls  #Clear the display area

    #Display the game board
    puts "\t\t\tWelcome to the Ruby Tic-Tac-Toe Game!\n\n\n\n"
    puts "\t\t\t      1      2      3\n"
```

```
puts "\t\t\t                |        |"
puts "\t\t\t    A    #{$A1}  |  #{$A2}  |   #{$A3}"
puts "\t\t\t                |        |"
puts "\t\t\t         --------------------"
puts "\t\t\t                |        |"
puts "\t\t\t    B    #{$B1}  |  #{$B2}  |   #{$B3}"
puts "\t\t\t                |        |"
puts "\t\t\t         --------------------"
puts "\t\t\t                |        |"
puts "\t\t\t    C    #{$C1}  |  #{$C2}  |   #{$C3}"
puts "\t\t\t                |        |"

#Prompt the player to enter a move
print "\n\n\n\n\nPlayer " + player + " turn. Please enter your move: "

move = STDIN.gets  #Collect the player's move
move.chop!  #Remove any extra characters appended to the string
move = move.upcase  #Convert to uppercase

#Terminate the loop if a valid move was entered
if move.length == 2 then  #Must be at 2 character long
  if move =~ /[A-C][1-3]/i  #Must be A1, A2, A3, B1, B2, B3, C1, C2, C3
    #Call method responsible for determining if the board square was
    #available
    validMove = validate_player_move(move)
    if validMove == true  #The move was valid
      break  #Terminate the execution of the loop
    end
  end
end

end

return move  #Return the player's move back to the calling statement

end
```

This method is controlled by a loop that has been set up to run forever. Each time the loop repeats, it displays the Tic-Tac-Toe game board. Embedded within the game board is a series of variable references. These variable references are filled in using variable interpolation during game play. After displaying the game board, the method displays a message prompting the current player, as specified by the value assigned to the player variable, to enter a move.

The player's input is converted to all uppercase and checked to see if it is two characters long. If it is, a regular expression is then used to further validate the player's input, ensuring that the first character is an A, B, or C and that the second character is a 1, 2, or 3. If the player's input passes these validation checks, it is passed as an argument to the validate_player_move method, which checks to see if the game board square selected by the player is available for selection (i.e., that it has not already been assigned). If the value returned by the validate_player_move method is equal to true, a break command is executed and the player's move is returned to the statement that called upon the method to execute. Otherwise, the player is prompted to make a different selection.

Step 8: Defining the validate_player_move Method

The next method to be added to the Game class is the validate_player_move method. This method is responsible for ensuring that the game board square specified by the player is available for selection. The script statements that make up this method are provided next and should be added to the Game class definition, immediately after the display_game_board method.

```
#Define a method that determines if the square selected by the player
#is still available
def validate_player_move(move)

  #Return a value of false if the square has already been selected
  return false if move == "A1" && $A1 != " "
  return false if move == "B1" && $B1 != " "
  return false if move == "C1" && $C1 != " "
  return false if move == "A2" && $A2 != " "
  return false if move == "B2" && $B2 != " "
  return false if move == "C2" && $C2 != " "
  return false if move == "A3" && $A3 != " "
  return false if move == "B3" && $B3 != " "
  return false if move == "C3" && $C3 != " "

  #Return a value of true if the square is available
```

```
    return true
```

```
end
```

When called, this method checks to see if the player's move, passed to the method as an argument, is available. This is accomplished by checking to see if the value assigned to the game board square is a blank space, which means the square is available.

A value of false is returned if the specified game board square is not available. Otherwise, a value of true is returned.

Step 9: Defining the play_game Method

The next method to be added to the Game class is the play_game method. This method is responsible for managing an individual round of play. The method's statements are shown next and should be added to the end of the class definition, immediately after the validate_player_move method.

```
#Define a method to control game play
def play_game

  player = "X"  #Make Player X the default player for each new game

  noOfMoves = 0   #Reset the value of the variable used to keep track
                  #of the total number of moves made in a game

  #Clear out the game board to get it ready for a new game
  clear_game_board

  loop do  #Loop forever

    Console_Screen.cls       #Clear the display area

    #Call on the method that displays the game board and collects player
    #moves
    square = display_game_board(player)

    #Assign the selected game board square to the player that selected it
    $A1 = player if square == "A1"
    $A2 = player if square == "A2"
    $A3 = player if square == "A3"
```

```ruby
    $B1 = player if square == "B1"
    $B2 = player if square == "B2"
    $B3 = player if square == "B3"
    $C1 = player if square == "C1"
    $C2 = player if square == "C2"
    $C3 = player if square == "C3"

    #Keep count of the total number of moves that have been made
    noOfMoves += 1

    #Call on the method that is responsible for determining if the game has
    #been won
    winner = check_results(player)

    #See if player X has won
    if winner == "X" then
      #Call on the method that displays the game's final results
      display_game_results("Player X Wins!")
      break  #Terminate the execution of the loop
    end

    #See if player O has won
    if winner == "O" then
      #Call on the method that displays the game's final results
      display_game_results("Player O Wins!")
      break  #Terminate the execution of the loop
    end

    #See if the game has ended in a tie
    if noOfMoves == 9 then
      #Call on the method that displays the game's final results
      display_game_results("Tie")
      break  #Terminate the execution of the loop
    end

    #If the game has not ended, switch player turns and keep playing
    if player == "X" then
      player = "O"
```

```
   else
     player = "X"
   end

  end

end
```

This method begins by assigning a value of X to a variable named player and a value of 0 to a variable named noOfMoves. The value assigned to player specifies the game's starting player. noOfMoves will be used to keep track of the total number of moves made by both players during game play.

Next, the clear_game_board method is called, resetting all of the game board's embedded variables to " ", thus readying the game for a new round of play. The rest of the method is controlled by a loop. Each time the loop repeats, the display_game_board method is called and passed the value assigned to the player variable. The display_game_board method returns a value representing the game board square selected by the player. A game board square is then assigned to the player based on the square that was selected, and the value of noOfMoves is incremented to keep track of the number of moves that have been made by both players.

Next, the check_results method is called. This method checks to see if the current player has won the game, returning a value of "X" or "O" if one of the players has won. If this is the case, the display_game_results method is called and a break command is executed, terminating the loop and ending the play_game method. If neither player has won the game, the value of noOfMoves is checked to see if it is equal to 9, in which case every game board square has been selected without either player winning the game.

If neither player has won the game and a tie has not occurred, the last thing the loop does before the loop repeats is switch the current player's turn from X to 0 or from 0 to X as appropriate.

Step 10: Defining the clear_game_board Method

The next method to be added to the Game class is the clear game method. This method is responsible for resetting the value of each variable embedded in the Tic-Tac-Toe game's game board. The method's statements are shown next and should be added to the end of the class definition, immediately after the play_game method.

```
#Define a method that is responsible for clearing out the game board
def clear_game_board
```

```
#Assign a blank space to each game board square
$A1 =   " "
$A2 =   " "
$A3 =   " "
$B1 =   " "
$B2 =   " "
$B3 =   " "
$C1 =   " "
$C2 =   " "
$C3 =   " "
```

```
end
```

When called, this method assigns each of the game board's nine embedded variables a value of " ", visually clearing each square and making it available for selection in the next round of play.

Step 11: Defining the check_results Method

The next method to be added to the Game class is the check_results method. This method is responsible for examining the squares on the game board to determine if the current player, passed to the method as an argument, has managed to line up three squares in a row. This method's statements are shown next and should be added to the end of the class definition, immediately after the clear_game_board method.

```
#Define a method to examine the game board and determine if the current
#player has won the game
def check_results(player)

  winner = ""  #Assign a default value

  #Check vertically
  winner = player if $A1 == player && $A2 == player && $A3 == player
  winner = player if $B1 == player && $B2 == player && $B3 == player
  winner = player if $C1 == player && $C2 == player && $C3 == player

  #Check horizontally
  winner = player if $A1 == player && $B1 == player && $C1 == player
  winner = player if $A2 == player && $B2 == player && $C2 == player
  winner = player if $A3 == player && $B3 == player && $C3 == player
```

```
#check diagonally
winner = player if $A1 == player && $B2 == player && $C3 == player
winner = player if $A3 == player && $B2 == player && $C1 == player

return winner   #Return the result back to the calling statement

end
```

The method checks vertically, horizontally, and diagonally for a winner. If a winner is identified, the method returns a letter representing the winning player (X or O). Otherwise an empty string is returned to the calling statement.

Step 12: Defining the display_game_results Method

The next method to be added to the Game class is the display_game_results method. This method is responsible for displaying the results of the current round of play when called at the end of each round of play. The method's statements are shown next and should be added to the end of the class definition, immediately after the check_results method.

```
#Define a method that will be used to display the game's final result
def display_game_results(message)

    Console_Screen.cls  #Clear the display area

    #Display the results of the game
    puts "\n\n\n"
    puts "\t\t\t      Game Over: " + message + "\n\n\n"
    puts "\t\t\t          1      2       3\n"
    puts "\t\t\t             |      |"
    puts "\t\t\t     A    #{$A1}   |   #{$A2}   |    #{$A3}"
    puts "\t\t\t             |      |"
    puts "\t\t\t          ----------------------"
    puts "\t\t\t             |      |"
    puts "\t\t\t     B    #{$B1}   |   #{$B2}   |    #{$B3}"
    puts "\t\t\t             |      |"
    puts "\t\t\t          ----------------------"
    puts "\t\t\t             |      |"
    puts "\t\t\t     C    #{$C1}   |   #{$C2}   |    #{$C3}"
    puts "\t\t\t             |      |"
    print "\n\n\n\n\nPress Enter to continue. "
```

```
    Console_Screen.pause          #Pause the game

end
```

As you can see, this method displays a message passed to it as an argument followed by a copy of the game's Tic-Tac-Toe board.

Step 13: Defining the display_credits Method

The last of the Game class's methods is the display_credits method, which when called will display the game's credits, including the author's URL. The statements that make up this method are shown next and should be added to the end of the Game class.

```
#This method displays information about the Ruby Tic-Tac-Toe game
def display_credits

  Console_Screen.cls  #Clear the display area

  #Thank the player and display game information
  puts "\t\t     Thank you for playing the Ruby Tic-Tac-Toe game.\n\n\n\n"
  puts "\n\t\t\t Developed by Jerry Lee Ford, Jr.\n\n"
  puts "\t\t\t\t  Copyright 2007\n\n"
  puts "\t\t\tURL: http://www.tech-publishing.com\n\n\n\n\n\n\n\n\n\n"

end
```

Step 14: Initializing Script Objects

Now that both of the custom classes have been defined, it is time to initialize objects based on these classes. This is done by appending the following statements to the end of the script file.

```
# Main Script Logic -------------------------------------------------

Console_Screen = Screen.new  #Instantiate a new Screen object
TTT = Game.new  #Instantiate a new Game object

#Execute the Game class's display_greeting method
TTT.display_greeting
```

```
#Execute the Game class's clear_game_board method
TTT.clear_game_board

answer = ""  #Initialize variable and assign it an empty string
```

In addition to instantiating the `Console_Screen` and `TTT` objects, these statements also execute the `Game` class's `display_greeting` method and define a variable named `answer`, which will be used to manage the execution of a loop that prompts the player for permission to begin a new round of play.

Step 15: Getting Permission to Start the Game

The following statements are responsible for prompting the player for permission to start a new round of play and should be appended to the end of the script file.

```
#Loop until the player enters y or n and do not accept any other input
loop do

  Console_Screen.cls  #Clear the display area

  #Prompt the player for permission to start the game
  print "Are you ready to play Ruby Tic-Tac-Toe? (y/n): "

  answer = STDIN.gets  #Collect the player's answer
  answer.chop!  #Remove any extra characters appended to the string

  #Terminate the loop if valid input was provided
  break if answer =~ /y|n/i

end
```

These statements are controlled by a loop. Every time the loop iterates, the player is prompted to enter a value of y or n, to instruct the game whether to start a new round of play or to terminate the execution of the game. Any input other than a y or n is rejected. Once valid input is provided, a `break` command is executed, terminating the loop and allowing the script to continue running.

Step 16: Controlling Game Play

The script's remaining statements are shown next. These statements are responsible for controlling the overall execution of the game.

```ruby
#Analyze the player's answer
if answer == "n"  #See if the player wants to quit

  Console_Screen.cls  #Clear the display area

  #Invite the player to return and play the game some other time
  puts "Okay, perhaps another time.\n\n"

else  #The player wants to play the game

  #Execute the Game class's display_instructions method
  TTT.display_instructions

  playAgain = ""  #Initialize variable and assign it an empty string

  loop do  #Loop forever

    #Execute the Game class's play_game method
    TTT.play_game

    loop do  #Loop forever

      Console_Screen.cls  #Clear the display area
      #Find out if the player wants to play another round
      print "Would you like to play another round? (y/n): "

      playAgain = STDIN.gets  #Collect the player's response
      playAgain.chop!  #Remove any extra characters appended to the string

      #Terminate the loop if valid input was provided
      break if playAgain =~ /n|y/i

    end

    #Terminate the loop if valid input was provided
    break if playAgain =~ /n/i

  end
```

```
#Call upon the Game class's determine_credits method
TTT.display_credits
```

end

The execution of these statements is controlled by an `if` statement code block. If the player decides not to play, a message is displayed encouraging the player to return and play another time and the game terminates. If the player decides to play, the `Game` class's `display_instructions` method is run. A loop then repeatedly executes the `Game` class's `play_game` method, allowing the players to play as many times as they want. The loop continues to iterate until the players decide to quit, at which time a `break` command is executed, terminating the loop and allowing the `display_credits` method to execute.

Running Your New Ruby Script Game

All right! Time to save and execute the Ruby Tic-Tac-Toe script and see how things go. As long as you followed along carefully and did not skip any steps or make any typos, everything should work as expected. If, however, you run into errors, read the resulting error messages carefully to ascertain what went wrong and, if necessary, crank up Ruby's debugger and use it to debug your script. In fact, even if your script runs just fine, you might want to go ahead and run it in the debugger anyway, just to get some additional experience working with the debugger.

SUMMARY

In this chapter, you learned how to debug your scripts using Ruby's built-in debugger. You learned how to set up error handlers to deal with errors when they occur. You learned about the differences among logical, syntax, and runtime errors. This chapter also introduced you to a number of debugger commands and demonstrated how to use them to set breakpoints, view variable values, and control the execution of your Ruby scripts.

Now, before you put down this book, I suggest you set aside one last block of time to make a few improvements to the Ruby Tic-Tac-Toe game by implementing the following list of challenges.

CHALLENGES

1. Currently, the Ruby Tic-Tac-Toe game rejects any invalid moves by redisplaying the game board and prompting the current player to try again. Consider modifying this behavior by displaying a message that explains precisely why the move is being rejected (e.g., move out of range, square already assigned, etc.).

2. Modify the Tic-Tac-Toe game so that it keeps track of the total number of games played as well as the total number of games won by each player and make these statistics available to the players upon demand so that they can see how well they are doing over time.

3. Rather than setting up the variables that represent game board squares as global variables, consider modifying the game to use local variables to represent these values and pass them as necessary to differentiate methods using an array.

4. Currently, the game is set up such that Player X always goes first. Consider changing things so that players must alternate to prevent either player from having the permanent advantage of always going first.

Part

IV

WHAT'S ON THE COMPANION WEBSITE?

As is the case with any programming language, to become proficient you must practice, practice, practice. While this may mean spending time creating new game scripts, like the ones demonstrated in this book, more than likely you'll want to begin focusing on developing all kinds of different scripts. For example, you may want to begin creating scripts that help you to become more efficient by automating tasks like file and folder management.

To get off to a good start, it helps to have a collection of sample code that you can reference and borrow from, copying and then pasting code statements into your new Ruby scripts. This book has provided you with hundreds of working examples, including everything from small one-liners to examples that demonstrate how to exercise specific language features and to perform specific tasks. For example, Chapter 6 is packed with examples of how to create and work with arrays and hashes, and Chapter 7 provides you with dozens of examples of how to work with regular expressions. Chapter 9, on the other hand, offers examples that demonstrate how to work with files and interact with system resources.

In addition to the code samples, each chapter in this book ended by providing you with a working example of a computer game. Within these game scripts, you will find no shortage of examples demonstrating how to work with many of the language features and programming techniques presented in this book. By drawing upon the script statements found in the script files, you have access to small templates that you can copy and then paste into new scripts to build more advanced and functional Ruby scripts.

If you have been creating and experimenting with this book's game scripts, then you already have access to a good collection of source code. However, if you have skipped around a bit when reading this book, then you may have also missed out on creating one or more of the game scripts. But don't fret; you can download all of the game scripts presented in this book from the book's companion website, located at www.courseptr.com/downloads.

Table A.1 provides you with a brief review of the game scripts that were presented in this book.

TABLE A.1	RUBY SCRIPT FILES AVAILABLE ON THE COMPANION WEBSITE	
Chapter	Application	Description
Chapter 1	Ruby Joke game	This Ruby script serves as the book's initial example on how to create and execute a Ruby script and demonstrates how to display text and perform basic user interaction.
Chapter 2	Ruby Tall Tale game	This Ruby script demonstrates how to collect and process user input through the development of an interactive storytelling game.
Chapter 3	Ruby Virtual Crazy 8 Ball game	This Ruby script demonstrates how to work with variables and to generate random numbers to create a game that provides randomly selected answers to player questions.
Chapter 4	Ruby Typing Challenge game	This Ruby script demonstrates how to apply conditional logic to analyze user input and control script execution flow through the development of a computer typing game that evaluates the player's typing skills.
Chapter 5	Superman Movie Trivia Quiz	This Ruby script demonstrates how to work with loops when collecting user input through the creation of an interactive quiz that evaluates the player's knowledge of the Superman movie series.
Chapter 6	Ruby Number Guessing game	This Ruby script is a number-guessing game that challenges the player to guess a randomly generated number in as few guesses as possible.

Chapter 7	Word Guessing game	This Ruby script demonstrates how to work with regular expressions through the development of a computer game that challenges the player to guess a mystery word after being first allowed to guess five consonants and one vowel.
Chapter 8	Ruby Rock, Paper, Scissors game	This Ruby game is a computerized version of the Rock, Paper, Scissors game in which the player goes head to head against the computer.
Chapter 9	Ruby Blackjack game	This Ruby game is a virtualized casino card game in which the player competes against the dealer (computer) in an effort to build a hand that comes as close as possible to 21 without going over.
Chapter 10	Ruby Tic-Tac-Toe game	This Ruby script is designed to bring together all of the programming concepts presented throughout the book through the development of a two player Tic-Tac-Toe computer game.

WHAT NEXT?

As you finish up your work with this book, you have no doubt learned a great deal about Ruby programming. However, there is still a lot left to learn. Rather than thinking of this book as the end of your Ruby education, I hope you view it as the beginning. In order to become an effective Ruby programmer, you need to learn as much about the language as possible.

A great place to go to find more information about Ruby is the Internet. However, the Internet is a big place and it is not always easy to find reliable and useful information without investing a lot of time and effort. To help make the most of your time and to assist you in honing in on some really useful and helpful information, this appendix provides you with the URLs of a number of great places that you can go to continue your Ruby education. You will also find information about Ruby books, mailing lists, newsgroups, and blogs.

RECOMMENDED READING

This book has provided you with a strong foundation upon which you can build and prepare to move on to advanced topics. To help you along your way, this section contains information about a number of books that focus on providing advanced coverage of Ruby programming, each of which makes for a good next step from this book.

Programming Ruby: The Pragmatic Programmer's Guide, **Second Edition**

by Dave Thomas, Chad Fowler, and Andy Hunt

ISBN: 0974514055, Pragmatic Bookshelf, 2004

This book, respectfully referred to as PickAxe by the Ruby community, serves as an excellent technical guide and reference manual and is an essential resource for professional programmers and dedicated Ruby enthusiasts.

The Ruby Way, Second Edition

by Hal Fulton

ISBN: 0672328844, Addison-Wesley Professional, 2006

This book serves as an excellent transition for beginning Ruby programmers looking to make a jump to the next level. It is packed with recipes for developing all kinds of Ruby scripts.

Ruby Cookbook

by Lucas Carlson

ISBN: 0596523696, O'Reilly Media, Inc., 2006

This book is packed with examples of Ruby scripts that address a host of real-world tasks and provide the reader with lots of source code. The sample scripts that you will find here include scripts that work with databases, the Internet, and web services.

If, on the other hand, you want to apply your new Ruby programming knowledge to web development, I recommend you read the following book.

Agile Web Development with Rails, **Second Edition**

by Dave Thomas and David Hansson

ISBN: 0977616630, Pragmatic Bookshelf, 2006

This book provides soup-to-nuts coverage of how to use Ruby on Rails to develop powerful applications that work with database back-ends.

RUBY WEB PAGES

Of course, books are not the only source of information for advancing your knowledge and understanding of Ruby programming. The Internet is packed with websites that address Ruby programming in one form or another. Some of these websites are better than others. To help you get off to a good start, the sections that follow provide you with information about some of the sites that are most worth visiting.

Ruby Programming Language

Ruby Programming Language, shown in Figure B.1, is located at http://www.ruby-lang.org/en/ and is the official Ruby website. From here you can stay up to date with what is going on in the world of Ruby as well as download the most current version of Ruby.

FIGURE B.1

Ruby Programming Language is the official website for Ruby.

RubyForge

RubyForge, shown in Figure B.2, is located at http://www.rubyforge.org/. It hosts information about Ruby open-source projects. In addition to learning about the work being done by other Ruby programmers, this website is a great place to show off your own Ruby scripts.

Ruby-doc.org

Ruby-doc.org, shown in Figure B.3, provides access to Ruby documentation. This documentation represents an effort by the Ruby community to develop a comprehensive set of Ruby documentation.

RubyForge provides a place for Ruby programmers to come together and share information and access each other's work.

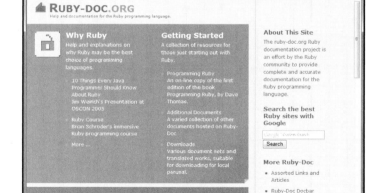

Ruby-doc.org represents a community effort to develop a comprehensive collection of Ruby documentation.

Ruby on Rails

Ruby on Rails (www.rubyonrails.org), shown in Figure B.4, is the official website for Ruby on Rails. From here you can learn how Ruby on Rails works and see examples of how it has been used to develop various professional websites.

FIGURE B.4

Ruby on Rails is dedicated to those who want to put their Ruby programming skills to use on the World Wide Web.

Ruby Mailing Lists

One of the very best and most convenient ways of exchanging information about Ruby and getting answers to problems that you are having difficulty solving on your own is to post information or questions on a mailing list to solicit conversation from other people. As you would expect, there are a number of mailing lists dedicated to Ruby. The two mailing lists covered in the sections that follow are of great help to beginner Ruby programmers.

ruby-talk

The ruby-talk mailing list provides discussions that address general Ruby questions and topics, and it is a great place to post a question and receive feedback from programmers facing similar challenges and receive help from programmers who may have already overcome the challenges you are facing. To join ruby-talk, send an email to ruby-talk-ctl@ruby-lang.org and enter the following line as the text message in the body portion of your e-mail.

```
Subscribe FirstName LastName
```

ruby-doc

If you have a question about a particular Ruby command or want to find where to go to get documentation for a particular topic, post a message on the ruby-doc mailing list. This mailing list is designed to facilitate discussion about all aspects of Ruby documentation and standards. To join ruby-doc, send an email to ruby-doc-ctl@ruby-lang.org and enter the following line as the text message in the body portion of your e-mail.

```
Subscribe FirstName LastName
```

RUBY NEWSGROUPS

Newsgroups are a type of forum in which individuals participate in an open, interactive discussion with one another. A number of newsgroups have been created for Ruby, and two of the best are discussed below.

comp.lang.ruby

comp.lang.ruby, shown in Figure B.5, is a mailing list with over 6,000 members. It provides a mirrored list of the topics discussed on the ruby-talk mailing list. Members can elect to either visit the website (http://groups.google.com/group/comp.lang.ruby/topics) or to receive e-mail containing each day's posts.

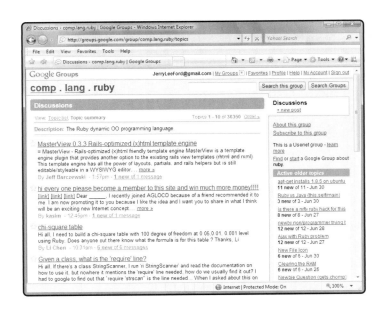

FIGURE B.5

By visiting comp.lang.ruby or signing up for its e-mail, you can keep an eye on what everyone is saying about Ruby.

Rails Weenie

Rails Weenie (http://www.railsweenie.com), shown in Figure B.6, is an online forum dedicated to discussing all things related to Ruby on Rails. As of the writing of this book, more than 1,300 people had participated in this forum, with over 5,600 posts.

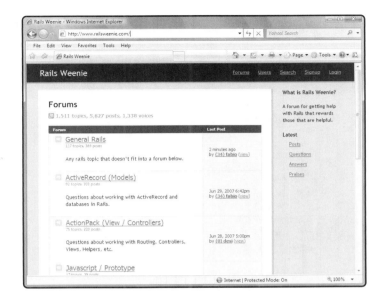

FIGURE B.6

Rails Weenie was set up to address the needs of Ruby on Rails programmers.

RUBY BLOGS

Blogs are web-based logs where content providers can post journal-like entries. There are many different blogs dedicated to Ruby; two of the best are outlined in the sections that follow.

Ruby Inside

Ruby Inside is a blog dedicated to Ruby and Ruby on Rails. It contains posts covering everything from tips and tricks to the most advanced programming topics. Ruby Inside is located at http://www.rubyinside.com/, as shown in Figure B.7.

Ruby Underground

The Ruby Underground blog is a general-purpose blog that hosts varied topics covering all aspects of Ruby programming. Ruby Underground is located at http://rubyunderground.org/, as shown in Figure B.8.

The Ruby Inside blog has over 8,000 subscribers.

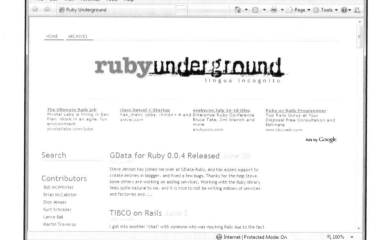

FIGURE B.8

The Ruby Underground blog has over 8,000 subscribers.

GLOSSARY

abstraction. A term that refers to the process of organizing program code into classes.

argument. Data that is passed to a script or method as input.

array. A collection of data that is stored as an indexed list.

Boolean. A value that represents a true or false condition.

breakpoint. A marker used to pause the execution of scripts run using the Ruby debugger.

call. The process of calling upon a method within a Ruby script.

case sensitivity. The differentiation of upper- and lowercase spelling in the formulation of Ruby variables and strings.

chaining. The process of passing one method's output to another method as input.

class. A template that can be used to create or instantiate individual objects based on definitions made within the class.

class variable. A variable with a scope that allows it to be referenced by all instances of the same class.

code blocks. A group of enclosed statements that are executed as a unit.

command prompt. A text-based interface used to accept commands and display the results of those commands.

comment. A statement embedded inside a script for the purpose of documenting the internal design and logic of the script.

compiling. The process that the Ruby interpreter goes through to convert a script into a format that can be executed by the operating system.

concatenation. The process of combining together two strings to create a new string.

conditional logic. The programmatic analysis of two or more conditions, providing the basis for controlling the logical execution of statements within a script.

debug. The act of tracking down and fixing an error within a script file.

decrement. The process of repeatedly decreasing a numeric value during the execution of a loop, method, or script.

delimiter. A marker that is used to identify different data items passed as input to commands, methods, and scripts.

dot notation. The syntax used when referencing object properties and methods.

element. An individual item stored in an array.

encapsulation. A programming technique that restricts access to one or more of the properties and methods defined within a class.

endless loop. A loop that repeats forever without means of terminating its execution.

error. A problem that occurs during the execution of a script.

escaping. A programming technique in which the \ character is pre-appended to a character within a string to instruct Ruby to interpret the character literally.

expression. A programming statement that when evaluated returns a value.

floating point. A real number containing a decimal point, representing a fractional value.

flowchart. A tool used to graphically represent some or all of a script's logical flow or design.

global variable. A variable that can be accessed from any location within a script.

hash. A collection of data stored using key-value pairs.

increment. The process of repeatedly increasing a numeric value during the execution of a loop, method, or script.

index. A numeric value used to specify the location of an element in an array.

inheritance. A term used to describe the process whereby one class is derived from another class. The derived class, sometimes referred to as the child class, inherits all of the properties and methods of the parent class.

input. An argument passed to a script or method for use as data.

instance variable. A variable with a scope that allows it to be referenced by all methods residing inside the class definition.

instantiation. A term that describes the process used to create a new object.

integer. A whole number.

interpolation. The process by which Ruby replaces a variable embedded within a string with the variable's assigned value.

interpreted language. A programming language used to develop scripts that must be compiled each time they are executed.

interpreter. An application that compiles scripts into a format that allows them to be executed.

irb (interactive Ruby). An interactive environment that can be used to submit Ruby statements for immediate execution and which is commonly used by Ruby programmers as a means of tinkering with Ruby and testing different language features to see how they work.

IronRuby. A Ruby environment that will facilitate the development and execution of Ruby scripts that interact with the Microsoft .NET Framework.

iteration. The process of repeating the execution of a loop.

iterator. A variable used to process the contents of a list of items during the execution of a loop.

JRuby. A Java-based Ruby environment being developed by Sun Microsystems.

key-value pair. An individual data item stored within a hash along with its associated label.

language constructs. Language commands that are part of the core Ruby scripting language.

Linux. An open-source computer operating system derived from UNIX.

list. A collection of data items that are stored and managed as a unit.

local variable. A variable that can be accessed only within the scope in which it is created.

logical error. An error that occurs when a mistake is made in the logic used to perform a task.

loop. A collection of statements that execute repeatedly as a unit.

Mac OS X. A proprietary operating system based on UNIX that is provided by Apple for use on Macintosh computers.

metacharacter. A character that alters the way a pattern match occurs in a regular expression.

method. A collection of statements defined within a class that can be called upon to interact with and control the operation of objects instantiating from that class.

modifier. An expression that alters the execution of a statement to which it is appended.

module. A structure used to store collections of classes, methods, and constants.

.NET Framework. A Microsoft-developed framework that supports the development of desktop, network, and Internet-based applications and scripts.

nil. A Ruby value that indicates a value of nothing.

object. A self-contained entity that includes information about itself in the form of properties and provides script code stored as methods that can be used to interact with and control themselves.

object-oriented programming. A method of program in which data, script code, and objects are stored together to define abstract representations of real-world concepts.

operator precedence. The process a programming language uses to determine the order in which mathematic operations are evaluated.

parameter. An argument passed to a command, method, or script for processing as input.

pattern matching. The process of identifying matching string values based on a search performed using a regular expression.

polymorphism. The ability to define something in different forms.

program. A collection of compiled code statements that make up an application.

properties. Characteristics that describe or characterize an object, such as size or type.

pseudocode. A rough, English-like outline of the logic required to develop all or part of a script.

RDoc. Provides access to documentation about Ruby classes and methods.

RegExp. A term used to refer to a regular expression.

Regular Expression. A pattern used to identify matching character data.

ri. A command line Ruby documentation viewer.

Ruby. A modern, interpreted, object-oriented scripting language.

RubyGems. A package manager that provides a standard format for distributing Ruby scripts.

Ruby on Rails. A web-based application-development framework, sometimes just referred to as Rails, that allows programmers to build website applications using Ruby.

runtime error. An error that occurs when a script attempts to perform an illegal action.

scope. A term used to refer to the accessibility of a variable within a script.

script. A group of statements stored in a plain text file that can be interpreted and executed.

script editor. A specialized text editor that is used to develop script files.

special variable. A variable that is automatically created and maintained by Ruby and which can be referenced by any Ruby scripts.

statement. An executable line of code within a script file.

STDIN (Standard Input). The default location where Ruby retrieves input (e.g., the keyboard).

STDOUT (Standard Output). The default location where Ruby sends output (e.g., the screen).

string. A group of text characters enclosed within matching quotation marks.

string interpolation. Variable substitution performed by embedding variables within text strings.

syntax. The rules that govern the formulation of commands and script statements.

syntax error. An error that occurs when you fail to follow the rules for formatting script statements.

terminal window. A software application that provides command line access to the operating system.

troubleshooting. The process of tracking down and fixing bugs in computer programs.

UNIX. A computer operating system created by AT&T Bell Labs in the 1960s that has been ported to every major computing platform.

validation. The process of analyzing data input to ensure that it meets required specifications.

value. The data assigned to a variable.

variable. A pointer to a location in memory where the objects that are created in your scripts are stored.

Windows. A proprietary operating system created by Microsoft for use on personal computers.

YARV (Yet Another Ruby VM). A Ruby environment designed to replace the current Ruby interpreter.

INDEX

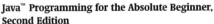

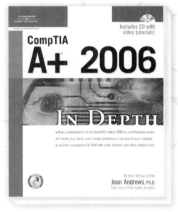